THE

PUBLICATIONS

OF THE

Lincoln Record Society

FOUNDED IN THE YEAR

1910

VOLUME 100

ISSN 0267-2634

WONDERFUL TO BEHOLD

A CENTENARY HISTORY OF
THE LINCOLN RECORD SOCIETY,
1910–2010

NICHOLAS BENNETT

The Lincoln Record Society

The Boydell Press

First published 2010

A Lincoln Record Society Publication
published by The Boydell Press
an imprint of Boydell & Brewer Ltd
PO Box 9, Woodbridge, Suffolk IP12 3DF, UK
and of Boydell & Brewer Inc.
668 Mt Hope Avenue, Rochester, NY 14620, USA
website: www.boydellandbrewer.com

ISBN 978–0–901503–88–6

A CIP catalogue record for this book is available
from the British Library

Details of other Lincoln Record Society volumes are available
from Boydell & Brewer Ltd

The publisher has no responsibility for the continued existence or accuracy of URLs for
external or third-party internet websites referred to in this book, and does not guarantee
that any content on such websites is, or will remain, accurate or appropriate.

This publication is printed on acid-free paper

Printed in Great Britain by
CPI Antony Rowe, Chippenham and Eastbourne

CONTENTS

LIST OF ILLUSTRATIONS

PREFACE

'Wonderful to behold': this sentiment was conveyed to the Lincoln Record Society (in the appropriately telegraphic Latin form *'Admirabile contemplatu'*) by its younger colleague, the Suffolk Records Society, on the occasion of the luncheon celebrating the completion of the monumental edition of the *Registrum Antiquissimum* in September 1973. It seems appropriate to use it again now, as the Society celebrates its Centenary with the publication of this, the one hundredth volume in the series inaugurated by its foundation in October 1910.

Many people have contributed, and are still contributing, to the success of the Society through the last century, and their achievements are chronicled in the pages of this volume. Two, however, stand out. The vision and commitment of Charles Wilmer Foster and Kathleen Major, whose combined involvement in the affairs of the Society spanned the first ninety years of its existence, provided the firm foundation which enabled it to flourish.

The thanks of the author are due to a number of people that have helped in the compilation of this volume. Rod Ambler undertook a survey of the changing nature of the membership of the Society. Ken Hollamby, whose enthusiasm for the Society knows no bounds, produced the catalogue of publications. Lynn Godson worked on the first draft of the list of members. Alice Kirke carried out the preliminary arrangement of the Society's archives, a rich resource which has underpinned the historical survey which follows. My wife Carol read the first draft of the text and removed many infelicities. Many others have assisted with their recollections of the Society, among them Sir James Holt, Dr Alison McHardy and Professor David Smith. The Society's President, Professor Michael Jones, has been greatly supportive throughout.

Nicholas Bennett
Nocton, 17 January 2010

ABBREVIATIONS

AASRP	*Associated Architectural Societies Reports and Papers.*
AHT	Alexander Hamilton Thompson
CWF	Charles Wilmer Foster
CYS	Canterbury and York Society
EHR	*English Historical Review*
FMS	Frank Merry Stenton
JWFH	James William Francis Hill
KM	Kathleen Major
LAO	Lincolnshire Archives
LCL	Lincoln Cathedral Library
LHA	*Lincolnshire History and Archaeology*
LNQ	*Lincolnshire Notes and Queries*
LRS	Lincoln Record Society
ODNB	*Oxford Dictionary of National Biography*
Reg. Ant.	C. W. Foster and K. Major (eds), *The Registrum Antiquissimum of the Cathedral Church of Lincoln*, 10 vols with 2 vols of facsimiles (LRS 27–29, 32, 34, 41–2, 46, 51, 62, 67–8, 1931–73)
Some Historians	C. J. Sturman (ed.), *Some Historians of Lincolnshire* (Occasional Papers in Lincolnshire History and Archaeology 9, 1992)
VCH	Victoria County History

ONE

THE ORIGINS OF THE SOCIETY

An eagle-eyed subscriber to the Lincoln Diocesan Magazine, leafing through the new issue for May 1910 over the rectory breakfast table, would have come across a few short paragraphs under the heading 'Proposed Lincolnshire Record Society'. Contributed by Canon C. W. Foster, the note alluded to the ongoing work of arranging the diocesan records, and the resolution of the Diocesan Conference, passed the previous year, 'That this Conference would welcome the formation of a Record Society ... to provide for the printing of unedited documents relating to the Diocese and County of Lincoln.' Those willing to become members of such a society were invited to send in their names.[1]

The Lincoln Diocesan Conference had given formal expression to its concern for the historic records of the see through the establishment in 1906 of a Records Committee, with the Bishop, Edward King, as Chairman and Canon Foster as Secretary. The purpose of the Committee was to endorse the work already begun of 'sorting, repairing, calendaring, indexing' the records and, by appealing for subscriptions, to enable its continuation. Reporting on the work of the Committee in 1907 the Dean of Lincoln, Edward Wickham, urged the need for action: '[These documents] contain the history of the Diocese; of families in the Diocese, and the general history of the county, and they are very important.'[2]

By 1909 it was reported that most of the documents had been arranged but that 'much remains to be done in the way of revision and calendaring and indexing'. Mr W. V. R. Fane had given much assistance with the parish register transcripts, while Revd R. E. G. Cole was contributing valuable work in calendaring. Presenting the report to the Conference in the Cathedral Chapter House on 14 October 1909, Canon Foster noted that

---

1   *Lincoln Diocesan Magazine* 26 (1910), 75.
2   *Report of the Lincoln Diocesan Conference 1907,* 67. It was Dean Wickham who brought Canon Foster's work to the notice of the Conference in 1906 (*Royal Commission on the Public Records 1910–19*, Vol. III Pt 2, para. 7809).

we have now almost got to the point that we might have something ready for the printer, but then the serious question arises who is to take the responsibility of printing … What would probably be the best would be the formation of a kind of Record Society such as they have in other Dioceses to undertake the issue of volumes. The great object of such a society is to get a band of people to subscribe for the volumes as they come out.

The formal proposal, duly laid before the Conference, was not universally welcomed. The Diocesan Magazine reported that the Revd R. E. H. Duke, Rector of Maltby-le-Marsh, 'vehemently opposed the motion on the ground that the past was often best left undisturbed'. He urged that 'Things that are past and gone had better be buried … Is it right for us to rake up all the misfortunes that have been in the lives of our forefathers?' His seems to have been a lone voice, however, and the motion was carried.[3]

Record Publishing in Nineteenth-Century England

What were the roots of this interest in publishing records? On the reverse of Lincoln Cathedral's copy of Magna Carta is written 'Transcribed October 1806'.[4] This endorsement, recording the work of members of the Record Commission first established by Parliament in 1800, led eventually to the publication of a facsimile of the charter in *Statutes of the Realm*. Between 1800 and 1837, six successive Record Commissions pursued the task of making the records of the nation more accessible, particularly through transcription and publication. Some of the resulting volumes, including the *Taxatio Ecclesiastica*, the *Valor Ecclesiasticus* and the Hundred Rolls, are still essential tools for the historian today.[5] The work of the Commissions led in turn to the establishment of the Public Record Office, with its new building constructed in Chancery Lane during the 1850s. Parallel with the opening of its search rooms went the launch of a new programme of publication of texts and calendars, beginning with the State Papers in 1856 and moving on by the end of the century to the great series of chancery rolls.[6]

At the same time as the records of central government were being opened up, interest was growing in records held locally. The Historical Manuscripts Commission was set up in 1869 to report on archives in private hands. The

[3] *Report of the Lincoln Diocesan Conference 1909*, 48–9, 103–5. As a member of the Royal Archaeological Institute, Mr Duke was by no means uninterested in the past: *Archaeological Journal* 66 (1909), xiv.

[4] Sotheby's, *The Magna Carta* (New York, 2007), 58.

[5] For the work of the Record Commissions, see Peter Walne, 'The Record Commissions, 1800–1837', *Journal of the Society of Archivists* 2:1 (1960), 8–16.

[6] John Cantwell, 'The 1838 Public Record Office Act and its aftermath: a new perspective', *Journal of the Society of Archivists* 7 (1984), 277–86.

reports of its inspectors provided guides, lists and calendars of such collections. Another means of making record texts available was through printing clubs. The earliest of these to begin work in England was the Surtees Society, founded in 1834 to print records relating to the north-east. Nationally the Camden Society was launched in 1838. Others followed, some following the lead of the Surtees Society in concentrating on a particular area or region. The Chetham Society, covering Lancashire and Cheshire, was founded in 1843; like the Surtees, it continues to flourish today, unlike the Berkshire Ashmolean Society (1840) or the Lincolnshire Topographical Society (1841), both of which had but a brief existence. Other printing clubs were established to publish specific classes of material: the Hakluyt Society (1846), for works of travel and discovery, survives today, having swallowed up its weaker rivals the Cabot and Columbus Societies. The Parker Society, founded in 1840 to publish works of the English Protestant divines of the sixteenth century, attracted a (still unsurpassed) membership of over seven thousand; it completed its work in 1853, having achieved its purpose of establishing 'a bulwark against Popish Error'.[7]

The 1840s were the golden age of the printing clubs. Thereafter the number of new foundations lessened. The later societies fall into the same two categories: some for particular classes of record, such as the Harleian Society for heraldic visitations (1869), the Pipe Roll Society for records of the medieval Exchequer (1884) and the Selden Society for legal records (1888), and others for specific localities, like the Lancashire and Cheshire Record Society (1878) and William Salt Archaeological Society in Staffordshire (1879). An indefatigable promoter of record societies both nationally and locally was W. P. W. Phillimore, the solicitor, genealogist and publisher, who was behind the establishment in 1888 of the British Record Society for the publication of indexes to series of records including wills and marriage licences. Phillimore argued that every county should have a record society; he was instrumental in the foundation of the Thoroton Society of Nottinghamshire in 1897 and its records series in 1903.[8]

In the wake of the early printing clubs came the foundation of the county archaeological societies. These arose from two enthusiasms of the early Victorian period: the ecclesiological movement, embodied above all in the Cambridge Camden Society of 1839, its roots in ecclesiastical architecture and its membership overwhelmingly Anglican, and the more broadly-based interest in archaeology, exemplified in the foundation of the Archaeological Association in 1843, subsequently divided into the rival factions of the

---

[7] For the printing clubs of the 1830s and 1840s, see Philippa Levine, *The Amateur and the Professional: Antiquarians, Historians and Archaeologists in Victorian England, 1838–1886* (Cambridge, 1986), 40–45.

[8] Kate Tiller, 'William Phillimore Watts Phillimore (formerly Stiff)' in *Oxford Dictionary of National Biography* (Oxford, 2004).

Archaeological Institute and the British Archaeological Association. Thereafter, few counties were without a local society embodying one or both
of these pursuits. The Lincoln and Lincolnshire Architectural Society was
established in 1844. It underwent periodic changes of name, emerging as the
Lincoln Diocesan Architectural Society in 1852. More importantly, in 1850 it
joined the group known as the Associated Architectural Societies, established
'to obtain a larger circulation for their papers and transactions'.[9]

Publishing Local Records in Lincolnshire

In Lincolnshire, interest in printing local records surfaced at the visit of the
Archaeological Institute to Lincoln in 1848. The published papers included
the text of the will and inventory of Richard Ravenser, Archdeacon of
Lincoln (1386), communicated by the Precentor, Richard Pretyman, from
among the muniments of the Dean and Chapter.[10] The first extended piece of
record publication in the county, however, was *Lincolnshire Church Furni-
ture* (1866), an edition of the returns made by Lincolnshire parishes in 1566
listing the 'superstitious' ornaments destroyed since the beginning of Elizabeth's reign. This was the work of Edward Peacock of Bottesford Manor, a
landowner whose strong taste for antiquarian matters was strengthened in
this instance by his reception into the Roman Catholic Church in 1854. The
publication of this work came at a time of sharpening debate about ritu-
alism in the conduct of Anglican worship; it was hailed in *The Ecclesiastic*
as 'important and timely … of equal value to the antiquarian, and to the
Ritualist', while the Catholic *Union Review* described it as 'remarkable and
most acceptable'.[11]

Although this pioneering work of Lincolnshire record publication had
been undertaken by a layman (and a Catholic layman at that), it was not
long before the established Church began to take an interest in the subject.

---

[9]   Levine, *The Amateur and the Professional*, 45–53. For the Lincolnshire society, see Sir
Francis Hill, 'Early days of a Society', *Lincolnshire History and Archaeology* 1 (1966),
57–63.
[10] *Memoirs Illustrative of the History and Antiquities of the County and City of Lincoln*
(London, 1850), 310–327. The actual editing of the documents was done by Albert Way,
Director of the Society of Antiquaries.
[11] *The Ecclesiastic* 28 (1866), 458–63; *The Union Review: A Magazine of Catholic Literature and Art* 4 (1866), 636–40. For Peacock, see Eileen Elder, 'Edward Peacock and his
family: an introduction to the Peacocks, collectors of north Lincolnshire dialect from 1850
to 1920', in *Some Historians*, 70–81. Peacock had discovered this manuscript 'among the
records in the Wills Office, within the Exchequer gate, Lincoln', by 1856, but at first was
only allowed to copy a few pages (see *Notes and Queries*, 2nd Series, 2 (1856), 185).
It was published in a cloth binding, uniform in appearance with the publications of the
Surtees Society, which Peacock had joined in 1857.

Christopher Wordsworth, who became Bishop of Lincoln in 1869, noted the absence of a standard history of the county and at his triennial visitation in 1873 suggested that, since 'the clergy in our county have usually much time at their disposal', they might employ it profitably 'in collecting the historical records of their various parishes'. In 1878 a committee was established to direct this undertaking, and in the following year details of the plan were circulated to the parish clergy with a copy of J. C. Cox's newly published *How to Write the History of a Parish*. Only a small number of incumbents are known to have taken up the Bishop's challenge. One who did so was William Oswald Massingberd, Rector of South Ormsby, who had taken over from his father in 1872 not only as incumbent but also as author of a projected history of the parish.[12]

The earliest published results of Wordsworth's stimulus tended to be based on the materials being uncovered in the national archives in London. In 1870 the Vicar of Boston, G. B. Blenkin, contributed an article on events in his parish in 1621, noting that

> The calendaring of the State Papers, now completed to the year 1638, and the opportunities of search afforded at the new Record Office have rendered the investigation of subjects of local interest comparatively easy and inexpensive.[13]

Not all local historians would have agreed with the word 'inexpensive', however. When Edward Peacock embarked on a study of the Lincolnshire Rising, eventually printed in 1873, he found it necessary to explain

> There is ... an immense mass of most interesting evidence relating to [the Lincolnshire Rising] in Her Majesty's Record Office, and thither I at once betook myself, to see what could be done. The result was, as I feared before I set out; the calenderers, who are hard at work on the reign of Henry VIII, had not got down so far as 1536, and, consequently, the papers I wanted could not be used, except by my spending many weeks in London.[14]

The answer, for those who could afford it, was to employ one of the growing number of record agents, who earned their living carrying out searches and making transcriptions at the British Museum and Public Record Office. When Edmund Venables published an account of Ravendale Priory in 1878,

---

12 Christopher Wordsworth, *Twelve Addresses delivered at his Visitation of the Cathedral and Diocese of Lincoln in the year MDCCCLXXIII* (London, 1873), 246–7; John Beckett, *Writing Local History* (Manchester, 2007), 46–7. For Massingberd, see Dorothy Owen, 'William Oswald Massingberd', in *Some Historians*, 40–44.

13 G. B. Blenkin, 'Notices of Boston in 1621', *AASRP* 10 (1869–70), 223.

14 Edward Peacock, 'Louth in the time of Henry VIII', *AASRP* 12 (1873–74), 26–40.

he included an appendix of documents 'which I have had transcribed from the returns in the Public Record Office'.[15]

Although only a handful of incumbents took up Wordsworth's suggestion to work on their parish histories, his concern for the preservation of historical evidence had a much greater impact on Lincoln Cathedral. In 1872, the Bishop brought Edward White Benson to Lincoln as Chancellor. Benson's principal task was to establish a theological college for the diocese, which he achieved in 1874, but he was also concerned to exercise his responsibility for the cathedral archives. The neglected state of the muniment room at this time was vividly described by Benson's son:

> deal boxes, shelves, pigeon holes, crammed with bundles of papers black with age, shrivelled parchments, deeds with huge beeswax seals attached, the whole thing incredibly filthy and neglected.[16]

Benson invited his old schoolfellow, Joseph Frederic Wickenden, 'an unbeneficed clergyman of retiring habits', to spend time at Lincoln engaged in work on the archives. From 1874 until his death in 1883, Wickenden worked on the cleaning, sorting, labelling and listing of the cathedral records. In 1875 he printed an account of the bequest of jewels to the cathedral by John of Gaunt and five years later he published a survey of the contents of the muniment room. [17]

Among those drawn in by Wickenden's labours to work on the cathedral records was a young Vicar Choral, A. R. Maddison. A member of a long-established Lincolnshire family, Maddison was inspired to investigate the history of the vicars choral and of the cathedral choir; his account of this was published in 1878. He then extended the boundaries of his research to include the records of the bishop as well as those of the chapter. In the diocesan registry, then housed in Exchequer Gate, Maddison found a treasure trove:

---

[15] E. Venables, 'The alien priory of Ravendale', *AASRP* 14 (1877–78), 166–178. Edmund Venables (1819–1895), who was appointed Precentor of Lincoln in 1867, had been a founder of the Cambridge Camden Society; by the 1870s his architectural and ecclesiological interests had widened to include historical records. See W. P. Courtney, rev. Nilanjana Benrji, 'Edmund Venables', *ODNB*.

[16] A. C. Benson, *The Trefoil: Wellington College, Lincoln and Truro* (London, 1923), 88.

[17] J. F. Wickenden, ' "Joyalx" of John of Gaunt, bequeathed to the Cathedral Church of Lincoln', *Archaeological Journal* 32 (1875), 317–25; *idem*, 'Contents of the muniment room of Lincoln Cathedral', *Archaeological Journal* 38 (1881), 309–15. Wickenden's work was later seen to a conclusion by Henry Bradshaw, Librarian of Cambridge University, and Christopher Wordsworth, son of the Bishop, who were engaged in producing their edition of the cathedral statutes. See Dorothy M. Williamson, *The Muniments of the Dean and Chapter of Lincoln* (Lincoln Minster Pamphlets 8, 1956).

Countless volumes of archidiaconal visitations; episcopal visitations; institutions to livings; ordinations; myriads of inventories of goods and effects from the year 1530; terriers; parochial enclosures, and much more …

An article on the memoranda register of Bishop Longland was the first result of this discovery, but Maddison quickly realised that work such as that carried out by Wickenden in the cathedral muniment room would be needed to bring some order to these records. In 1882 he published an account of the parish register transcripts and the work he was doing towards their cleaning, sorting and boxing, concluding with an appeal for help:

But what remains? *A great deal.* When I look at what has been done, and contemplate the mass of material yet untouched, a feeling of despair creeps over me. I can only hope that some one more able than myself will speedily come and join in the good work.[18]

Three years after the publication of this article, Edward King was appointed Bishop of Lincoln. He was concerned about the neglected state of the diocesan records, and as a result he 'spent a considerable sum' in having some of them properly sorted.[19] A key figure in this work was Alfred Gibbons. Born in Lincolnshire (his father was Lord Yarborough's estate agent at Brocklesby), Gibbons had qualified as a solicitor and worked for a time in London. During this time, he had compiled *Gibbons Family Notes* (privately printed in 1884), an extensive collection of references to the name Gibbons including extracts from parish registers and wills from all over England and in particular Lincolnshire. By the end of 1887, he had given up the practice of the law and established himself at 4 Minster Yard in Lincoln where he was evidently working energetically on the Bishop's records. During the following year, with astonishing rapidity, he published *Early Lincoln Wills* (a calendar of the wills found in the medieval episcopal registers), the *Liber Antiquus* of Bishop Hugh of Wells (containing records of the ordination of vicarages in the early thirteenth century) and *Lincoln Marriage Licences* (an abstract of the allegation books from 1598 to 1625). These books were all printed by James Williamson of 290 High Street, Lincoln, and were marketed together as volumes in the 'Lincoln Record Series'. Potential subscribers were encouraged to send in their names to Alfred Gibbons himself. Although early reviews were encouraging ('We must … conclude with the hope that Mr

---

18 Nicholas Bennett, 'A. R. Maddison and the development of local history in Lincolnshire' in *Some Historians*, 27–31; A. R. Maddison, *A Short Account of the Vicars Choral, Poor Clerks, Organists and Choristers of Lincoln Cathedral From the 12th Century to the Accession of Edward 6th* (London, 1878); 'Extracts from Bishop Longland's Register', *AASRP* 15 (1880), 167–79; 'The transcripts in the Bishop of Lincoln's Registry' *AASRP* 16 (1882), 163–6.
19 *Royal Commission on the Public Records 1910–19*, Vol. III Pt 2, para. 7808.

Gibbons will soon give us, in print, some more of the priceless documents to which he has access'), a fourth volume, advertised as a 'Calendar of Bishop Chedworth's Register of Memoranda, 1452–1472', never appeared.[20]

Thus from the 1860s to the 1880s there was a growing awareness in Lincolnshire of the value of archive material in underpinning the writing of local histories. Work based on these records, whether held locally or nationally, had appeared in the *Archaeological Review* and increasingly in the *Reports and Papers* of the Lincoln Diocesan Architectural Society. Then in January 1888 a new publication appeared on the scene. This was Lincolnshire Notes and Queries, edited by E. L. Grange, a Grimsby solicitor and antiquary, and printed by W. K. Morton of Horncastle. In the first number, the editors nailed their colours firmly to the mast:

> In the present age of enquiry and research – when so much is being done to place on record by means of County 'Notes and Queries' the immense store of antiquarian treasure that still remains hidden in documents which are perishing, in monuments that are being 'restored' off the face of the earth, in provincialisms which are gradually being lost by the advance of education – it certainly seems that some endeavour should be made in Lincolnshire to preserve these memorials of the past by means of a [similar] publication.[21]

By the time the second number was issued in April 1888, nearly 400 subscribers had signed up for the new journal. Many were clergy and gentry and some lived well beyond the county boundaries (including two in the United States). Contributors included Gibbons, Peacock, Venables and Maddison. From the outset, a particular emphasis was placed on record publication. Among the potential contributions that would be welcomed, the editors suggested

> Extracts from Diocesan and County Records, Parochial Registers, Church-wardens' Accounts, Manorial Rolls and similar documents.

They did not ask in vain. The first four numbers included instalments of a handlist of manorial court rolls contributed by Alfred Gibbons, extracts from

---

[20] Alfred William Gibbons: born 16 April 1853 at Brocklesby; articled clerk at Grimsby; moved to Norwood (Surrey) where he married (1877) Elise Ligear Weightman; working at 68 Lincoln's Inn Fields, 1883; resident in Lincoln c.1887–93; living in York (Heworth Green) from c.1895. See A. W. Gibbons, *Gibbons Family Notes: A Collection of Memoranda relating to the Gibbons Families* (Westminster, 1884), 72–3; Census Returns, 1871; *Notes and Queries,* 6th Series, 8 (1883), 389; Census Returns, 1891, 1901; Alfred Gibbons, *Early Lincoln Wills: An Abstract of all the Wills and Administrations Recorded in the Episcopal Registers of the Old Diocese of Lincoln* (Lincoln, 1888); *Liber Antiquus de Ordinationibus Vicariarum tempore Hugonis Wells, Lincolniensis Episcopi* (Lincoln, 1888); *Lincoln Marriage Licences: An Abstract of the Allegation Books between 1598 and 1625* (Lincoln, 1888); *LNQ* 1 (1888–89), 94–6; *LNQ* 1, Part 2 (April 1888), iii.
[21] 'Editorial Notice', *LNQ* 1, Part 1 (January 1888), iii-iv.

the estate book of Sir Thomas Cony of Bassingthorpe transcribed by Edward Peacock, and (from the same author) a few extracts from the Louth church-wardens' accounts accompanied by the editorial comment that 'suggestions have been made from more sources than one that these ... Accounts should form one of the early volumes of the proposed Lincolnshire Record Society'.[22]

The Lincolnshire Record Society

With the successful launch of *Lincolnshire Notes and Queries* and the appearance of Gibbons' 'Lincoln Record Series', the time must have appeared ripe for the establishment of a local record publishing body. Similar societies were springing up in other counties: the Oxford Historical Society began publishing in 1885, the Somerset Record Society in 1887 and the Worcestershire Record Society was to appear in 1893. The two prime movers behind the proposed Lincolnshire society were Hudson, the joint editor of *Lincolnshire Notes and Queries*, and Gibbons himself. They secured the patronage of an unexpected supporter, the Dean of Lincoln. Well known as the founder of an Anglican sisterhood, the Community of St Mary the Virgin at Wantage, William John Butler was a prominent high churchman who was busily engaged as Dean in restoring something of the beauty of holiness to the cathedral worship. Although he was an early subscriber to *Lincolnshire Notes and Queries* and would, no doubt, have come across Gibbons as a near neighbour in Minster Yard, he is not known previously to have had any strong interest in local history and records. The clue to his involvement in the projected records society may lie in his friendship with Maddison, a close ally of the Dean and one on whose support he relied in cathedral business.[23]

The brief history of the new society may be followed through the regular advertisements it placed in *Lincolnshire Notes and Queries*. An inaugural meeting was held at the Deanery in Lincoln on 4 January 1889, at which 'it was unanimously resolved that a *Lincolnshire Record Society* should be established'. It was announced that the names of about sixty potential subscribers had been received but that more were needed, since 'the support of 300 members *at least* will be required to place the Society on a permanent basis'. The annual subscription was fixed at 10s 6d, a sum 'resolved on as most likely to meet the views of all classes interested in the matter'. The Dean was appointed Provisional Chairman, and Hudson and Gibbons were chosen as Provisional Honorary Secretaries. A report of the meeting was placed in *Lincolnshire Notes and Queries* in April 1889, inviting the interest

---

[22] *LNQ* 1, Parts 1–4 (1888), esp. 104. The lists of subscribers and advertisements, both for local publications and for the Lincolnshire Record Society, were printed among the preliminary material and are consequently often missing from bound sets.
[23] A. J. Butler, *Life and Letters of William John Butler* (London, 1898), 318, 346–7.

of new subscribers and setting out a long list of potential subjects for future volumes: a calendar of wills and administrations, the civic and borough records of the county, episcopal and archidiaconal visitations, bishops' registers, the charters of bishop and chapter, monastic cartularies, inquisitions post mortem, feet of fines, heraldic visitations, marriage bonds, parish registers and churchwardens' accounts.[24]

Three months later in July, a further notice announced that 'The Council propose to commence operations by printing a General Account of Lincolnshire Records and the Chronicle of Louth Park Abbey'. It is not clear who was to be responsible for the first of these two works, although it may have been the London record agent W. K. Boyd, since it appears from a subsequent advertisement that the 'Lincolnshire Records' involved were to be principally those in the Public Record Office and British Museum. Boyd had recently been publicising his own project ('preparing for early publication') under the title *A Series of Records in English, Illustrative of the History of Lincolnshire Anterior to A.D. 1400,* of which Volume I, *Selections from Lincoln Assize Roll, A.D. 1218–1219,* was said to be in the press. It would have made sense to bring this possible rival into the fold by offering him the first volume in the new society's series.[25]

In the event, when another advertisement appeared in January 1890, the *General Account* had been relegated to second place on the list of forthcoming publications: 'The Council are now prepared to print, as the first volume, *The Chronicle of Louth Park Abbey,* a fifteenth century MS., edited by the Rev. Precentor Venables. Considerable progress has been made with the MS. of the volume containing a *General Account of Lincolnshire Records.*' Original members were reminded that their subscriptions were now due. Three months later, the General Account had disappeared altogether, being replaced as the proposed second volume by Canon Harvey's *Abstracts from the Bishops' Rolls of the Thirteenth Century.*[26] Meanwhile the Louth Park volume was said to be 'in the press'. Thereafter, the Society's periodical announcements remained unchanged until two years later, in April 1892, *The Chronicle of Louth Park Abbey,* edited by Venables with a translation by Maddison, was advertised.[27]

---

[24] *LNQ* 1, Part 6 (April 1889), back cover.
[25] *LNQ* 1, Part 7 (July 1889), back cover. William Keown Boyd: son of William Keown of Ballydugan House, co. Down, who assumed the surname Boyd in 1873 under the will of his great-uncle; born 1854; educated Rossall School and Trinity College, Dublin; served in 5th Battalion, Royal Irish Rifles; studied law and became a record agent in London; died 1938 (Burke, *Landed Gentry*, 6th edn (London, 1879), 900; Walter Rye, *Records and Record Searching*, 2nd edn (London, 1897), 124; *The Times*, 12 February 1938).
[26] George Tyson Harvey: born 1837; educated Christ's College, Cambridge; Priest Vicar of Lincoln Cathedral, 1865–93; Canon of Lincoln, 1889–1907; Rector of Navenby, 1893–1907; died 1907 (J. Peile, *Biographical Register of Christ's College 1505–1905*, Vol. II (Cambridge, 1913), 544–5).
[27] *LNQ* 2–3 (1890–93), *passim.*

This volume, which in reality had been published the previous year, proclaims on the reverse of the title-page 'The Publications of The Lincolnshire Record Society. Vol. I. For the Year 1889.' It comprised an edition of the Chronicle of this Cistercian house from a manuscript in the possession of William Allison of Louth, the only copy known to exist. Printed by W. K. Morton of Horncastle, it included an introductory account of the history of the abbey with architectural notes contributed by W. H. St John Hope. One enthusiastic reviewer welcomed the publication with the hope, 'If [the Society's] future volumes be as well selected and as carefully edited as the one before us, we may safely promise it a long career of usefulness.'[28] Sadly, this book remains as the only tangible result of the work of the Society. No further notices of its activities or future plans were placed in *Lincolnshire Notes and Queries*. There were, no doubt, several reasons for the Society's demise. The delay of nearly three years in bringing out the first volume would not have encouraged the new subscribers on which its future was known to depend; there may have been difficulties in extracting subscriptions from existing members. Of the two Secretaries, Hudson's time was taken up with editing *Lincolnshire Notes and Queries*, while Gibbons was increasingly seeking work further afield. He had already in 1888 produced a volume in the series of Calendars of York Wills issued by the Yorkshire Archaeological Society and another followed in 1893. In addition, he was preoccupied with his monumental guide to *Ely Episcopal Records*, which appeared in 1891. By 1895, when he was appointed editor of the *Northern Genealogist*, he had left Minster Yard and moved to York.[29]

Despite the failure of the Lincolnshire Record Society, editions of Lincolnshire material continued to appear independently. They included volumes which might well have been issued by the Society, had it survived. The edition by G. S. Stephenson, a local doctor, of the parish registers of Grimsby (1889) marked the first appearance in print of any complete Lincolnshire registers. It was swiftly followed by volumes of registers for Irby on Humber (1890), Horncastle (1892–1912), Holbeach (1892), Horbling (1895), Haydor (1897), Doddington (1898) and Coleby (1903). Some of these were issued by the Parish Register Society; others were printed privately for subscribers.[30] Other

---

[28] E. Venables (ed.), with a translation by A. R. Maddison, *Chronicon Abbatie de Parco Lude* (Lincolnshire Record Society 1, 1891); *Notes and Queries* 8th Series 1 (1892), 285.

[29] Alfred Gibbons (ed.), *The Northern Genealogist*, 6 vols (York, 1895–1903). This publication, printed by John Sampson of 13 Coney Street, York, was more diverse in its content than the title might imply. In addition to material relating to Yorkshire and Durham, it included a Grimsby burgess roll, Ely marriage allegations and the Kingerby parish register transcripts, all resulting from work that Gibbons had done elsewhere.

[30] G. S. Stephenson (ed.), *The Register Book of the Parish Church of Saint James, Great Grimsby* (Grimsby, 1889); F. A. Crisp (ed.), *The Parish Register of Irby-upon-Humber* (London, 1890); J. Clare Hudson (ed.), *The First (-Fifth) Register Book of the Parish Church of Saint Mary, Horncastle* (5 vols, Horncastle, 1892–1912); G. W. Macdonald (ed.),

genealogical sources were not neglected. Gibbons himself began in 1890 to issue in instalments his *Notes on the Visitation of 1634*, including, besides extensive annotations on the history of the families, a calendar of Dean and Chapter wills from 1534 to 1780. Only sixty subscribers put their names down for the first part, which consisted of twenty pages only. A warm review in *Lincolnshire Notes and Queries* ('we only trust that his subscribers will soon be counted in hundreds') helped to spread the word and subsequent parts were considerably larger. Others assisted with contributions on particular families: Mrs Tempest on Lister of Coleby and Scrope of Cockerington, J. K. Floyer on Ayscough of Fulstow, A. R. Maddison on Totheby of Totheby and Moigne and W. O. Massingberd on Skipwith. The work was eventually completed in 1898.[31]

Maddison was also working on genealogical sources, and in April 1888 he offered to subscribers, at a price of 21 shillings, a volume of *Lincolnshire Wills: First Series, A.D. 1500–1600*. Printed by James Williamson of Lincoln, the book included abstracts of selected wills of members of some of the county families of the sixteenth century. In excusing the use of abstracts, the editor pointed out that

> the Wills in the Lincoln Registry run up to tens of thousands, and the costliness of doing the work of such a Society as the Surtees is quite beyond the means of a single individual.

A second series of abstracts, for the years 1600 to 1617, appeared in 1891 (the considerably shorter period covered being the result of much fuller abstracts). It was Maddison's intention to go on to produce a third series, but in the event he undertook a much larger project. This was the revision and expansion for publication of the collection of pedigrees of Lincolnshire families originally compiled earlier in the nineteenth century by A. S. Larken, Richmond Herald and the brother-in-law of the sixth Lord Monson. Maddison's edition of these materials was issued in four volumes by the Harleian Society between 1902 and 1906. The completed work owes much to Maddison's tireless labours on the wills and parish register transcripts in Exchequer Gate.[32]

The Holbeach Parish Register (Lincoln, 1892); Henry Peet (ed.), *The Baptismal, Marriage and Burial Registers of the Parish of Horbling* (Liverpool, 1895); *The Register of Haydor* (Parish Register Society, 1897); R. E. G. Cole (ed.), *The Registers of Doddington-Pigot* (Parish Register Society, 1898); E. B. Tempest and W. F. D. Curtoys (eds), *The Registers of Coleby* (London, 1903).

[31] Alfred Gibbons, *Notes on the Visitation of Lincolnshire, 1634* (Lincoln, 1898); *LNQ* 2 (1890–91), 63–4.

[32] A. R. Maddison (ed.), *Lincolnshire Wills, First Series A.D.1500–1600 (Second Series 1600–1617)*, 2 parts (Lincoln, 1888, 1891); *Lincolnshire Pedigrees*, 4 vols (Harleian Society 50–52, 55, 1902–06).

The publication of civic and borough records, another element in the Lincolnshire Record Society's 1889 prospectus, was by no means neglected. R. W. Goulding brought out in 1891 a selection of *Louth Corporation Records*, which was printed in Louth by the family firm of J. W. Goulding. It included extracts from the records of the Warden and Assistants and of King Edward VI School. Gibbons produced a report on the records of the Borough of Grimsby for the Historical Manuscripts Commission (1895), including a calendar of royal charters and letters, court rolls and books, chamberlains' accounts and leases. For Lincoln, W. de Gray Birch published an edition of *Royal Charters and Grants* (1906).[33]

Perhaps the most energetic of those engaged in printing the historical records of the county during the last decade of the nineteenth century and the first decade of the twentieth was W. O. Massingberd. In 1893 he published his monumental *History of the Parish of Ormsby-cum-Ketsby*. The painstaking industry that went into this history was noted with satisfaction by a reviewer:

> Mr Massingberd has given to the world what, so far as Lincolnshire is concerned, is unique, viz., a complete History of his Parish compiled from *original sources* … Since the throwing open to the public of treasures, which in old days were jealously guarded, facilities have existed for diving into the past which former generations in vain sighed for. The student has now but little difficulty in finding what he wants in the Record Office, as yet a mine of almost unexplored wealth, while in Somerset House an order for the Literary Enquiry Department gives him access to wills, without any cost, which not many years since were stowed away in Doctors' Commons, and only grudgingly submitted to the inspection of genealogists, who were allowed to note down a few particulars in return for the payment of a shilling.[34]

In his Preface, Massingberd noted that he had based his work on, *inter alia*, charters, court rolls, deeds, accounts and letters at Ormsby, feet of fines, assize rolls, inquisitions and chancery rolls at the Public Record Office, the diocesan records at Lincoln, charters, deeds and other manuscripts at Gunby Hall and in the British Museum, parish registers at Ormsby and other places, and wills at Somerset House. He expressed his thanks to Maddison and to William Boyd for help with documents. The completion of such a lengthy project evidently stimulated him to further work on records and he

---

33 R. W. Goulding, *Louth Old Corporation Records* (Louth, 1891); Alfred Gibbons, 'The Records of the Corporation of Great Grimsby' in *The Manuscripts of Lincoln, Bury St Edmund's, and Great Grimsby Corporations, etc.* (Historical Manuscripts Commission 14th Report, Appendix, Pt 8), 237–91; W. de Gray Birch, *Catalogue of the Royal Charters and other Documents belonging to the Corporation of Lincoln* (Lincoln, 1906).

34 W. O. Massingberd, *History of the Parish of Ormsby-cum-Ketsby* (Lincoln, 1893); review in *LNQ* 3 (1892–93), 222–3.

proceeded to publish in the two local historical journals a thirteenth-century survey of the manor of Stow, a series of early Lincolnshire inquisitions post mortem, a roll of the wapentake of Yarburgh, an account of the charters of Lincoln Cathedral and a survey of the barony of Bayeux in 1288. In 1902 he published *Court Rolls of the Manor of Ingoldmells*, a pioneering work which is still the only printed edition of medieval court rolls of a Lincolnshire manor. Reviewing the book, F. W. Maitland wrote that it

> deserves perusal by all who are studying the rural economy of medieval England. In the first place we must always be grateful to those who will give us the substance of legal records that are in private hands, so great is the danger of their remaining unknown and even of their perishing. In the second place Mr Massingberd is right in thinking that the rolls of Ingold-mells have some special claims upon our attention. The manor lay in the extreme east of England, its lord was not a religious corporation … What Mr Massingberd gives us is enough to show that from such manors we yet have much to learn.[35]

The other edition by Massingberd to appear as a separate volume was his *Abstracts of Final Concords temp. Richard I, John and Henry III*, privately printed in London in 1896. This, described in the Preface as 'the first volume of Lincolnshire Records preserved at the Public Record Office ever printed', was a joint work produced by Massingberd (who contributed the Introduction and Index) and William Boyd (who contributed the abstracts). Although it was described as 'Volume I', the second volume was not forthcoming until the project was revived by Canon Foster in 1920. Like the Ingoldmells Court Rolls, this volume was reviewed in the *English Historical Review*, this time by the forthright J. H. Round who gave it but modest praise:

> The county record societies founded of recent years represent a phase of the growing movement in favour of the documentary method in local as in general history. Hampered, as a rule, by narrow means, they have succeeded, nevertheless, in accomplishing some valuable work … It is always a matter of some difficulty to know by what standard one should judge the work of amateurs. The gratitude that is rightly due to those who voluntarily undertake an arduous and valuable work makes one loth to insist on the highest standard of exactitude; yet it must be observed that the 'forinsec service' which occurs so regularly in these records, and is so difficult to define, is not happily termed 'foreign service', nor rightly explained in the brief introduction.[36]

---

[35] W. O. Massingberd, *Court Rolls of the Manor of Ingoldmells* (London, 1902); F. W. Maitland, review in *English Historical Review* 18 (1903), 780–2.

[36] W. O. Massingberd and W. K. Boyd, *Lincolnshire Records: Abstracts of Final Concords temp. Richard I, John and Henry III* (London, 1896); J. H. Round, review in *EHR* 12 (1897), 549–50.

During these years, W. K. Boyd himself was contributing to *Lincolnshire Notes and Queries* some of the fruits of his work among the public records, and Lincolnshire historians were treated to further series of final concords and inquisitions post mortem, as well as extracts from assize rolls and a calendar of Exchequer lay subsidies. Despite the failure of the Lincolnshire Record Society, then, these years of record publishing demonstrated that the underlying interest in historical sources was still there. In 1905 Maddison and Massingberd, as editors of *Lincolnshire Notes and Queries*, wrote:

> More and more people are learning the value of original records. Never, perhaps, at any rate in the same time, have so many been published for this county as in the last 20 years, and Lincolnshire Notes and Queries, through the kindness of contributors, has done its fair share in the work. The process must be slow so long as there is no Record Society, but the Editors hope that in the future, as in the past, their endeavours will be assisted by willing hands.[37]

This, then, was the background that led to the formation in 1906 of the Diocesan Records Committee, whose deliberations in turn led to the proposal for the formation of a Record Society announced in May 1910. It was hoped to secure a minimum of 120 names, subscribing a guinea each. The announcement was followed up by a circular, and in September of the same year a second notice was placed in the magazine, reporting that the response had been 'fairly encouraging'. On 8 October, Canon Foster issued a circular to all those who had promised to join, indicating that a meeting to discuss the formation of the Society would be held, by consent of the Bishop, Edward Lee Hicks, at the Old Palace on 19 October at 5.15 p.m., and that 'The Bishop has kindly offered to provide tea.'[38]

---

[37] 'Preface', *LNQ* 8 (1904–05), iii.
[38] LRS Archive, printed circulars: 'Proposed Lincoln Record Society'.

TWO

CHARLES WILMER FOSTER AND
THE FOUNDATION OF THE SOCIETY

The proposed meeting took place on 19 October 1910 at the Bishop's Palace in Lincoln, the Bishop himself taking the chair. Among the other prospective members who attended were the Bishop of Grantham (Welbore MacCarthy), the Dean of Lincoln (T. C. Fry), the Archdeacon of Stow (John Bond), Chancellor Crowfoot, nine canons of Lincoln, M. H. Footman (Chapter Clerk) and A. E. T. Jourdain (Diocesan Registrar). Apologies were received from, among others, the Bishop of Salisbury (John Wordsworth), Lord Heneage, Sir Hickman Bacon, Lady Elizabeth Cust and Mrs Tempest. Canon Foster explained the background to the meeting, the resolution of the Diocesan Conference and the subsequent announcement, as a result of which he had received 133 promises of membership. The motion was then proposed by the Archdeacon of Stow, seconded by the Dean of Lincoln and carried unanimously, 'That it is desirable to found a Record Society to provide for the printing of inedited documents relating to the Diocese and County of Lincoln and that the name of the Society be "The Lincoln Record Society".' It was further resolved that the annual subscription be one guinea. The Bishop was elected Chairman and a Council appointed, to hold office until the first annual meeting in October 1911. Canon Foster was elected Editor, Canon Bell Secretary and Mr G. L. Simpson Treasurer. It was also resolved that the Lincolnshire Church Notes of the seventeenth-century antiquary Gervase Holles should form one of the earliest volumes.[1]

What were the prospects for the fledgling Lincoln Record Society in 1910? The history of the 'Lincolnshire Record Society' in the 1890s was not encouraging, and would have served as a reminder that record publishing societies could fail. Local printing clubs, lacking the social attractions of their architectural and archaeological counterparts, were more likely to struggle for survival. The Hampshire Record Society, whose creation in 1889 had been heralded in *Lincolnshire Notes and Queries*, ceased to publish after 1897. And, while it was true that some of the older-established societies – the

---

[1]   LRS Minute Book I, 2–4.

Surtees and the Chetham – continued to flourish, some of the more recent foundations tended to shelter as a branch or section under the wing of a more broadly-based – and 'sociable' – county society such as the Yorkshire Archaeological or Thoroton Societies.

From a wider perspective, too, 1910 was perhaps not the best of years to be embarking on such a venture. Locally, the Diocese of Lincoln suffered the loss of its much-loved Bishop, the saintly Edward King, who as Chairman of the Records Committee had done much to support Canon Foster's work. Later in the year, Lincoln Cathedral mourned the death of its Dean, E. C. Wickham, whose forthright advocacy of the work of the Committee has already been noted. Out in the diocese, that stalwart pioneer of the publication of local records, W. O. Massingberd, died on 11 September at his rectory in South Ormsby.[2] All three of these men would have championed the new society and encouraged others to become members.

Nationally, too, it was a time of pressing concern. There were two general elections during the year, as the country found itself gripped by a constitutional crisis arising from the rejection by the House of Lords of Lloyd George's budget in November 1909. The international situation was deteriorating, the Irish were demanding Home Rule, the suffragettes were becoming increasingly strident and in the middle of it all, on 6 May, the King, Edward VII, died. All in all, it would not appear to have been a good time to attempt to persuade people of the importance of printing historical records.

Charles Wilmer Foster

This difficult background serves to highlight the importance of the contribution made by Canon Foster in the founding of the new Society. It is improbable that, without him, it would have been started at all. Professor Stenton said of him, 'Few men have surpassed him in imperturbable consistency of will', and added:

> it was the industry and practical ability of Canon Foster which first made possible the establishment of a permanent and organised society for the publication of such documents.[3]

The conclusion is inescapable that it was Canon Foster's enthusiasm and quiet but unshakeable persistence that ensured the successful foundation of the Lincoln Record Society.

---

[2]   A. R. Maddison, 'William Oswald Massingberd', *Lincoln Diocesan Magazine* 26 (1910), 159–60; Owen, 'William Oswald Massingberd' in *Some Historians*, 43.
[3]   F. M. Stenton, 'Charles Wilmer Foster' in *Reg. Ant. IV*, xi–xvi.

Charles Wilmer Foster was born on 3 June 1866 at the Parsonage House in Dalton Parva, a village just outside Rotherham.[4] His father, Charles William Foster, had been instituted to the Perpetual Curacy of Dalton in 1856; he was himself a son of the parsonage, having been born at the neighbouring village of Wickersley where his own father, John Foster, had served as Rector for sixty years. Although Canon Foster was thus a Yorkshireman by birth and the son of a Yorkshireman, the Fosters were by origin a Lincolnshire family whose forebears could be traced at Dowsby near Bourne back to the sixteenth century. The earliest recorded clergyman in the family was Thomas Foster (1672–1719), Warden of Browne's Hospital in Stamford; another Thomas (Canon Foster's great-grandfather) was Rector of Careby from 1789 to 1825.[5]

His mother, Isabella, was the daughter of Francis Wilmer Watkins, a Civil Surgeon in the service of the East India Company. There was a strong clerical influence on this side of the family as well: two of her uncles, her grandfather and great-grandfather were all clergymen. Isabella was born at Poona on 30 May 1838 and, like so many British children born in India, was sent home for her education. Her mother, who had come back with her, died in 1849 at the age of 34; her father died in Bombay in 1853, aged 43. Isabella was therefore brought up by other members of her family, among them her uncle, Revd Frederick Watkins, who as an Inspector of Schools for Yorkshire, Nottinghamshire and part of Lincolnshire resided at Thrybergh, not much more than a mile from Dalton.[6] The marriage of Charles William Foster and Isabella Watkins took place at Thrybergh on 21 June 1864. Charles Wilmer was their first child; he was followed by a daughter, Margaret Charlotte, born on 22 July 1867. Another daughter, Mary, was born on 29 November 1869.[7]

The young Wilmer's education appears to have been dogged by persistent ill-health.[8] He attended Aysgarth Preparatory School in Wensleydale and went in 1880 to Rossall School in Lancashire, but his stay there lasted one term only. Afterwards, he was educated at Sheffield Collegiate School whence he gained a place at St John's College, Oxford, matriculating on 16 October 1884. Here, too, his work was affected by illness and he read for a pass degree, graduating BA in 1887 and MA in 1891.[9] It is likely, too, that his

4 'June 3, the wife of Rev. C. W. FOSTER, Dalton Parsonage; a son' (*Guardian*, 6 June 1866).
5 'Foster of Dowsby' in A. R. Maddison, *Lincolnshire Pedigrees* (Harleian Society, 1902–06), 1226–1230. For Canon Foster's father, see Peile, *Biographical Register of Christ's College*, 493.
6 She was staying with her uncle at Thrybergh at the time of the 1861 Census.
7 Information about the family can be found in C. W. Foster and J. J. Green, *History of the Wilmer Family* (privately printed, Leeds, 1888), 316–328.
8 His family appears always to have used his middle name.
9 L. R. Furneaux (ed.), *Rossall School Register 1844–1923* (Godalming, 1923); Joseph Foster, *Oxford Men 1880–1892* (Oxford, 1893). Doris Stenton recalled that 'He went up to St John's College, Oxford, with an income suitable to his station and a modest cellar

university career was affected by the death of his father on 23 May 1886; he remembered him as a man 'chiefly remarkable for his trustworthiness and justice'. His mother and sisters had to leave Dalton Parsonage, moving to Grosvenor Terrace in York.[10]

There does not appear to have been any question but that he would follow his father, grandfather and great-grandfather into the Church.[11] It may be that at this point, no longer having his father to advise him, he turned to his uncle, Revd John Watkins. Vicar of Gamlingay in Cambridgeshire, Watkins had served his curacy at Leeds Parish Church under James Russell Woodford, later Bishop of Ely. There is evidence that Wilmer spent some time with his uncle, learning at first hand the daily routine of a busy parish priest. He was not too preoccupied, however, to neglect the history of his mother's family, on which he had been working for the past few years; a notice of this forth-coming work in the *Archaeological Journal* invited subscribers to send in their names to C. Wilmer Foster, Gamlingay Vicarage.[12]

It may also have been John Watkins who suggested the next step for the prospective clergyman; at any rate, Wilmer enrolled in 1888 in the Leeds Clergy School. This School had been established in 1876 by the Vicar of Leeds, John Gott, but it drew its inspiration from the work of his predecessor, Woodford, and would have been well-known to Watkins.[13] On Trinity Sunday 1889 in Worcester Cathedral, Charles was ordained deacon by the Bishop of Worcester and was licensed to serve as curate of St Michael's Coventry (later to become Coventry Cathedral). He was ordained priest on St Matthew's Day, 21 September 1890.[14]

It was at this point in his career that a second curacy brought him to the Diocese of Lincoln, to the church of St Andrew in Grimsby. Built in the Early English style between 1867 and 1870, the church was given a district parish in 1871. The incumbent in 1890, Revd Richard Meddings, was in charge of a busy team. One curate, Revd John Evans, had charge of St Luke's Mission Church in Wellington Street. There was also a new church, dedicated to St John the Divine and built, with money given by Revd Beauchamp St John Tyrwhitt, as a chapel of ease to St Andrew's. It was used as the church of St Andrew's Waterside Church Mission, in the charge of two 'chaplain-curates', Revd Byrom Holland and Revd Arthur Nunn-Rivers, who spent much of their

---

provided by his father so that "he could offer a friend a bottle of wine for luncheon or dinner".' (Doris M. Stenton, 'Canon C. W. Foster of Timberland, Lincolnshire, 1866–1935', *Amateur Historian* 6 (1963–65), 157).

[10] Peile, *Biographical Register*, 493; Census Returns, 1891.

[11] 'His destiny as a parish priest was decided for him by his family history and it never occurred to him to challenge it': Stenton, 'Canon C. W. Foster of Timberland', 157.

[12] *Archaeological Journal* 44 (1887), 213. For John Watkins, see J. and J. A. Venn, *Alumni Cantabrigienses* (2 parts in 10 vols, Cambridge, 1922–54), Part II, Vol. 6, 365.

[13] Alan Haig, *The Victorian Clergy* (Beckenham, 1984), 86–87.

[14] *The Guardian*, 19 June 1889; 24 September 1890.

time ministering to the men of the Grimsby fishing fleet. Charles Wilmer Foster thus became the fourth curate in the team, moving into 'St Andrew's House' in Strand Street with two of his fellow curates, Holland and Nunn-Rivers.[15]

On 5 September 1893 Wilmer was licensed to the curacy of Navenby where the Rector, John Hays, was in ill health. In the event, Hays died on 3 October and Wilmer remained in the parish only to cover the short period of vacancy. The new Rector, George Tyson Harvey, was instituted on 28 December and on 10 February 1894 Wilmer moved to a curacy at Epworth.[16] Here he came under the wing of Canon John Henry Overton, a church historian of some distinction and one of the few of his time who wrote about the eighteenth-century Anglican Church from a sympathetic viewpoint. In 1878 he had published, with C. J. Abbey, *The English Church in the Eighteenth Century*, which became a standard work on the period. He also produced biographies of John Wesley, John Hannah and William Law, as well as a life of Bishop Christopher Wordsworth. There is no doubt that Wilmer's own development as an historian benefitted greatly from close association with his new Rector.[17]

Overton resigned the living of Epworth in 1898, whereupon Wilmer moved back to St Andrew's, Grimsby. Finally, on 7 March 1902, he was instituted to the vicarage of Timberland, a parish situated on the western edge of the Witham fens, midway between Lincoln and Sleaford. This became his home for the rest of his life. It was not long before he began to fill key administrative positions in the diocese. He was Secretary of the Diocesan Board of Education from 1904 until 1910, helping to guide the church schools through a time of reorganisation occasioned by the Education Act of 1902. In 1908 he became the first Secretary of the Lincoln Diocesan Trust and Board of Finance, a position he continued to fill until 1926. His work in these roles was characterised by that spirit of persistent inquiry which he brought to his historical work. Reporting to the Diocesan Conference in 1910 on the work of the Diocesan Trust and Board of Finance, he urged those who had responsibility for small parochial trusts to vest their property in the hands of the Diocese, to avoid misadventure:

The property of the premises of the Burgh Missionary College was vested in two private trustees to begin with, and the last surviving trustee died and it was found that by his will he had left everything he possessed in the world to a certain lady. It was necessary to find this lady and she had

---

15 Census Returns, 1891; White's *History, Gazetteer and Directory of Lincolnshire*, 5th edn (Sheffield, 1892), 401–2, 418.

16 *Lincoln Diocesan Calendar 1894*, 115; *Lincoln Diocesan Calendar 1895*, 117.

17 Stenton, 'Canon C. W. Foster of Timberland', 157. For Overton, see B. W. Young, 'John Henry Overton' in *ODNB*.

entirely disappeared. I employed a detective to try and find her, but the detective did not succeed, and I remained at a standstill until I saw a bill for the Wesleyan Harvest Thanksgiving in my village and the name of the preacher was the same as the name of this lady. She had changed her name by that time. I am glad to say I found her very accommodating indeed, and she agreed to execute a deed vesting the property in the Diocesan Trust.[18]

His work for the diocese was recognised by Bishop King who conferred on him in 1908 a canonry and prebend in Lincoln Cathedral.[19]

By the time he moved to Timberland Vicarage, his mother and sisters were also settled in south Lincolnshire. Margaret had married in 1896 George Ingoldby, a Spalding man who followed in his father's footsteps by becoming a bank manager; in 1901 they were living in Sleaford. Meanwhile his mother and younger sister Mary had taken up residence in Dowsby, the village where their Foster ancestors had lived, a circumstance which no doubt pleased Wilmer greatly. In 1902 his younger sister Mary was married to Edmund Gilchrist Wilson, a London solicitor; they went to live in Hampstead. Six nieces (two from Margaret and four from Mary) arrived in due course. Wilmer himself remained a bachelor until 1911, when he married Annie Constance Wimbush at Brandsby Church in North Yorkshire.[20]

The Early Historical Work of C. W. Foster

Throughout this period, at Oxford, Leeds, Coventry, Grimsby, Epworth and Timberland, his involvement in historical research was growing. As early as 1884 he was pursuing inquiries into the Forsters of Aldermaston, a branch of the Wilmer family. His monumental *History of the Wilmer Family* was printed privately for subscribers in 1888. The work was written jointly with Joseph Green who contributed the sections on the Quaker branches of the family, but Wilmer was responsible not only for writing the bulk of the chapters but also for compiling the index and seeing the book through the press. It represents a considerable achievement for a twenty-two year old, not only in the extent of the research he carried out in parishes and diocesan registries across the country but also in the confident way he wrote up and arranged his material, scrupulously referencing his sources.

The history of his Foster ancestors in Lincolnshire was another project of great interest to Wilmer and this was no doubt one of the reasons why he

---

[18] *Report of the Lincoln Diocesan Conference 1910*, 54.

[19] His prebend of Leicester St Margaret was, appropriately, that once held by Robert Grosseteste.

[20] Census Returns, 1901 and 1911; *The Times*, 18 November 1911. Dean Fry officiated at the wedding.

put down his name as one of the earliest subscribers to *Lincolnshire Notes and Queries* in January 1888.[21] It also occasioned his first contributions to that journal, as he inquired about the first marriage of Augustine Earle of Stragglethorpe and the marriage of William Foster of Bourne in 1733.[22] By this time, however, his historical interests had undergone a decisive transformation. The history of families continued to be of interest, but he now became increasingly absorbed in the history of the Church. His association at Epworth with Canon Overton provided a strong stimulus for this and it was given a particular focus when he was recruited to the cause of the Church Defence Institution. Founded in 1859–60 to counter the (primarily noncon-formist) pressure for disestablishment, the Institution worked through local associations to publish pamphlets and provide lectures in support of the cause. The Lincoln Diocesan Secretary for Church Defence was James Goulton Constable of Walcot in the parish of Alkborough, a squire with strong ecclesiastical and antiquarian interests. He reported in 1896 that

> much has been done in the way of lectures … Rev. W. E. Varah of Scunthorpe, Rev. C. W. Foster of Epworth and Rev. G. S. Lee of Cleethorpes … have all done good work lecturing.[23]

It was noted that during the previous year more than 1,300 lectures, 'of which a large number were illustrated with limelight dissolving views', had been given in England and Wales under the auspices of the Institution. A series of three lectures which Wilmer gave in the Market Hall at Crowle in November 1895 elicited a published response from a member of the local Roman Catholic community. The content of Wilmer's lectures is not known but they appear to have emphasised ('aided by splendid magic lantern views') the continuity between the medieval Church and the post-Reformation Church in England. This claim was contested in two further lectures given in the Market Hall by Revd W. M. Smith, a Premonstratensian Canon of St Norbert's Priory in Crowle. Despite the divergence of his views with the previous speaker, Smith acknowledged that

> Where the convictions of the lecturer would allow of it, he spoke of [Roman Catholics] with kindness and consideration, I therefore wish publicly to acknowledge and to thank him for his kind sentiments towards us.[24]

[21] 'List of Subscribers', *LNQ* 1, Part 1 (January 1888), viii.

[22] *LNQ* 5 (1896), 60–61.

[23] *Lincoln Diocesan Magazine* 12 (1896), 121. For the Church Defence Institution, see M. J. D. Roberts, 'Pressure group politics and the Church of England: The Church Defence Institution, 1859–1896', *Journal of Ecclesiastical History* 35 (1984), 560–82.

[24] *English Church History: A reply by the Rev. W. M. Smith, Canon Regular of Prémontré, to the Lectures given in the Market Hall, Crowle, by the Rev. C. W. Foster, M.A.* (Market Weighton, 1896).

His historical energies now focussed on the Reformation period, Wilmer unearthed in the Diocesan Registry at Lincoln 'four thin manuscript volumes' which went some way towards filling up the gap in the Lincoln Episcopal Registers after 1547. He produced a full calendar of these books and embarked on its publication, partly in *Lincolnshire Notes and Queries* and partly in the *Reports and Papers* of the Diocesan Architectural Society. He noted that, should his decision to publish be in need of justification, 'it meets with the approval of so eminent an authority as Canon Overton'.[25]

It was Wilmer's move to Timberland in 1902 that enabled him to extend his work on the records in the diocesan registry. When the Committee on Diocesan Records met for the first time on 28 December 1906, it was noted that

> About £350 has been expended upon the undertaking during the last four years. The work of sorting the great masses of documents into classes and periods is all but finished; all the damaged records have received what may be called 'first aid', while a very large number have been finally repaired; and considerable progress has been made with the work of calendaring and indexing.

This work was not done without help. The sorting and calendaring was materially assisted by, among others, W. V. R. Fane of Fulbeck and Revd R. E. G. Cole of Doddington, while the 'first aid' was carried out at a workshop established for the purpose in Timberland. The efforts of the Committee were encouraged by the favourable comments of those who came to Lincoln to use the records:

> several workers, who have visited diocesan registries in different parts of the country, have expressed the opinion that owing to the work done by the Committee information is more readily obtainable at Lincoln than in almost any other diocese.[26]

Through the regular reports of the Committee, and the willing endorsement of its work by Bishop King and Dean Wickham, the issue of the diocesan records was kept in the public eye.

By 1910, therefore, Canon Foster's reputation as an authority on the archives of the diocese was firmly established in Lincolnshire. His election in

---

[25] The books are now bound together as LAO, Episcopal Register 28. The calendar was printed in C. W. Foster, 'Institutions to benefices in the diocese of Lincoln in the sixteenth century', *LNQ* 5 (1896–98), 129–44, 164–81, 194–209, 227–43; *LNQ* 6 (1900–01), 3–19, 45–53, 78–85, 102–11, 142–7; C. W. Foster, 'Institutions to benefices in the diocese of Lincoln, 1540–1570', *AASRP* 24 (1897–98), 1–32, 467–525 and *AASRP* 25 (1899–1900), 499–505.

[26] *Report of the Lincoln Diocesan Conference 1909*, 48.

that year as a Fellow of the Society of Antiquaries brought him wider recognition in the world of scholarship. He was fully aware of the support both locally and nationally for the publication of records but his experience would have taught him that such support needed to be nurtured and encouraged. The piecemeal printing of records, such as hitherto had been achieved through *Lincolnshire Notes and Queries* and the *Associated Architectural Societies Reports and Papers*, would not achieve this; a more permanent organisation was needed. The Lincoln Record Society was the answer.

The Founding of the Lincoln Record Society

The inaugural meeting of the Society was followed up on 25 November by the first meeting of the Council, which was also held at the Old Palace with the Bishop in the Chair. Of those who had taken part in the work on the diocesan records during the period leading up to the Society's foundation, Maddison, Cole and Fane were all on the Council along with Foster himself. It was reported that 173 people had joined the new Society. It was resolved that two volumes be issued in respect of the years 1910–1911, that one of these should be, as previously agreed, *Holles' Church Notes*, and that the other would be a calendar of the acts of Bishop Cooper (1571–1584), to be edited by Canon Foster. A list of prospective publications was put forward, including episcopal registers, lay subsidy rolls, final concords, charters, indexes of wills and administrations, marriage licences, episcopal and archidiaconal visitations, abstracts of wills, documents relating to monasteries and compositions for first fruits. Nearly all of these classes were to feature in the Society's subsequent publications.[27]

By July 1911, the new Society numbered 183 members. The nature of the membership can be seen in the list printed in the first Annual Report, for 1910–11.[28] As might be expected, some two-thirds of individual members were resident in Lincolnshire. The Society's origins in a resolution of the Diocesan Conference are reflected in the number of clergy members, although their proportion, at 40%, was markedly lower than their comparable strength in the sister Archaeological Society. It might also have been expected that more than thirty-eight members of that Society would have joined the new venture. The LRS indeed was not unsuccessful in attracting members from outside Lincolnshire. Some, like J. T. Spalding and F. A. Wadsworth, both of Nottingham, were members of the neighbouring Thoroton Society; others, such as William Brown of Thirsk, William Farrer, Christopher Wordsworth and Dean Purey-Cust of York, belonged to the veteran Surtees Society.

---

[27] LRS Archive, Minute Book I, 5–7.
[28] For a survey of the membership, see Appendix One.

T. M. Blagg of Nottingham belonged to both of these Societies as well as
to the Royal Archaeological Institute. There were ten overseas members,
including individuals from Milwaukee, Brooklyn, Philadelphia, Manhattan
and New Zealand, and six institutions (all American). The presence among
the membership of nine ladies – Lady Elizabeth Cust, Mrs Henry Cook of
Milwaukee, Miss H. L. Garbett of East Keal, Miss Hemmans of Cottingham,
Mrs Little of Heckington, Mrs Nevile and Mrs Scott of Lincoln, Mrs Tempest
of Broughton and Mrs Weigall of Petwood in Woodhall Spa – gave a hint of
the significant part to be played by women in the Society's work.

The first annual meeting of the Society was held at the Old Palace on
25 October 1911, with the Bishop in the Chair. Twenty-seven members were
present. A report for the first year of the Society's existence was read and
adopted; it included the assurance that the first volume, *Gervase Holles'*
Lincolnshire Church Notes, was ready to be issued to members. Officers and
a Council were elected, the Bishop becoming President, while Canon Foster
took on the joint roles of Secretary and Editor. A set of rules was agreed and
ordered to be printed with the report.

The Lincolnshire church notes of Gervase Holles furnished ideal material
for the first volume to be issued by the new Society. The descriptions covered
most of the county, including the cathedral, and they treated of those subjects
– church buildings, heraldry, county families and genealogy – which were
of overwhelming interest to the clergy and gentry who made up the great
majority of members. The editing was not perfect. H. E. Salter noted that 'it
is unfortunate that this volume has been prepared not from the original but
from a transcript in Lincolnshire, which has introduced some errors of which
Holles was innocent'. Despite this, he declared that 'No volume could be
more fit as a commencement of the Lincoln Record Society.'[29]

---

[29] H. E. Salter, review in *English Historical Review* 27 (1912), 620.

1. Charles Wilmer Foster and his sister Margaret, *c*.1870.

2. Charles Wilmer Foster as a young man.

From CANON FOSTER, F.S.A.,
TIMBERLAND VICARAGE, LINCOLN.

17 August, 1910.

PROPOSED RECORD SOCIETY
FOR THE DIOCESE & COUNTY OF LINCOLN.

The work of arranging the Lincoln Diocesan Records, which has been in progress for six years, has now reached a stage which makes it possible to begin printing calendars of the documents. There is also a vast mass of material in the Public Record Office, in the muniment room of the Dean and Chapter of Lincoln, and in private hands. There are, too, the registers of important parishes which it is desirable to print. In many cases where parish registers have disappeared it is possible to a large extent to supply their place from the Bishops' transcripts at Lincoln. The various records supply a great body of interesting matter relating to Church, parochial, manorial and family history, which for the most part is at present inaccessible.

Books of this class have only a very limited circulation and it seems desirable to secure a permanent body of subscribers by forming a Record Society, as has been done in other dioceses and counties.

The Lincoln Diocesan Conference last year passed the following resolution :

" That this Conference would welcome the formation of a Record Society or the adoption of some other arrangement to provide for the printing of inedited documents relating to the diocese and county of Lincoln."

The Lincoln and Nottingham Architectural Society also has passed a resolution commending the proposed Society.

It would be possible to print two volumes a year if a minimum number of 120 people each subscribed a guinea annually ; and if the number of copies was limited the books would become more valuable as time went on.

The chief part of the Society's work would be devoted to Lincolnshire ; but some of the volumes would probably include matter relating to the counties of Bedford, Buckingham, Hertford, Huntingdon and Leicester, which were until about 1840 in the diocese of Lincoln.

The Rev. R. E. G. Cole has kindly offered to edit Gervas Holles' Lincolnshire Church Notes for one of the early volumes of the Society ; and an account of the Lincolnshire chantries at the time of their dissolution is nearly ready for the printer.

The object of this circular is to obtain the names of persons who would be willing to join such a society and, if the response is sufficiently encouraging, it is proposed that a meeting should be held to promote the scheme.

I am, yours faithfully,

C. W. FOSTER.

[P.T.O.

3. Circular advertising the Lincoln Record Society, August 1910.

4. Design for the Seal of the Lincoln Record Society, 1912.

5. Unused design for the Society's Seal.

6. Edward Lee Hicks, Bishop of Lincoln: First President of the Society.

South Place

Gretton

Kettering

2 March 1916

My dear Foster:

My vicar wants to know some means of cleaning and smoothing out his letters of orders, which have been in a damp place and are nearly illegible. I told him that I would write to you and ask what he had better do.

Will you be at home early in Holy week or during the week before? I am thinking of coming to Lincoln about then, and should be glad if I might come to you for two or three days.

My wife and I were at Firton last week, and I was very pleased to meet Miss Power. She

7. Letter from Alexander Hamilton Thompson to Canon Foster, 1916.

8. Exchequer Gate, Lincoln, *c*.1925.

THREE

THE EARLY YEARS OF THE SOCIETY

With the appearance of Volume I, the new Society could be said to be well and truly launched. Early on in its existence, the suggestion was made that it needed to strengthen its corporate identity, and in August 1912 the Council discussed two designs that had been put forward for a seal. One of these was offered by Everard Green, Somerset Herald; the other, proposed by Christopher Turnor of Panton Hall, was the work of Winckworth Allen. Neither of these was considered suitable and it was decided to ask Mr Allen to produce another design, using the figure of St Hugh with his swan. This was to be submitted to Colonel Welby and Canon Foster for approval. At the Annual Meeting in October of that year, a resolution was passed thanking

> Mr Christopher Turnor for his generosity in providing a design for the seal of the Society and a block for printing the same, and to Mr Winckworth Allen for the care that he has taken in designing the seal.[1]

The successful issue of *Holles' Church Notes* itself emphasised the importance of a regular supply of new editions, competently edited. The example of the earlier Lincolnshire Record Society, with its one published volume, would have served as a warning against complacency. What were the prospects for Canon Foster, as General Editor, of securing such a supply of future volumes?

He had a faithful lieutenant in Robert Eden George Cole. A member of the Jarvis family of Doddington, he had served that parish as its rector for nearly forty-nine years, retiring in 1909 to live in the Cathedral Close at 3 Pottergate. He had for many years devoted much of his leisure to historical studies, producing a *Glossary of Words used in South-West Lincolnshire* (1886), an exemplary *History of the Manor and Township of Doddington* (1897) and an edition of *The Registers of Doddington* in the following year. As well as these works, he had contributed numerous articles to the *Reports and Papers* of the Associated Architectural Societies and to *Lincolnshire Notes*

---

[1] LRS Minute Book I, 13–14, 18.

and Queries. He made regular visits to work on the diocesan records and had amply demonstrated his industry and ability in the work of calendaring.

Canon Foster was also in contact with an energetic extra-mural lecturer of the University of Cambridge, Alexander Hamilton Thompson. Between 1903 and 1905, Hamilton Thompson had lived at Exchequer Gate Lodge in Lincoln and it was during these years that he first came to know both Canon Foster and the Lincoln diocesan records. Although his early academic interests tended towards literary and architectural subjects, he was by 1911 working on chantry certificates, English monasteries and similar studies necessitating research in medieval episcopal registers and other ecclesiastical records. He joined the LRS in 1912 but even before that, in July 1911, the Council had resolved 'that one of the Publications for the year 1912 and 1913 be "The Monastic Injunctions of Bishop Repingdon", edited by Mr Hamilton Thompson'.[2] The recruitment of such an editor, well-known in academic circles far beyond the boundaries of Lincolnshire, did much to introduce the work of the Society to a national audience.

The lynch-pin of the editorial team would inevitably be Canon Foster himself. Already in 1911 he had the Society's second volume in hand, an edition of records covering the episcopate of Bishop Thomas Cooper between 1571 and 1584. This represented further fruits of his work on the history of the sixteenth-century diocese, begun during his curacy at Epworth. The material included an impressive collection of volumes unearthed in the diocesan registry and repaired in the workshop he had established in the vicarage garden at Timberland.[3] These were supplemented by other sources, some at Lincoln, such as the series of presentation deeds which Cole had worked on, others in London, such as the Crown presentations.

Working with Other Societies

It was clear, however, that the combined efforts of these three editors, industrious though they undoubtedly were, would hardly be enough to supply a new publication each year, let alone the two volumes which had been held out as a prospect to the membership. Foster and Hamilton Thompson both had many other commitments, limiting the time they could spend on editing, and, while Cole had retired from parish work, he had now passed his eightieth birthday. At a meeting of the Council in July 1911, Foster therefore proposed that the

---

[2]   LRS Minute Book I, 9. See also David M. Smith, 'Alexander Hamilton Thompson', in *Some Historians*, 61–66.

[3]   'The records needed not only to be arranged, but to be cleaned, pressed and repaired, and therefore I set up a workshop and trained women, who presently became highly skilled in the work' (*Royal Commission on the Public Records 1910–19*, Vol. III Pt 2, para. 7809).

Society enter into arrangements with the Canterbury and York Society and the British Record Society, either for the exchange of publications or for the joint issue of volumes. This proposal was accepted, and it was subsequently confirmed at the first annual meeting of the Society in October that year.[4]

These arrangements were put into practice in different ways. The agreement with the British Record Society eventually resulted in the joint publication in 1921 of *Calendars of Administrations in the Consistory Court of Lincoln A.D. 1540–1659*, edited by Canon Foster himself. This was in fact the third volume which Canon Foster had brought out in the British Record Society's Index Library series, following on from two earlier calendars of Lincoln wills published in 1902 and 1910. With the Canterbury and York Society, on the other hand, it was decided to effect an exchange, so that appropriate volumes from each Society would also appear in the 'livery' of the other Society. Under this arrangement, the *Lincoln Episcopal Records* of Bishop Cooper and the three volumes of *Visitations of Religious Houses* edited by Hamilton Thompson all appeared as publications of both Societies, as did the episcopal rolls of Bishops Hugh of Wells and Robert Grosseteste. While this system of exchange undoubtedly boosted the output of the LRS in the short term, it was to cause the Society problems in the long term, as will be seen.

The Parish Register Section

Another way in which it was attempted to broaden the range of the Society's activities was through the printing of parish registers. The first proposal to undertake this was brought forward at a meeting of the Council in July 1910, when it was decided not to proceed with the printing of a transcript of the early Boston registers which had been prepared by Revd Frank Besant. In the following year, however, the Council reversed this decision, and the project was added to the list of forthcoming volumes. Then, at the Annual Meeting of the Society on 16 October 1912, it was resolved to form a 'Parish Register Section' for the purpose of printing such documents, the Boston registers among them. The annual subscription was fixed at one guinea, 'persons being allowed to become members without subscribing to the general publications of the Society'. A small committee, consisting of Canons Bell, Foster and Cole, was appointed to deal with the work of the Section.[5]

Shortly afterwards, a circular was issued inviting subscriptions to the new Section:

The RECORD SOCIETY have resolved to obtain, with the consent of the incumbent in each case, a copy of as many of the Lincolnshire parish

---

4 LRS Minute Book I, 8–9, 13–14.
5 LRS Minute Book I, 20–21.

registers as possible and, further, to print as many of these copies as their resources will permit. It is proposed that market towns shall be taken in hand first, since they often contain notes of historical interest and entries relating to families residing in the country-side. It is hoped, however, that, when local support is forthcoming, it may be possible at an early date to deal with some of the country parishes.[6]

There seems to have been some pressure for this development from members of the Society with a particular interest in genealogy. One such was the Nottinghamshire historian T. M. Blagg, who had already edited a volume of seventeenth-century parish register transcripts for the Thoroton Society and was heavily involved in W. P. W. Phillimore's marriage register project. Canon Foster himself had come from a thorough grounding in family history and he was in no doubt about the importance of registers, declaring that 'there is no class of documents that is more valuable for the purposes of parochial and family history than parish registers'. He was clear, however, that there was to be no selection of material: 'It is one of the principles of the Society that whatever is done should be done thoroughly; and therefore nothing will be omitted.' This did not mean printing the entries *literatim*. In the interests of economy, it was decided to set out the material in tabular form, retaining the names in full but omitting repetitive phrases such as 'were married' or 'was baptised'. It was also resolved that the registers should be collated with the bishop's transcripts in the Diocesan Registry, so that the evidence might be presented as fully as possible.[7]

The first volume of the Parish Register Section was the earliest part of the Boston registers, issued in 1914. Besant's original transcript had been checked against the register itself by Canon Foster, who had also collated it with the bishop's transcripts and compiled the indexes. An early indication that all was not well with the Section, however, was given at a Council meeting in February 1914, when Canon Foster reported that the number of subscribers to the Section 'was barely enough to justify the Society in printing one volume a year, much less the two volumes a year which they wished to issue'. He had therefore reached a provisional agreement with the printers, Messrs W. K. Morton of Horncastle, who had offered to bear the cost of producing two volumes a year, supplying a copy to each member of the Section and receiving all their subscriptions in return. In addition, they would be allowed to sell additional copies to members of the public, at a price not less than 20% above the subscription value. This offer was accepted by the Council and confirmed at the Annual Meeting in December of that year.[8]

[6] LRS Archive, printed circulars: 'Proposed Parish Register Section', 25 October 1912.
[7] C. W. Foster (ed.), *The Parish Registers of Boston, Volume I: 1557–1599* (LRS Parish Register Section 1, 1914), vii-ix.
[8] LRS Minute Book I, 26–7, 34–5.

Thereafter, register volumes appeared regularly: Lincoln St Margaret and the second Boston volume in 1915, Grantham in 1916, Alford in 1917. Indeed, during the dark years of the First World War, it was the Parish Register Section that continued to issue volumes; the main Society published no volume in 1916. The exceptionally high cost of printing after the War, however, made it impossible for W. K. Morton to continue with the arrangement. In February 1919, it was resolved

> that since it is no longer possible for the Society to finance the Parish Register Section, the Council are obliged with much regret to discontinue, until happier times, the printing of volumes as soon as the books which are now in the press have been completed and issued.[9]

Existing commitments were met. Volumes for Gainsborough (1920) and Bourne (1921) were issued, but when the registers of St Peter at Gowts, Lincoln, were published in 1923, the volume was prefaced by the statement that

> The present volume is unfortunately almost the last which the LINCOLN RECORD SOCIETY will be able to issue in its Parish Register Section. This department of its work has never been supported by a sufficient number of subscribers to justify its continuance and, but for the generous help of Messrs W. K. Morton and Sons, it would have been impossible to print the eight volumes which have now appeared.

One last volume, *Lincoln City Marriages 1538–1754*, was issued to members of the Section in 1925 but thereafter its work ceased. In 1926, as the result of an offer of financial help, it was agreed to print the Epworth parish register as a volume in the Parish Register Section 'without cost to the Society' but by 1931 the prospective benefactor had withdrawn, 'since it had been found that the expense would be greater than he had thought'.[10]

While it was undoubtedly Morton's financial backing that made the work of the Parish Register Section possible, the high quality of the published volumes was due largely to Canon Foster's involvement. He himself edited seven of the nine volumes issued; his care and vigilance have already been seen in his polishing of Besant's Boston transcript. A minor point in the introduction to his edition of the Bourne registers prompted a letter of inquiry to Hamilton Thompson who replied with detailed information on mortuaries and funeral oblations.[11] In the case of the two registers edited by R. C.

---

9   LRS Minute Book I, 79–80.
10   R. C. Dudding (ed.), *The Parish Registers of St Peter at Gowts* (LRS Parish Register Section 8, 1923), vi; LRS Minute Book I, 110, 125–6.
11   C. W. Foster (ed.), *The Parish Registers of Bourne* (LRS Parish Register Section 7, 1921), viii; LRS Archive, Hamilton Thompson correspondence: AHT to CWF, 27 August 1920.

Dudding (Alford and Lincoln St Peter at Gowts), Canon Foster insisted on retaining overall editorial control, as Dudding, the Vicar of Saleby, recalled in an obituary:

> The chief editor always kept an anxious eye upon his assistant editors. When I was reading the proofs of the Alford Parish Register he suddenly asked me to send him the original volume. I explained that I was using it to check the proofs, and as I had probably transcribed more registers than any other man in Lincolnshire I did not see the utility of sending away this particular volume. I heard no more at the moment, but two days later Canon Baron, then vicar of Alford, had a letter asking him if he would kindly oblige Canon Foster by sending him the Alford Parish Register. Canon Baron neglected to reply promptly, as I had the register, and a few days later he had a letter from Dr Hicks, the Bishop, 'Will Canon Baron kindly let Canon Foster have the loan of the Alford Parish Register?' Canon Baron then hastened to Saleby, exclaiming, 'We must let Foster have that register, or I shall soon get a letter from the Archbishop of Canterbury.'[12]

R. E. G. Cole

A steadfast supporter of the Parish Register Section was Canon Cole, who remained a member of its Committee to the end of his life (two of its meetings in 1915 were held in his house) and contributed the introduction to the registers of St Margaret in the Close, Lincoln. Cole made a major contribution to the work of the Society in its early years. He followed his volume of *Holles' Church Notes* with an edition of the early eighteenth-century *Speculum Diocesis* of Bishops Wake and Gibson. This proposal was accepted by the Council in August 1912, and Part I, covering the archdeaconries of Lincoln and Stow, appeared during the following year. It was welcomed as 'a valuable piece of work', throwing light on the state of the Church at that time. [13]

---

[12] R. C. Dudding, 'Canon Foster', *LNQ* 24 (1936), 3. Dudding's somewhat waspish obituary gave great offence to Canon Foster's friends; Doris Stenton wrote 'Mr Hill is sending us a N[otes] and Q[ueries] with the obnoxious article. I take it that R. D. has given his subconscious full rein' (LRS Archive, Major correspondence: Doris Stenton to KM, 1 February 1937). Miss Major was still annoyed by it some fifty years later (personal knowledge).

[13] LRS Archive, Minute Book I, 16; review in *EHR* 30 (1915), 375–6. Although Canon Cole completed his transcript of the remainder of the *Speculum*, this second part was never published. In 1941 Miss Major, at the suggestion of Rosalind Hill, approached Professor Norman Sykes with a view to his doing this; he replied 'I am most glad to hear from Rosalind Hill that you hope to honour Oxford with a visit next term … But what has that wicked person said to convey the impression that I am leading a life of leisure which would give opportunities for work on your unrivalled *Speculum*?' (LRS Archive, Major correspondence: Norman Sykes to KM, 5 January 1942).

Cole's next project was to undertake an edition of the *Liber Crassus*, the great register of the chapter acts of Lincoln Cathedral from 1520 to 1559. A resolution to publish this was agreed at the Annual Meeting held on 15 October 1913. In view of the size of the volume, it was decided to publish the Latin text in the form of a calendar, on the model of those published by the Public Record Office, while transcribing any English documents in full. The first part of the edition, covering the period 1520–1536, appeared towards the end of 1915. Hamilton Thompson, to whom Canon Foster had sent the proofs, commented:

> I have looked through the proofs which I am sending back, and think that it is a very valuable and interesting volume. The notes, like everything of Canon Cole's, are very clear and full of his lively interest in his subject. It is rather difficult to suggest any methods of abbreviating these occasionally long and verbose documents, but I think that, in cases of constant recurrence such as inductions, installations and protestations of residence, all merely formal matter might be taken for granted after the first specimen of the kind, and only notable additions or omissions recorded.[14]

The second part, bringing the work to the end of the reign of Henry VIII in 1547, was sent to the printer in September 1914.[15] The delays of wartime made progress slow; the book was in the hands of the binder by September 1917 but it was still awaited a year later.

Even after the second volume of the *Chapter Acts* appeared, delays continued to affect the third and final part of the edition. Cole's health was deteriorating and it began to look as though he would not live to see the work completed. He suffered a setback in January 1919. Canon Foster reported on 28 January 1919 that 'Poor Cole has had a stroke, I am grieved to say; but he seems to be coming round again.'[16] Hamilton Thompson noted that 'I saw Canon Cole twice last week: he is looking very feeble' and added a few days later:

> As Canon Cole, I am afraid, will not be with us very long, I think that, in the question of precedence of volumes, what remains to be printed of his *Chapter Acts* should be taken in hand as soon as possible. He spoke rather anxiously to me about this last week.[17]

Cole himself wrote disconsolately in April 1919 to Canon J. T. Fowler (who was working on the earlier Chapter Acts):

---

[14] LRS Archive, Hamilton Thompson correspondence: AHT to CWF, 20 October 1915.
[15] *Annual Report 1913–14*, 6.
[16] LAO, Longley 5/31/6.
[17] LRS Archive, Hamilton Thompson correspondence: AHT to CWF, 20 January 1919, 23 January 1919.

They began my 3rd vol[ume] of the 16th cent. Chapter Acts before the end of 1917, and have only just got 64pp. in type, so it is very doubtful if I shall see the end of it. Indeed my illness in the middle of January was a very serious one, – a stroke of some kind, – which I am only getting over very slowly. The Doctors think I shall when the weather gets warmer, but the exceptionally cold winds and the provoking shortness of coal and gas are all against me, and I am still very much of an invalid.[18]

In the event, although Canon Cole had to hand over to Canon Foster the work of seeing the book through the press, he did live to see it published. He wrote to thank Foster for bringing an advance copy to Pottergate:

It is a great satisfaction to me to have seen the work completed during my life-time, and I am greatly obliged to you for all the trouble you have taken about it, and for the help you have given me for so many years. It has caught my eye that Mr Dudding and the printer between them have converted my 'John Pope' the Chancellor into 'the Pope' in the Index, but of course it can't be altered, and I hope it will not be noticed.[19]

He died on 9 January 1921 and Canon Foster paid tribute to his fellow-worker:

He will be long remembered as a faithful parish priest, as a capable man of affairs, as a ripe scholar who specialized in the field of historical research, and as one who was distinguished by a charming old-world courtesy.[20]

The First World War and its Aftermath

The early years of the War did not bear heavily on the work of the Society. There are occasional references in Canon Foster's correspondence that something extraordinary was going on, and those left at home shared in the general anxieties of the time. Writing to Thomas Longley on 10 March 1915, Foster reported, 'We heard signs of the firing here yesterday, but I understand that it was only practice.' In August 1916 Hamilton Thompson reported from Oxford, where he had been examining, that 'St John's is mostly barracks, and Christ Church is given up to a flying corps'.[21]

As the War dragged on, its effects began to spread through the British economy. These were years of extreme difficulty for the Society. Attendance

---

[18] Lincoln Cathedral Library, Fowler MSS.
[19] LRS Archive, Foster correspondence: R. E. G. Cole to CWF, 3 October 1920.
[20] 'Canon Cole', *Lincoln Diocesan Magazine* 39 (1921), 18–19.
[21] LAO, Longley 5/30/91; LRS Archive, Hamilton Thompson correspondence: AHT to CWF, 14 August 1916.

at Annual Meetings was very low. Ten members were present at the 1916 meeting and only seven the following year; both gatherings were held in the confined surroundings of the Common Chamber of the Cathedral.[22] The Annual Report for 1916–17 noted that only one publication had been issued during the previous year. This was Volume 8, *The Visitation of the County of Lincoln in 1666*, edited by Everard Green, Somerset Herald of Arms. The Report continued:

> The fact that volume VIII consisted of no more than 100 pages has led to some complaints being received from members who considered that they were not getting a fair return for their subscription. These complaints, however, rest on no solid ground; for the whole of the Society's funds are spent in printing volumes, and if the members get a smaller slice on one occasion, the Society is enabled to give them a bigger slice next time.[23]

A year later in September 1918, there were still problems to report:

> The War has caused much delay in the editing and printing of the Society's volumes; and it has not been found possible to issue any books to members … These difficulties, in so far as they are due to lack of labour and shortage of paper, will probably soon pass away, but a more formidable problem remains; for it now costs just twice as much to print and bind a book as it did before the War.[24]

The delays in printing meant that a backlog of volumes had built up, among them the final volume of Cole's edition of the Chapter Acts, the second volume of Lincoln Wills and the second volume of Hamilton Thompson's Visitations. It was noted, however, that these volumes were 'so nearly finished that there is a good prospect of their being sent out before the annual meeting is held'. Canon Foster's edition of Lincolnshire Final Concords was promised as a double volume for 1919.

In the event, only *Lincoln Wills II* and *Visitations of Religious Houses II* appeared before the end of 1918; as has been seen, Canon Cole's volume did not appear until 1920. The Final Concords were also held up. In June 1919 Thomas Longley wrote to Canon Foster:

> I am not surprised that the Concords are at a stand still. Peace seems to be worse than war, and the whole world seems to have gone mad.[25]

Looking back from the vantage point of 1923, Canon Foster noted that 'The years 1919 and 1920 proved to be the most critical period in the Society's

22 LRS Minute Book I, 47, 57.
23 *Annual Report 1916–17*, 7
24 *Annual Report 1917–18*, 9.
25 LRS Archive, Domesday correspondence: Thomas Longley to CWF, 6 June [1919].

history.' At a Council meeting in February 1919 it was decided that it would not be possible to complete the volumes that were in hand and also to print Canon Longley's work on Domesday Book. It was therefore agreed to launch an appeal to members to contribute to a special fund for Longley's volumes. Hamilton Thompson was quick to promise his support:

> It is certainly undesirable to increase the subscription for all members, and I think that asking for voluntary donations is the best way. I will gladly increase my own subscription by a guinea a year for the present, if this course is decided on. Guineas are not very plentiful just now and do not go very far, but one should do all one can to help one's own branch of industry.[26]

Economies had to be made. Replying to an enquiry from Lord Monson on 19 January 1921, Canon Foster wrote:

> The Society has not printed an Annual Report since the one dated 1916–18. Printing is so expensive that we have to save where we can.[27]

The period from 1914 to 1923 also saw a net loss in the membership, which fell to 169. It was not until 1924 that a more optimistic note began to emerge:

> The years from 1919 to 1922 were a critical and anxious time, and brought some, though not serious, loss of members. The experience of the last year fortifies the hope that a gradual increase of membership may be looked for.[28]

Alexander Hamilton Thompson

Although Alexander Hamilton Thompson was not based in Lincoln during these years, and indeed his historical interests were spread generously across much of the Midlands and Yorkshire, the work he did for the LRS was of crucial importance. The first volume of his monumental *Visitations of Religious Houses*, comprising material from the registers of Bishops Fleming and Gray, was accepted for publication by the Society in July 1911. He was in the final stages of the work in September 1913, when he wrote that he was sending the printer the last batch of injunctions (numbers xlvi-lii) and was going to Lincoln the following day to revise and look up scattered refer-

---

[26] LRS Minute Book I, 80–1; LRS Archive, Hamilton Thompson correspondence: AHT to CWF, 1 February 1919.

[27] Letter from Canon Foster to Lord Monson, dated 19 January 1921 (in the writer's possession).

[28] *Annual Report 1923–24.*

ences in registers.[29] The volume was published in 1914 and had a considerable impact on the study of late medieval monasticism. The *Times Literary Supplement* was enthusiastic:

> There is indeed, up and down this book, an immense amount of entertaining reading; and the reader may make himself happy that as he reads he is learning history without knowing it; and the many valuable details will no doubt in time find their way into the heads of the gentlemen who write perspicuous histories, and the medieval Church will not be left to the tender mercies of controversialists with a case to prove.[30]

The publication of the *Visitations* followed a recent article by the influential G. G. Coulton on monastic visitations; Hamilton Thompson commented to Canon Foster in September 1913 that

> I have just been reading the proofs of an article by [Coulton] for the E[nglish] H[istorical] R[eview] on 'the Interpretation of Visitation Documents', in which he has given a useful advertisement for the Record Society by announcing my edition of Alnwick's Visitations, and quoting a long passage from a letter which I wrote to him on the subject of Flemyng and Gray. I hope that it may have the effect of bringing in a few subscribers.[31]

The study of monasticism in late medieval England had become sidetracked by the feud between the anti-clerical Coulton on one side and the popular but inaccurate Cardinal Gasquet on the other. Hamilton Thompson's work had the effect of focussing attention away from their rivalry onto the records themselves. His success in doing so can be demonstrated by Coulton's praise on the one hand and the plaudits of the *Catholic World* ('a fine example of the scholarly work done by the Historical Societies of England') on the other. He wrote to Canon Foster in August 1916:

> The remark about my dependence on Gasquet is rather amusing; but it is better in the long run to be polite to Gasquet than to follow Coulton's lead in tilting against him.[32]

Meanwhile, he was working on the next two volumes, an edition of the visitation manuscript (then unbound) of Bishop William Alnwick. He had

---

[29] LRS Archive, Hamilton Thompson correspondence: AHT to CWF, 14 September 1913.

[30] Review in *Times Literary Supplement*, 3 June 1915.

[31] LRS Archive, Hamilton Thompson correspondence: 21 September 1913.

[32] LRS Archive, Hamilton Thompson correspondence: AHT to CWF, 14 August 1916. The review had claimed: 'The editor acknowledges his dependence upon Gasquet's *English Monastic Life*' (*Catholic World* (1916), 549–51).

started work on this as early as 1913, copying from the sheets of the original manuscript which seem to have passed freely between Lincoln and Hamilton Thompson's house at Gretton in Northamptonshire. In June of that year he wrote:

> I am sending back the sheets of Alnwick's visitations, which I have now quite finished with, and shall be greatly obliged if I can have the rest, as I am anxious to get my transcript done by the end of the summer, if possible. These sheets were terribly stained, and the middle of many of the pages was practically illegible …[33]

The absence of part of the manuscript from Lincoln created a difficulty shortly afterwards when Eileen Power, newly appointed Director of Studies in History at Girton College, Cambridge, asked to see it.[34] Responding to Canon Foster's request, Hamilton Thompson wrote:

> If you prefer to have the *whole* original for Miss Eileen's (I do not know her other name) inspection, I will send it in time for her coming; but I have more time at my disposal to work at it just now, and she cannot possibly study the MS with any profit in a few days, unless she is working at one particular religious house. I will, however, gladly lend her my transcript, and send it to her either to your care or straight to Girton; and, if to your care, she can take it back to Cambridge with her. The transcript is partly annotated, and the textual notes are complete; but I have not yet punctuated it properly or filled up the *lacunae*, where they can be supplied. She can have the rest of the transcript, when I have finished it. My only conditions are that she returns it directly she has done with it, and makes full acknowledgement of her use of it, if she is publishing anything.[35]

The young researcher was evidently happy to use the transcript. Hamilton Thompson wrote a few days later (now in a more chivalrous and protective tone):

> I send the transcript for Miss Eileen… I find that I shall want it back as soon as she can let me have it, as it is useful to refer to for the glossary to Flemyng and Gray… The visitation of Newarke College, Leicester, contains some very unpleasant and disgusting evidence; and, unless she

---

[33] LRS Archive, Hamilton Thompson correspondence: AHT to CWF, 3 June 1913.

[34] Eileen Power, who joined the Society in 1912, proposed in 1914 an edition of the accounts of the nunnery of St Michael, Stamford (LRS Minute Book I, 33); this was accepted as an LRS volume but was never completed. For Hamilton Thompson's influence on her great work *Medieval English Nunneries* (Cambridge, 1922), see Maxine Berg, *A Woman in History: Eileen Power 1889–1940* (Cambridge, 1996), 73–4, 116.

[35] LRS Archive, Hamilton Thompson correspondence: AHT to CWF, 21 September 1913.

specially wants it, it need not, I think, be delivered to her with the rest. In fact, although I do not like expurgation, I do not think that any possible service can be done by printing it, even in Latin.[36]

By the end of 1916, it had been agreed that the Alnwick visitations would be divided into two volumes. The printing of the first of these was nearly complete in August 1918 and it was published later in the year. Although much of the work of transcribing and translating the remainder of the text had already been completed by this stage, the final volume did not appear until 1929, a gap of eleven years largely explained by Hamilton Thompson's successive moves to Professorships at Newcastle and Leeds, and the new responsibilities that these entailed. The completed three volumes have proved to be of lasting value to the study of the late medieval Church in England. The significance of the work was encapsulated in a footnote by David Knowles:

> Edited in three volumes, with notes and admirable introductions, they are perhaps the most outstanding of the many that go to make up the heavy debt that all students of medieval religious history owe to the industry and judgement of the late A. H. Thompson. Moreover, their format, as analysed by their editor, has made clear once and for all the significance of the various stages and documents of a visitation. In addition, they are a mine of information on the daily life and organization of the monasteries and on the social life of the times.[37]

The Rolls of Bishop Gravesend

Another factor behind the delayed appearance of the final volume of *Visitations of Religious Houses* was the problem that arose over the editing of the episcopal rolls of Bishop Gravesend. Under the arrangement with the Canterbury and York Society, their editions of the rolls of Hugh of Wells and Robert Grosseteste had appeared as LRS volumes. Gravesend's rolls were the next chronologically and they were edited for publication by Revd F. N. Davis, Rector of Crowell in Oxfordshire and General Editor of the CYS. When Canon Foster saw the proofs of the volume in the summer of 1918, it was immediately apparent that there were errors and omissions. He discussed the difficulty with Hamilton Thompson, who replied:

> Davis' treatment of Gravesend is very annoying, and I am dismayed to hear of his omissions. I identified a large number of his places for him, presum-

---

[36] LRS Archive, Hamilton Thompson correspondence: AHT to CWF, 26 September 1913.
[37] David Knowles, *The Religious Orders in England, II: The End of the Middle Ages* (Cambridge, 1961), 208n.

ably for the index, and incidentally read through his proofs and sent him a list of suggestions. On looking through the Leicester part of the volume, I find that he has not paid much attention to what I wrote, but has allowed many obvious mistakes to remain. Such errors as the attribution of the patronage of Wytham-on-the-Hill to Bullington are precisely points which I queried and which he ought to have corrected.[38]

To make matters worse, Davis was now suggesting that he should go on to edit the rolls and register of Bishop Sutton. Foster and Hamilton Thompson reluctantly decided that the matter would have to be raised with the Council of the Canterbury and York Society. Hamilton Thompson wrote on 23 January 1919:

I think that it is a very awkward matter to have to write to the C. and Y. Society about Davis' work. It was, however, a distinct breach of trust to edit the rolls so carelessly. As I told you, in looking over his proofs, I did not think his editing ideal and suspected him of spelling much as he chose; but I thought at any rate that he was not missing entries. I shall try and go to the April council meeting… I should have thought that it could have been done by private correspondence instead of by making the matter public; but of course the C. & Y. council will have to realise somehow why Davis can have no more registers.[39]

Foster duly wrote a letter which does not appear to have been taken amiss:

Your letter to the C. and Y. Society was quite merciful, and I am glad that Davis, who, if inaccurate, is cheerful and good-tempered, took it well. His habits of mind and methods of editing are illustrated by his pronunciation of Grosseteste as Grotay, which is a feature of C. and Y. meetings.[40]

The result of these discussions was that Foster and Hamilton Thompson undertook to produce a section of addenda and corrigenda for the volume. Hamilton Thompson agreed to go through the original rolls, checking them against Davis's proofs. On 18 February he wrote, 'Gravesend's Northants Roll arrived quite safely this morning, for which many thanks.' A week later he reported:

I am about half-way through the Northampton roll: the omissions are very serious – e.g. a document about Catesby priory, which goes far to prove what I have always held, that English Cistercian nunneries were in their origin Gilbertine houses, is dismissed in a mere line or two – and there is

---

[38] LRS Archive, Hamilton Thompson correspondence: AHT to CWF, 5 August 1918.
[39] LRS Archive, Hamilton Thompson correspondence: AHT to CWF, 23 January 1919.
[40] LRS Archive, Hamilton Thompson correspondence: AHT to CWF, 1 February 1919.

no system about the whole thing. The details of recoveries of presentations are very slovenly.[41]

By May he was returning the Northampton roll and asking for that of Leicester. He had attended the Canterbury and York Society Council meeting but the matter had not been raised:

> Jenkins was there, but, as old Lindsay, who is a rather intractable person, was in the chair, he did not raise the question of editing. Davis was very urbane: he seems neither to repent nor to bear malice. He has accepted a new cure of souls somewhere.[42]

The compilation of the corrigenda and addenda continued for the next two years, leading Hamilton Thompson to wonder whether it might not have been simpler to abandon the whole edition and start again:

> I wish that [Davis] had never been allowed to take the thing in hand: the work ought really to have been scrapped after the first part was in proof, and a new edition prepared.[43]

By the autumn of 1921 the revisions were completed but then a new difficulty arose: the officers of the Canterbury and York Society began to have second thoughts about the increased expenditure that would be involved in printing the corrections. Hamilton Thompson expressed his views forcefully:

> The printers' charges, as stated by Davis, seem to me very heavy. I do not see, however, what can be done: the titles of the years might be left out, and there are perhaps certain trifling points which might be omitted here and there, where they are not absolutely vital to the right understanding of the document... I shall hardly be able to attend the next Council meeting; but I owe Jenkins of the Lambeth library a letter, and, as he feels strongly upon the necessity of printing registers with the strictest accuracy, I might mention the matter to him and ask him to press it at the Council. I think also that Johnson would take our side. You may be seeing both of them before the meeting, which should be on the last Wednesday in this month; and I think it would be desirable to let them know that the corrections and additions are really important. Of course, the whole business reflects upon Davis' competence; but the Council may be unwilling to incur expense in printing matter which shows that it was mistaken in its choice of an editor.

---

[41] LRS Archive, Hamilton Thompson correspondence: AHT to CWF, 18 February, 26 February 1919.

[42] LRS Archive, Hamilton Thompson correspondence: AHT to CWF, 21 May 1919. Claude Jenkins (1877–1959) was then Librarian of Lambeth Palace Library and Professor of Ecclesiastical History at King's College, London (*ODNB*).

[43] LRS Archive, Hamilton Thompson correspondence: AHT to CWF, 25 May 1921.

As the edition will appear eventually, with a host of corrections, it will not be to the credit of the Society; and I really think that the best thing would have been to cancel the printed numbers and wait until it was possible to issue an accurate edition. Meanwhile, I think that we must press for the retention of all corrections which involve necessary points, and that the necessity of these should be interpreted in the strictest sense.[44]

Canon Foster wrote back in full agreement, remarking that 'there is very little that we can cut out'. Hamilton Thompson, writing during a train journey to approve some further alterations, observed prophetically that 'The whole business, however, is most unsatisfactory, as no-one will be able to use Davis' imperfect calendar and check it by the errata without some irritation.'[45]

In the end, the protracted affair of Bishop Gravesend's rolls was settled by Canon Foster travelling to London to interview the senior figures in the Canterbury and York Society, and making it abundantly clear that the corrigenda and addenda must stand. He reported in triumph on 13 December 1921:

I had a conference last week with Johnson and Flower and they agreed that our corrections cut down in the way I suggested to you must stand. At first they talked about cutting our items down wholesale and I suggested to them that they should take the text and I should read a few pages of the corrections. They then saw that most of what we had put in was absolutely necessary. The fact was that they had not in the least realised how bad the work was. At last we arrived at a very amicable agreement and it was arranged that I should try to see Jenkins with a view to getting him to agree also. Jenkins came to the Palace Hotel on Friday at 9.45 p.m. and stayed till 11.15 p.m. and we talked to the strains of a band which was playing for a dance in the adjoining room. We went through a lot of stuff and Jenkins entirely agreed with what I had settled with Johnson and Flower.[46]

The volume was finally published at the end of 1925, some ten years after it had been first announced, with a preface by Canon Foster alluding tactfully to a 'change of plan in 1922'. The whole business brought to an end the arrangement for exchange of volumes with the Canterbury and York Society, although it should be added that the replacement of F. N. Davis as General Editor by the redoubtable Rose Graham soon established the latter Society with a reputation for academic excellence.

---

[44] LRS Archive, Hamilton Thompson correspondence: AHT to CWF, 4 October 1921.
[45] LRS Archive, Hamilton Thompson correspondence: CWF to AHT, 8 October 1921; AHT to CWF, 6 December 1921.
[46] LRS Archive, Hamilton Thompson correspondence: CWF to AHT, 13 December 1921. Charles Johnson (1870–1961) and Cyril Thomas Flower (1879–1961) were both members of the staff of the Public Record Office (*ODNB*).

The Contribution of Canon Foster

The first meeting of the Council of the Society in November 1910 resolved that the second volume to be published was to be Canon Foster's edition of the records of Thomas Cooper, Bishop of Lincoln from 1571 to 1584. In the event, publication was delayed by the negotiations for joint publication with the Canterbury and York Society, but the volume duly appeared towards the end of 1912. Its quality and significance were fully recognised in a perceptive review by W. H. Frere, himself a master in the editing of documents (his *Visitation Articles and Injunctions of the Reformation Period* had appeared in 1910).[47] Noting that Canon Foster's volume was 'very much more than the reprint of an episcopal register', comprising information derived from a variety of sources to present a full picture of the bishop's work, he suggested that

> A representative episcopate such as that of Bishop Cooper was well worth the labour and skill thus ungrudgingly bestowed upon it; and the result is a very interesting collection of first-hand evidence bearing on the administration of the largest diocese in England by one of the better sort of Elizabethan bishops.

Frere drew attention to the valuable information furnished on such subjects as the standard of learning among the clergy and the exercise of church discipline, concluding with an endorsement of the importance of such editions for the study of the Elizabethan church:

> Cooper's connexion with the diocese of Lincoln had ceased by his translation to Winchester (1584) five years before he was in the thick of the controversy with Martin Marprelate. But, in reviewing his work at Lincoln, one cannot help asking oneself, which is the truer picture of the aims and methods of the better Elizabethan episcopate – that which was painted by the brilliant and reckless satirist, or that which emerges by degrees from the musty pages of official registers? Who shall say? But, at least, such evidence as this must not be neglected in the future.[48]

Another reviewer concluded that the volume

> throws a flood of light on church conditions under Elizabeth, and is admirably indexed. The subject index shows the presence of not a few unexpected matters, as, for instance, Armour, Astrology, Cards and Dice, Latin Dictionaries, Physic and Surgery, Sorcery, and Whipping for Profanity.[49]

---

[47] W. H. Frere (ed.), *Visitation Articles and Injunctions of the Period of the Reformation, 1536–1575*, Alcuin Club 14–16 (1910).
[48] Review in *EHR* 28 (1913), 569–71.
[49] Review in *The Athenaeum*, 5 July 1913.

Foster originally planned to follow this volume with an edition of thirteenth-century final concords for Lincolnshire and with a collection of *Libri Cleri* or clergy lists from visitations of the late sixteenth century. However, the death in April 1912 of the veteran Canon Maddison, who was to have undertaken an edition of the cartulary of the vicars choral of Lincoln, meant that an alternative volume had to be brought forward quickly. At a meeting of Council in August 1912, therefore, it was decided that a volume of Lincolnshire wills, edited by Canon Foster, should be issued to members for the current year's subscription.[50] Although this was evidently material which he had in readiness, any hope of early publication was dashed by his prolonged illness during the early part of 1913. Hamilton Thompson wrote in some concern during the summer of that year:

> I understand from various sources that you are much better: I hope that this is true. I did not care to write while I knew you were ill, as I could not come to inquire in person, and felt that Mrs Foster would not want to be troubled by answering letters; but I have been anxious, and shall be glad to know that you have really recovered.[51]

Foster was apparently working on the notes and glossary in September 1913 when Hamilton Thompson wrote, returning the proofs with some annotations and recommending that he consult Coulton about the identification of certain books ('His acquaintance with medieval literature is very large').[52] The finished volume, *Lincoln Wills I: 1271–1526*, was issued to members in November 1914. It broke with precedent by aiming to be exhaustive rather than selective (as, for example, Maddison's two volumes had been) and also by printing full abstracts of each will, omitting only common form and undue repetition. A helpful glossary was included, to elucidate archaic or technical terms. For the *Times Literary Supplement*, it consolidated the favourable impression that the Society's publications were giving:

> A great deal of excellent work is being done by local antiquarian and record societies. Notable ... [is] the work of the young, but healthy, Lincolnshire Society, directed by Canon Wilmer Foster. There is now before us a volume of Wills from the last-named body, which is an admirable example of the usefulness of such learned societies.[53]

The Annual Report for 1914–15 noted that *Lincoln Wills* was one of the volumes that had proved to be very popular, and that a second volume was in the press. This appeared as Volume 10 in the autumn of 1918 and carried the

---

50 LRS, Minute Book I, 16.
51 LRS Archive, Hamilton Thompson correspondence: AHT to CWF, 3 June 1913.
52 LRS Archive, Hamilton Thompson correspondence: AHT to CWF, 21 September 1913.
53 Review in *Times Literary Supplement*, 31 December 1914.

series of published wills forward to 1530. The procedures involved in probate jurisdiction were outlined in an introduction. The book was reviewed enthusiastically by H. E. Salter ('The Lincoln Record Society is to be congratulated on this volume') and the *Church Times*, in a detailed notice, extolled it:

> Volumes of mediaeval wills are therefore welcome to the student, and of them the collections issued by the Lincoln Record Society are the very model. Edited with scholarly care by the Rev. C. W. Foster, excellently printed in the little town of Horncastle, the volume before us is fully worthy of the distinguished series in which it appears, and there can be no higher praise.[54]

Canon Foster went on to produce a third volume in the *Lincoln Wills* series, covering the years 1530–1532; this was issued as Volume 24 in 1930.

The long-delayed edition of *Final Concords of the County of Lincoln* made its appearance in 1920. It was conceived as a continuation of the volume, published by Massingberd and Boyd in 1896, which had dealt with the period from 1193 to 1244. For this reason, the new publication, which brought the series to the end of the reign of Henry III in 1272, was described as 'Volume II'. A series of appendices printed additional fines for the earlier period which had been omitted from the previous volume, together with a list of errata. The index included references to final concords printed in Volume I, where many of the place-names had been left unidentified. Some members, unaware of the previous publication, wondered whether they might have missed a Record Society volume; Canon Foster had to write to explain:

> Volume I of Final Concords was not one of our Society's volumes, but was privately printed by the late W. O. Massingberd in 1896. If you want a copy you could probably buy one from George Harding, Bookseller, Great Russell Street, W.C.1., for about 10s or 12s.[55]

The fines printed in the LRS volume were prepared from abstracts made by Miss Burdett Butcher, a native of Timberland whom Canon Foster had instructed in palaeography. She did a great deal of work for him in the Public Record Office, at which institution she was a regular attender. Doris Stenton described a wintry visit to London, when

> the cold was most trying. Neither B.M. nor R.O. had its pipes working and there were draughts. They lighted a fire on Tuesday in the Round Room and it warmed Miss Butcher nicely but the radius of a fire is limited.[56]

---

[54] H. E. Salter, review in *English Historical Review* 34 (1919), 449; review in *Church Times*, 27 June 1919.

[55] Letter from CWF to Lord Monson, dated 19 January 1921 (in the writer's possession).

[56] LRS Archive, Stenton correspondence: undated letter from D. M. Stenton to CWF. For Miss Butcher, see *Lincolnshire Archives Committee: Archivists' Report* 7 (1955–56), 8.

William Brown of Sowerby near Thirsk, a Record Society member who had done much work for the Surtees and Yorkshire Archaeological Societies, wrote enthusiastically about the volume:

> I keep looking at your Lincolnshire Concords and wish there was something from Yorkshire to set against it. The Lost Vills and other Forgotten Places must have involved a lot of work. The index of subjects is the fullest I have ever come across.[57]

The reputation of the publications of the Lincoln Record Society continued to grow and reach a wider audience. As Canon Foster was to note in 1923:

> The Society's credit as a serious contributor to historical knowledge is steadily growing, and scholars of repute take increasing account of its work.[58]

An illustration of the interest taken in the Society's volumes by established historians can be seen in the review of *Final Concords* by the great J. H. Round:

> It is a hopeful sign for the future of local historical research in England that even the general impoverishment following on the great war has failed to arrest the work of those meritorious societies which are striving to publish, on sound lines, the materials needed for writing – or, in some cases, writing anew – the history of our ancient counties. Unfortunately, the most valuable of such records for the scholar are also, as a rule, the least attractive to the average member of such societies, on whose pecuniary support they are dependent for their existence. In spite of this difficulty and of the almost prohibitive cost of producing their volumes at the present time, they have hitherto contrived to carry on their work and have even increased in number.

Round gave high praise to 'this admirable volume', observing that Canon Foster had 'provided the student with an apparatus of elaborate learning. All future editors of fines should carefully examine his work and profit by his labours.' He commended the introduction, particularly the section on 'Lost Vills and other Forgotten Places', and admired the indexes, concluding:

> One can but express the hope that the Lincoln Record Society may be able to produce many volumes of no less scholarly character.[59]

---

[57] LRS Archive, Domesday correspondence: William Brown to CWF, 13 February 1921.
[58] *Annual Report 1922–23*, 6.
[59] Review in *EHR* 37 (1922), 426–8.

The substantial work published in 1926 under the title *The State of the Church in the Reigns of Elizabeth and James I as Illustrated by Documents relating to the Diocese of Lincoln* had its origins in the continuation of Canon Foster's work on the history of the Elizabethan Church, begun in his calendars of institutions and admissions to benefices and continued in his volume on the episcopate of Bishop Thomas Cooper. Early Reports issued by the Society refer to a forthcoming volume of *Libri Cleri*, the lists of the clergy compiled during the regular visitations carried out by bishop or archdeacon. By 1916, however, Canon Foster had decided to broaden the scope of the edition to include other material casting light on the state of the Church in that period. The size of the resulting volume – 562 pages plus nearly 150 pages of introductory material – is itself a testimony to the energy and thoroughness with which he had mastered the contents of the Diocesan Registry. The introduction discussed many of the key issues of the times – the learning of the clergy, clerical marriage, Puritanism and recusancy. Statistics (in the compilation of which Canon Foster had been assisted by his secretary, Miss F. E. Thurlby) provided evidence on education, preaching, pluralism and hospitality. A reviewer summed up the whole achievement:

> Canon Foster's massive volume, though it contains much that is only of local interest in such matters as the succession of the parish clergy, is also an important contribution to general history. The great diocese of Lincoln, with its unequalled records … is typical of all England, and the editor has not only added to knowledge but illuminated his collections by an admirable introduction.[60]

The review concluded by looking forward to 'the pleasant prospect of at least one further volume'. In the event, this never appeared (though some of the material survives among Canon Foster's transcripts). For during the previous ten years, the focus of his historical energies had shifted from the records of the sixteenth-century Church to the medieval charters of Lincoln Cathedral and in particular to its ancient cartulary, the *Registrum Antiquissimum*.

---

[60] E. W. Watson, review in *EHR* 42 (1927), 429–30.

FOUR

THE STENTONS, DOMESDAY BOOK AND THE *REGISTRUM ANTIQUISSIMUM*

In May 1916 Canon Foster, who was contemplating an edition of early Lincolnshire charters, heard that another scholar, Professor Frank Stenton of the University of Reading, was at work in this area. He lost no time in writing to enquire:

> I have been planning a calendar of Lincolnshire charters prior to the year 1201, and I have begun to collect material for the volume. Mr C. Johnson of the Public Record Office has just told me that you are working at a similar volume relating to a part of Lincolnshire. I have no wish to cover ground which you have already trodden, and so I am writing to ask you kindly to tell me what you are doing – what period and what locality and what classes of documents, what sources, you are dealing with.[1]

Stenton was in fact working on the collection of monastic charters, mostly from the British Museum, which was published in 1920 by the British Academy as *Danelaw Charters*. The son of a Southwell solicitor, Stenton had steeped himself in the history and topography of the Danelaw. Since graduating from Keble College, Oxford, he had combined schoolmastering at Llandovery College in Wales with writing on Domesday for the *Victoria County History*. In 1908 he was appointed Research Fellow in Local History at University College, Reading, where he became Professor of Modern History in 1912.[2]

The two men met at Reading to discuss their different projects, and shortly afterwards Stenton paid a visit to Lincolnshire. Canon Foster later described their inspection of the records: 'it will be long before I shall forget his wonder and delight as I opened before his eyes box after box of the original charters'. Moving with characteristic speed and decision, he persuaded Stenton to undertake a volume for the Lincoln Record Society, a proposal which was

---

[1] University of Reading, Stenton Papers: CWF to FMS, 13 May 1916.
[2] D. M. Stenton, 'Frank Merry Stenton', *Proceedings of the British Academy* 54 (1970), esp. 348–368.

agreed at a Council meeting on 16 June – exactly one month after the initial letter of enquiry quoted above.[3] This was to be an edition of monastic charters relating to the possessions of five Lincolnshire Gilbertine houses (Sixle or Sixhills,[4] Ormsby, Catlcy, Bullington and Alvingham), which were copied on to the Memoranda Roll of the King's Remembrancer between 1407 and 1411 as evidence for the (successful) claim of these priories to exemption from taxation. Stenton had been working on these charters since 1908; by the beginning of 1917 Stenton was able to send transcripts of the whole of the Sixhills series and was looking forward to starting on Catley.[5]

Stenton had not only offered to edit a volume for the LRS but had also offered the services of a research pupil. This was Miss Doris Parsons, whose name also appears in the minutes of the Council meeting of 16 June as the editor of a forthcoming volume of *Early Assize Rolls*. Stenton also volunteered her services as an assistant to help with the copying of the Cathedral charters. Miss Parsons wrote to Canon Foster on 24 October:

> I must thank you and Mrs Foster very much indeed for your invitation to me. It will give me great pleasure to see the Lincoln records and still greater pleasure to help copy some of them.[6]

She spent part of the Christmas vacation at Timberland. Stenton wrote from Southwell, where his sister had recently died:

> I hope you are finding [Miss Parsons] useful and, which is equally important, are not hesitating to exploit her, and that you really feel she is helping you to make headway with the series.[7]

The young Miss Parsons was soon absorbed in the daily routine of Timberland Vicarage:

> By the time that I first stayed at Timberland in 1916 his study there had become not only the retreat where his sermons were thought out and the records of the church at Lincoln were analysed and edited, but one of the business centres of the diocese. In the parish room next door his three young clerks, practised in shorthand and beginning to learn to copy medieval manuscripts, were proving how much talent the children in a village

---

3   *Reg. Ant. I*, i–ii; LRS Minute Book I, 44.
4   The modern spelling 'Sixhills' did not commend itself to medievalists who preferred the earlier 'Sixle'. Hamilton Thompson thought 'Sixhills is a very debased form, which I suppose has arisen from the likeness of the name to the Leicestershire Sixhills' (LRS Archive, Stenton correspondence: AHT to CWF, 9 January 1917).
5   D. M. Stenton, 'Frank Merry Stenton', 382–3; LRS Archive, Stenton correspondence: FMS to CWF, 2 January, 6 January 1917.
6   LRS Archive, Stenton correspondence: Doris Parsons to CWF, 24 October 1916.
7   LRS Archive, Stenton correspondence: FMS to CWF, 2 January 1917.

school possessed and could develop under proper guidance. As Secretary of the Lincoln Diocesan Trust and Board of Finance, Foster had an enormous correspondence. He dealt with it immediately after breakfast every morning with the aid of one of his secretaries, but his day had begun before his early breakfast, when he walked across the field to his church to read matins. Sitting in a corner of his study and working at the Lincoln charters I was filled with admiration of the skill with which he organised his work and the amount he achieved in a day. As he dictated his letters and answered numerous telephone calls I could not but become familiar with the problems of dilapidations on which his advice was continually sought. He was in touch with his fellow clergy and benefice holders all over the county and when he took an historical guest out to see the countryside there was generally a bit of diocesan business to be dealt with during the excursion. Throughout the county he was a well-known figure and, until overwork forced him to curtail his activities, he maintained to the full this administrative burden.[8]

A regular correspondence began between Timberland and Reading, in which the progress of the Gilbertine charters featured regularly. Stenton wrote in April 1917:

> I hope to start another season ticket to London in about a fortnight, if the Sixle set therefore could be printed within some six weeks I could get the whole set read through with the original enrolment straightaway, which would perhaps save time... I think we agreed that the Latin and English should face each other on opposing pages.[9]

On 21 August 1917 Stenton wrote from Southwell, sending the first revise of Sixle, and thanking Foster for his comments. The correct translation of legal terminology and the identification of place-names were among the problems that cropped up:

> I agree altogether about Aisthorpe. I had identified the place so at first, but did not know whether the good Thomas son of William son of Hacon held any land there. But your note is conclusive.

More complex matters could be dealt with by a meeting:

---

[8]   Doris M. Stenton, 'Canon C. W. Foster of Timberland, Lincolnshire, 1866–1935', *Amateur Historian* 6 (1963–65), 158. Canon Foster's clerks played an essential role in his work, not only at the Vicarage but also travelling into Lincoln on Fridays to copy documents. The names of some of them are known: Miss E. Kettleborough and Miss Doris Ainsworth. The longest-serving among them was Miss Florence Thurlby, who became his secretary; after his death, she continued to look after the Foster Library until her retirement in 1961. See *Lincolnshire Archives Committee: Archivists' Report* 7 (1955–56), 6.

[9]   LRS Archive, Stenton correspondence: FMS to CWF, 25 April 1917.

Are you still coming to Lincoln every week? If so, I can easily bicycle over and see you if you can suggest a place of meeting. There will certainly be one or two things we could settle more easily in that way than by letter.[10]

Meanwhile, Hamilton Thompson had been drafted in to help with the proofs. On 7 August 1917 he wrote to Foster:

I have delayed answering owing to the pressure of examination work, which is gradually coming to an end; but in the intervals of looking over papers I have read these Sixle charters and send a set of notes on small points in the translations, some of which I hope may be useful… Any more of this sort of thing you can send me I shall be delighted to see: it is a real relief to turn to it in spare moments from the deadening work of reading the valueless opinions of youths and maidens on the character of Esmond and the difference between a ballad and a poem.[11]

In 1920 Stenton began work on the introduction, a work of lasting value which included the first survey of the diplomatic of the medieval private charter since Madox's *Formulare Anglicanum* of 1702. Although later in life he considered that he had been unwise to base such a study on documents which were not originals but merely fifteenth-century transcripts, the introduction to Gilbertine Charters remains nonetheless a groundbreaking work. The edition was published in 1922. Its significance was recognised by F. M. Powicke who noted that, while the charters cast little light on the domestic life of the Gilbertines,

the twenty pages … which [Stenton] gives to the written instruments as such are a most important addition to the neglected history of English diplomatic. Nobody appreciates better than Mr Stenton the relation between social change or circumstance and the forms of documents. He explains how feudal ties required specific epistolary greetings in a charter in one case and not in another; how the movement towards precision, as for example in charters recording the grant of a church, corresponded to a change in contemporary thought… how thought developed on the problem of land held in free alms, how old symbolism survived – the symbolism which was more important than the document which recorded the act of

---

[10] LRS Archive, Stenton correspondence: FMS to CWF, 21 August 1917. Stenton was a prodigious bicyclist at that time. On 11 July 1911 he rode from Southwell to Leicester, noting that 'The Foss cannot yet be ridden' and recalling later that he had to push his way through bushes; he returned the same day via Mount Sorrel and Nottingham, arriving home at 8.10p.m. Shortly after his marriage to Doris, they cycled from Reading to Southwell in two days (D. M. Stenton, 'Frank Merry Stenton', 365, 379).

[11] LRS Archive, Hamilton Thompson correspondence: AHT to CWF, 7 August 1917.

gift or transfer … Under Mr Stenton's care the stoniest ground becomes fruitful.[12]

Meanwhile, Doris Parsons had been at work on the plea rolls, later published under the title *Earliest Lincolnshire Assize Rolls*. This was an edition of legal proceedings before justices hearing pleas in Lincolnshire, largely contained in three Assize Rolls of 1202 and 1206. As such, they are 'among the earliest judicial records of England, and for that matter of Western Europe'. They are also extremely difficult to decipher. C. G. Crump, editor of many of the *Curia Regis Rolls*, commented that 'The writing of these rolls is generally bad, and the contractions often hard to understand.' Stenton himself wrote that

It is execrable stuff to read, but Miss Parsons has squinted at it till she has I should think got everything that can be made out by a sympathetic imagination. Her reading is wonderfully good: I am now reduced to asking her meekly to read things that I can't. She always does it. The younger generation knocking on the door.[13]

Stenton indeed was full of enthusiasm for the publication of the rolls. In February 1918, when it looked as though some of the archives in the Public Record Office would have to be evacuated to a place of greater safety, he wrote to Canon Foster:

The Plea Rolls are certainly going, some time within the next three weeks. Miss Parsons, with an heroic effort, has copied her two rolls – the criminal one is packed with interesting details often of a lurid sort. I hope the Society will like them and the bishop find them toothsome.[14]

When he heard that Canon and Mrs Foster had played the part of the Good Samaritan in rescuing an injured young lady by the roadside near Grantham, he wrote:

It was very good of you, but it must have hung you up badly. The episode would go well into a plea roll. *Quedam puella inventa fuit sanguinolenta in via regis apud Sichestan. Nullus inde malecreditur. Iudicium infortunium. Primus inventor fuit W. canonicus ecclesie Linc' qui eam transtulit ad domum hospitalem apud Graham.*[15]

---

[12] F. M. Powicke, review in *EHR* 38 (1923), 269–70.
[13] LRS Archive, Stenton correspondence: FMS to CWF, 17 February 1918.
[14] LRS Archive, Stenton correspondence: FMS to CWF, 13 February 1918.
[15] 'A certain young woman was found bleeding in the king's highway at Syston. No one is suspected. Judgement: misadventure. The first finder was W[ilmer] canon of the church of Lincoln who took her to the hospital at Grantham' (LRS Archive, Domesday correspondence: FMS to CWF, 2 November 1920).

The marriage of Frank Stenton and Doris Parsons in November 1919 cemented an historical partnership that had begun several years earlier. Doris wrote to Canon Foster from Southwell on 4 January 1921:

> We are both labouring at our respective Introductions. The Gilbertines is nearly finished and mine won't take long. You will like the Gilbertines, I think. It is coming out well. Mine is too but it's getting longer and longer and longer. I shall have to amputate here and there, perhaps.[16]

We catch another glimpse of the volume in preparation in a letter sent by Stenton to Foster on 2 May 1922, enclosing the preface to *Gilbertine Charters* ('Doris has got up steam on the Plea Roll'). There comes a time, however, when any editor needs time for relaxation, and the Stentons were no exception. At the end of 1922 Canon Foster received an unexpected request from Doris:

> It has occurred to me that if you do not use, or expect to want to use your bagatelle board, you might not mind lending it to us. Ours is very ancient and for years was unused and kept in an outer place where it warped rather. It requires skill to play on and although it gives us pleasure a less warped one would give us more. We have become very keen on bagatelle. It seems [a] waste of time but if we work all day we find we do not do much good after supper.[17]

It was, however, a weightier matter than bagatelle that delayed the completion of *The Earliest Lincolnshire Assize Rolls*. Stenton and Foster had become concerned about the moribund state of the Pipe Roll Society, which had not published a volume since 1914. As Doris Stenton recalled:

> Some members had gone on paying their subscriptions. Others had paid a few before stopping. No attempt had been made to find additional members. The reverse process was followed. We had acquired the early printed volumes but were advised not to join the Society. Canon Foster and Frank were both in urgent need of the rolls, partly in order to help them date undated twelfth- and thirteenth-century charters. After a Lincoln Record Society meeting in the early twenties we discussed the matter in the café on High Bridge, Lincoln, and the Canon said: 'Something must be done.'[18]

---

[16] LRS Archive, Stenton correspondence: Doris Stenton to CWF, 4 January 1921.
[17] LRS Archive, Stenton correspondence: Doris Stenton to CWF, 30 December 1922. Canon Foster appears to have retained his bagatelle board; at any rate, in 1923 Doris was presented by S. A. Peyton with 'a large Bagatelle Board which he possesses but scorns to use' (Stenton Correspondence: Doris Stenton to CWF, 5 May 1923).
[18] D. M. Stenton, 'Frank Merry Stenton', 386.

The date of this meeting has never been established. Kathleen Major put it in 1922 and suggested that, besides the Stentons and Canon Foster, Professor L. V. D. Owen of Nottingham (a former pupil of Frank Stenton's at Llandovery College) was present. If this was the case, the minute book of the LRS indicates that it could have taken place after the Annual Meeting on either 20 April 1921 or 28 September 1923, when all four people were present. Doris Stenton recalled that it was Canon Foster 'who introduced her to Sir Henry Maxwell-Lyte and secured her appointment in December 1923 as Organizing Secretary'. Given the speed at which Canon Foster worked when he wanted 'something to be done', it is hard to resist the conclusion that the conversation in the High Bridge Café took place in September 1923.[19]

The need to produce a new Pipe Roll Society volume swept all other work aside. By June 1924, the roll for the second year of Richard I was ready for the press and it duly appeared, as Volume I in a New Series, in 1925. Only then was it possible for the final touches to be put to the Assize Rolls. The indexes were compiled by R. R. Darlington, then a colleague of the Stentons at Reading. A delighted Doris wrote to Timberland:

> You will be pleased to hear that Darlington thinks that 'much may be learned of indexing from a consideration of the corrections Canon Foster has made'!![20]

In February 1926 she wrote: 'When is Hereford going to disgorge the Assize Rolls? They are slow.' Although the publication date on the title-page is 1926, the volume does not seem to have been issued until the following year. When Doris wrote to Canon Foster in May 1927, she had not only received her parcel of copies but was planning to market them among her students:

> Many thanks for the volumes. They have arrived safely but I have not yet unpacked the Hereford bundle. You suggested 16s as a price for students. Is that right? I shall tell them that volumes are on no account to be sold to second hand booksellers. I do not know how many will be wanted this year yet. The other people have not made up their minds about their specials … I am much pleased with the volume. It looks well and is not too unwieldy or too thin. Much of its usefulness is due to you. Flower tells me that he has already used it for identifications. I am very grateful for all the help you gave. Have you sent out review copies yet?[21]

---

[19] Kathleen Major, 'Doris Mary Stenton', *ODNB*; LRS Minute Book I, 89, 97; *Liber Memorialis Doris Mary Stenton*, Pipe Roll Society, New Series 41 (1976), 16.
[20] LRS Archive, Stenton correspondence: Doris Stenton to CWF, 26 December 1925.
[21] LRS Archive, Stenton correspondence: Doris Stenton to CWF, 7 May (year not given, but datable from internal evidence to 1927).

The edition was welcomed by C. G. Crump, who prefaced his review with high praise for the work of the Society, which gives a clear indication of the sterling reputation it had achieved in the academic community:

> In any review of a publication of the Lincoln Record Society it is or should be common form to begin with a paragraph praising the work of that society and making special mention of the merits of Canon Foster. There was a time when the feudal history and the topography of Lincolnshire appeared to those who had to deal with it as a dark and horrible jungle full of places called Carlton and hamlets undiscoverable on any map, a county where Scampton and Stainton lay not very far apart for the confusion of medieval scribes and the vexation of later students, a county which, like the forerunners of Agamemnon, lacked a meritorious antiquary, and was in consequence without a county history in the proper number of folio volumes. In those days Professor Stenton had not begun to write or publish documents, and the Lincoln Record Society was unborn. In these happier times the feudal history of Lincolnshire, its institutions and its topography, are gradually coming out of the darkness that used to cover them.[22]

By 1926, the Society had issued twenty-two volumes over a period of sixteen years. Of these, ten related to the early modern period, one to the early eighteenth century, and the remaining eleven to the middle ages. The adoption of a publication programme involving so much medieval Latin was a bold move for a local record society. As Doris Stenton pointed out:

> The Lincoln Society was in composition much like any other county record society of those days. Its members were very largely Lincolnshire country gentlemen and clergymen of the Church of England. Its rare meetings were held on a Friday because that was market day when everyone went to Lincoln. Members preferred English documents, not that they could not read Latin, for most of them had been through the public school mill, but they liked parish registers, wills, and, in general, English documents, of which the record repositories in Lincoln could offer an immense store.[23]

One way of making a Latin text palatable to the membership was to issue the volume with an English translation on the opposite page. This was done in the case of Hamilton Thompson's *Visitations of Religious Houses* and Stenton's *Gilbertine Charters*. In the case of the Chapter Acts and again with the Final Concords, an English summary was given in place of the original Latin. The early volumes taken by way of exchange from the Canterbury and York Society were published in the Latin text of the original; the volume of

---

22 C. G. Crump, review in *EHR* 43 (1928), 97–9.
23 D. M. Stenton, 'Frank Merry Stenton', 376.

Gravesend's rolls was a mixture of Latin text and English summary. When it came to the early Assize Rolls, it was felt that

> while, on the one hand, the rolls as they stood in Latin might not be readily intelligible to readers unversed in medieval law and Latin, on the other hand, if they were literally translated into English they would not be a great deal more intelligible. The real difficulty lies in the form in which the entries are cast, rather than in the language that clothes them.[24]

There was also the difficulty that the increase in printing costs had made it uneconomic to include a full translation. Here, therefore, it was decided to print the Latin text with notes to explain cases of particular difficulty, and to include an introduction setting out the legal background.

Domesday Book

In the autumn of 1915, a new prospective edition was announced to LRS members; this was described as 'A volume of exceptional interest, namely, *Domesday and other Feudal Surveys*.' This project was to occupy the Society, and Canon Foster in particular, for more than two decades, and although it resulted in the publication of a notable volume, it never achieved its original purpose. The editor of the work was Revd Thomas Longley, a Yorkshireman by birth who, after a brief period as Master of the failing King's School at Pontefract, spent nearly forty years as incumbent successively of the Lincolnshire marsh parishes of Grainthorpe and Conisholme. Here he developed his interest in local history, starting with the identification of individual fields in his parish (apparently for the practical purpose of tithe collection) and developing, through the study of maps, awards, acre-books and title-deeds, into an attempt to trace the history of the successive owners of the land.[25]

To set this into context, Longley began to construct an outline of manorial descents, using the evidence of Domesday Book, the Lindsey Survey and the feudal returns of 1212 and 1243 then known by the title *Testa de Nevill* and available in an edition printed by the Record Commissioners in 1807.[26] As early as 1895, he contributed an article on the *Testa* to *Lincolnshire Notes and Queries* and this led to a correspondence with W. O. Massingberd, raising the possibility that his work might be published as part of the Lincolnshire VCH. After Massingberd's death in 1910, Longley found a new source of

---

[24] D. M. Stenton, *The Earliest Lincolnshire Assize Rolls A.D. 1202–1209*, LRS 22 (1926), xi.
[25] See [D. M. Williamson], 'Longley Deposit', *Lincolnshire Archives Committee: Archivists' Report* 6 (1954–55), 24–6; C. Sturman, 'Thomas Longley', in *Some Historians*, 32–9.
[26] J. Caley and W. Illingworth (eds), *Testa de Nevill sive liber feodorum* (London, 1807).

encouragement in Canon Foster and the Lincoln Record Society. Once the project had been accepted by the Society, the two men began a regular correspondence, discussing the identification of place-names ('I had not forgotten Osgodby in Beltisloe but I thought that was rather far away for suit of court at Barrow') and the setting-out of the proposed volume ('I am relieved by your growing preference for the paragraph form').[27] An external stimulus to the project came in September 1915 from the Public Record Office:

> I have an exciting piece of news for you! I have been in communication with the Deputy Keeper of the Records about a new edition of the *Testa* which the Commissioners are bringing out, and he has lent me the sheets of Lincoln as far as printed, and has promised me the remaining sheets as they come out. Unfortunately the Inquest of 1242 will not be in print for a good while to come, and on the whole I am inclined to think that we cannot wait for it. The earlier Return, however, is most valuable … A comparison with the *Testa* shows that it is even worse edited than I thought.[28]

Foster sent the proofs on to Longley and later went up to London to confer with the Deputy Keeper. He reported to Longley on 21 October:

> Sir Henry Maxwell Lite and his two assistants were most gracious, and I spent a long time with them puzzling out difficult names. The rolls are very bad to read. They accepted most of your suggestions and two or three of mine. I will tell you about this another time. They would be very glad of any suggestions for filling up further blanks if you know what they ought to contain.[29]

The isolation in which Longley was working at Conisholme is starkly illustrated through casual remarks in the correspondence. Foster, attempting to arrange a meeting, writes:

> We are probably going to Sutton or Mablethorpe tomorrow. Shall you be at home on Tues. or Weds. afternoons? Could you send me a p[ost] c[ard] to the Post Office at both places?

A few days later, in the middle of a discussion of abbreviations and other conventions, Longley reveals:

> I am writing this in Louth, where I am waiting for a R[ural] D[istrict] Finance Committee this afternoon. Pity me! as I had to come in by the carrier, who started at 8 o'clock.

---

[27] T. Longley, 'Testa de Neville', *LNQ* 4 (1894–95), 172–8; LAO, Longley 5/30/91, 95.
[28] LAO, Longley 5/30/97–8.
[29] LAO, Longley 5/30/100.

Two months later, when Foster had completed checking the *Testa* against the Book of Fees, he wrote:

> as I have to go to Louth on Thursday I propose to take it with me. Should I leave it at Gouldings for you? ... PS I suppose there is no chance of your being in to Louth on Thursday. I arrive at 11.58 and am to lunch with Duncan Jones.[30]

In view of Longley's obscurity, Foster took the precaution of sending samples of his work to a number of scholars, including Charles Johnson and J. H. Round. Stenton's view, after initial hesitation, was enthusiastic:

> After much thought it seems to me that Longley's work is quite first class. I think it is the best piece of assessment reconstruction that anyone has carried through ... It is a full work for a lifetime to have brought Domesday Book into line with the Lindsey Survey, and to have demonstrated in detail what the assessment of the county was and how it was distributed.[31]

By the autumn of 1917, Canon Foster reported to members that

> It was hoped that a valuable work on *Domesday Book* and other early feudal surveys upon which the Rev. T. Longley has been engaged for many years, might have been ready this year. The book is eagerly awaited by students of medieval history, and though its appearance is delayed, it is satisfactory to be able to report that Mr Longley is making steady progress.[32]

The project, indeed, was expanding and, in outline at least, had outgrown the confines of a single volume. In 1918 members were told that 'The volumes on *Domesday Book* and other early feudal inquests, at which Mr Longley has been working for more than thirty years, have been delayed by the immense difficulties of his task; but there is good reason to hope that part of the work may be in print by the time of the annual meeting in 1919.'[33] The work was now to consist of three volumes. The first of these would be a translation of the Lincolnshire portion of the Domesday Book together with the early twelfth-century Lindsey Survey, with an introduction by Professor Stenton and appendices. The second volume would be Longley's reconstruction of the medieval villages of the county by collecting together the entries for each place scattered among the feudal holdings of Domesday. It would also examine the evidence for the assessment of the county. A third volume would

---

30 LAO, Longley 5/30/92, 96, 102.
31 LRS Archive, Domesday correspondence.
32 *Annual Report 1916–17*, 7.
33 *Annual Reports 1914–15*, 6; *1916–18*, 7, 9.

trace the descent of Lincolnshire estates from Domesday to the middle of the thirteenth century.

Such an ambitious programme was beyond the ordinary resources of the Society, particularly in the difficult economic circumstances of the post-war years. Canon Foster therefore organised the launch of a special Domesday Book Fund, aimed at raising £400 to print the three volumes. Some members made one-off donations, others increased their subscriptions for a period of two or three years. By September 1923 the Fund stood at £347.[34] Longley, however, was becoming despondent about the slow progress of the project. Much of the delay had been on his own account. One letter to Foster began:

> Twice (on Thursday and Saturday) have I tried to answer your letter, and each time I have been stopped by visitors who stayed for tea ... The whole of Friday I had to spend in Louth. All last week we had my wife in bed, and we have not yet met with a likely maid, so that Olga and I have not much spare time, especially as she is provider-in-chief of entertainments for the soldiers in the district ... I am sorry to say that my rheumatism or sciatica or whatever it is still troubles me more than I like, and it is not lessened by the fact that I cannot get a man even occasionally, so that I have had to do all my gardening myself, with the result that in the evenings I have been so tired that I could not settle down to serious reading.[35]

A combination of wartime difficulties, illness, and an ingrained perfectionism that bogged him down in details, prevented Longley from seeing the work through to completion. In the spring of 1923 he wrote to Canon Foster, expressing concern about the project and suggesting that he was unlikely to see it in print. He also appears to have been aggrieved that the first volume, which comprised Foster's translation of the Lincolnshire Domesday and the Lindsey Survey with Stenton's introduction, was likely to appear without his name on the title page.

Foster consulted Stenton, who suggested that Longley, 'in view of his age and infirmities', should appear as joint editor of the volume, but that it should be made clear that the appendix on lost vills was Foster's work.[36] Foster then replied at length to Longley on 11 April 1923:

> Joint editorship, as you suggest, is quite clearly the best course. Thus both our names will appear on the title page and the cover. It is unfortunate that there has been a misunderstanding, and I am glad that it has not resulted

[34] LRS Archive, printed circulars: 'Special Fund: Domesday Book and Afterwards' (10 May 1919); *Annual Report 1922–23*, 6–7.

[35] LRS Archive, Domesday correspondence: T. Longley to CWF, 17 June (year not given). Another of Longley's letters recounts his difficulties resulting from the loss of his teeth in transit between Norwich and Conisholme.

[36] LRS Archive, Stenton correspondence: FMS to CWF, 5 April 1923.

in any real difficulty. I do not quite know how it arose. I, and others too, were fascinated by your reconstruction of the Domesday Book vills and the new light which you have shed on medieval assessment. The work is so important that our Society decided to make a special appeal for funds to print the volumes.

In considering the form in which your work could best be expressed in print, I became convinced that we ought to have a new translation of D.B. and L.S. to which reference from your tables would be easy. In order that you might concentrate on your reconstruction (i.e. volume 2), I undertook to do the translation (i.e. volume 1). The identifications of places in volume 1 were professedly to be based on volume 2. At that time I hoped that volume 2 might appear at the same time as volume 1, or even before it. In talking the matter over with the printer I told him that the copy for volume 2 was to take precedence of all the other work of the Society.

As things have turned out, not a single page of volume 2 is in print, and that alters the case about the identifications in volume 1. You have not the credit of having produced volume 2, as I hoped. Anyone could have edited volume 1 if he had volume 2 to help him. I am doing all I can to get the volume finished. Stenton has just completed the introduction, which will add greatly to the value of the book.

I am finishing an appendix on *Extinct Villages*, and a list of medieval places arranged under wapentakes.

The short preface should, I think, apportion responsibility, explaining that the identifications are based on your work, and that they will be justified in volume 2; fixing responsibility on me for the Extinct Villages, indexes, etc. Stenton's name will appear on the title page as the writer of the introduction, to which his responsibility is limited. His help throughout must, however, be acknowledged.

Canon Foster also expressed his concern about the future of the whole project:

I am very much concerned about volume 2, and my anxiety is increased by your letter in which you express a doubt as to whether you will see it in print. Apart from the loss to scholarship, its non-appearance would really knock the bottom out of the Society's scheme, and I doubt whether we could keep the money of the special fund which I have collected with so much effort. It would be a deep disappointment to the members, and a blow to the Society.

I know that the last few years you have had a hard struggle with trouble and pain; but do not be despondent. Your long labours have brought the task nearly to an end, and there seems to be but little more to be done than to polish the material for the printer. Do not wait till every difficulty is solved. You must handle the printed volume before you give up work. I am, as you know, ready to help, and even to have the MS recopied for the printer, where necessary, with a uniform plan of capitals, headings, stops, signs, numbers, and the other various details of printing. I will also make the index if you wish. Stenton will give any help he can.

The responsibility for the book must, however, be solely yours, and yours will be the name on the title-page. In the preface you can acknowledge any help, as you may see fit.

I feel that unless you can make a push now, and we can begin printing soon, we shall never see the volume.[37]

The first volume in the series, *The Lincolnshire Domesday and the Lindsey Survey*, appeared in 1924. Part of the cost of printing was met from the Domesday Book Fund.[38] The edition was warmly received. T. F. Tout, noting the 'excellent work done by the Lincoln Record Society', looked forward to the fulfilment of the 'ambitious undertaking' represented by the projected three volumes on Domesday:

When this task is completed, we shall be nearer than we have ever been before to an adequate county history of medieval Lincolnshire and a stage nearer to the definitive history of the northern Danelaw.

He gave especial praise to Stenton's 'admirable introduction' and to Foster's appendix of extinct villages. His observation, 'It is remarkable how numerous these forgotten places are,' serves as a reminder of how little was known about this subject before Canon Foster's groundbreaking work.[39]

Longley's death on 24 November 1926 effectively put an end to the rest of the project. For a while it was hoped to find someone who might complete Longley's work on the reconstruction of Domesday villages, although it was acknowledged that the volume recording the descent of Domesday estates to 1250 would have to be abandoned, not least because 'estates cannot be satisfactorily treated by the county in which parts of them happen to lie, but rather they must be dealt with under the great feudal unit of the honour of which they formed a part, and which generally extend over several coun-ties'.[40] In August 1934 a possible editor for the second volume came forward, Miss Nancy Spilman of Kirmington Vale in north Lincolnshire. Canon Foster wrote to enquire of Doris Stenton:

She took a 1st in history at St Andrew's (is that good enough?) and worked for several years on the staff of the V.C.H.; and for the last part of the time on Lincs. manorial history till they had to close down on the county. I wrote asking Page about her, but of course he died in February … I have

---

[37] LAO, Longley 5/31/1.
[38] *Annual Report 1923–24.*
[39] T. F. Tout, review in *EHR* 40 (1925), 120–1.
[40] *Annual Report 1924–31*, 5–6.

written to the Inst[itute] of Hist[orical] Research about her. Do you know anything?[41]

Frank Stenton wrote back to Foster:

> The difficulty about Longley's remains is that to make them intelligible, even to experts, two different qualifications are wanted. No one could tackle them profitably who wasn't soaked in OE finance & the detailed organisation of the Danegeld. On the other hand, unless the editor had what seems to be an unusual faculty of clear writing, the result would be really useless … the production of a volume which could not be read & would only be used for reference after much exegesis would really mean wasted labour.[42]

This was effectively the end of the Lincolnshire Domesday scheme. Canon Foster suggested an alternative topic to Miss Spilman:

> I have choked Miss Nancy Spilman off the D.B. work, and have offered her rotographs of the Bardney cartulary and charters.[43]

Thereafter, the Domesday volumes disappeared from the list of the Society's future publications.

The *Registrum Antiquissimum*

Canon Foster's work on the Lincolnshire Final Concords, his collaboration with Longley and Stenton on the Domesday edition, and above all his increasing mastery of Lincolnshire place-name forms, were all strengthened by his extensive work on the medieval charters of Lincoln Cathedral. Ever since his first meetings with Frank Stenton in 1916, Foster had been making plans for an edition of these charters. The size of the task was immense: Foster estimated that there were in the muniment room some 4,200 original charters for the pre-Reformation period, together with more than 3,600 others copied into cartularies, of which the original was lost. The earliest complete cartulary, known as the *Registrum Antiquissimum*, would form

---

[41] University of Reading, Stenton Papers: CWF to Doris Stenton, 19 August 1934. William Page (1861–1934) was editor of the Victoria County History from 1904; in 1928 he became the proprietor of the work (*ODNB*).

[42] LRS Archive, Stenton correspondence: FMS to CWF, 27 August 1934. For a modern view of Longley's work, see David Roffe, *Domesday: The Inquest and the Book* (Oxford, 2000), 62n.

[43] University of Reading, Stenton Papers: CWF to Doris Stenton, 29 November 1934.

the basis of any publication. In September 1923, the Annual Meeting of the Society agreed to Stenton's proposal that

> by the leave of the Dean and Chapter, arrangements be made for the printing of the Registrum Antiquissimum of Lincoln Cathedral, with other early relevant charters, and that the Secretary be asked to edit the work.[44]

Foster then worked up a detailed proposal, which he put to the next Annual Meeting in April 1925. Stenton was unable to attend but wrote to express his firm support:

> I think the Society has a unique opportunity in the work you have done on the RA and the charters. At present, there is not a single English cathedral of which the charters have been adequately edited. The Rolls Series published a volume of the Salisbury documents, but I remember many years ago when I first began to read Diplomatic this edition was quoted to me as an illustration of the way in which texts should not be produced. Although originals exist at Salisbury in great number, the editor printed the texts from Cartulary copies! There are I think two chief features of interest in the Lincoln material – the large number of charters by kings and great men – interesting to everybody – and the charters which prove that a considerable part of the cathedral endowment came in from contributions from small people – the free peasants, e.g. of east Lindsey. An edition would be of great value to all students of English medieval society, and I know it would please our Scandinavian and other academic subscribers.

> The difficulties I think are twofold. There is the question of money, for these texts would demand a certain amount of comment and introduction and this will send up the cost of printing. A special fund I should think would be necessary. Perhaps even more serious is the amount of work an edition would require. But for your previous work it would of course be impossible and no one who knew the county less well than you could possibly settle the topographical and genealogical questions involved. You would earn everyone's gratitude if you felt you could carry an edition through. I needn't say that I will do whatever I can to help, but the Society ought to realise how much it is asking of you if it proposes to go forward with an edition.

> I think not the least of the reasons for an edition is the example it would set to other cathedral chapters. Think of the unprinted Norwich cartularies that you have seen, and of the Durham originals that we went through together. Also, as a teacher of history, I think an edition would do something material to correct the general impression that all medieval religious foundations were monastic![45]

---

[44] LRS Minute Book I, 100.
[45] LRS Archive, Stenton correspondence: FMS to CWF, 26 April 1925.

The meeting approved the proposal, and agreed to establish a special 'Registrum Antiquissimum Fund' to help the Society meet the cost of the edition.

A circular was printed inviting contributions to the special fund; it was hoped that this would also bring the work of the Society to the attention of potential new members. The plan of the edition, following the framework of the *Registrum Antiquissimum* itself and using the texts of the original documents where these survived, was set out. It was suggested that the edition, which would be the work of Canon Foster and Professor Stenton, would extend to four volumes, corresponding to the arrangement of the cartulary itself: (1) charters of kings, popes, bishops and magnates; (2) and (3) charters relating to the several wapentakes of Lincolnshire and to other counties; (4) charters relating to the city of Lincoln. The scheme was endorsed by J. P. Gilson, Keeper of Manuscripts at the British Museum ('We want the originals [of twelfth-century charters] … edited and, with them, the (few) really good early cartularies'), by Sir Henry Maxwell-Lyte of the Public Record Office ('I heartily wish all success to the scheme for printing the *Registrum Antiquissimum* and early charters of Lincoln Cathedral. What a wealth of them you have there!'), and by Professor T. F. Tout, then the President of the Royal Historical Society:

> The scheme of the Lincoln Record Society seems to us of the utmost interest, and of importance far transcending most of the enterprises of local societies. It is the more impressive since we know that its creation will be in the hands of scholars of rare competence for such editorial work. It deserves the warmest support from all interested in medieval history, whether they belong to the wide limits of the old diocese of Lincoln or not.[46]

More than £200 was donated to the special fund, and for the next six years Canon Foster concentrated his editorial work on the new edition. Much had already been done; all of the charters had been copied by Canon Foster or his clerks, and many of the originals had been collated with the cartulary copies. Much work was still needed, however, to prepare the manuscript for the press, in writing the English summary of each document and in dating the undated charters. Although Stenton's advice continued to guide the project (and he contributed detailed notes on four of the earliest charters), it became clear that the bulk of the editing would need to be done by Canon Foster. Accordingly, he was the sole editor of the first volume, which appeared in October 1931. It was already becoming clear that the size of the edition would be more extensive than had been thought; this first volume included only the royal, papal and the earlier episcopal charters, those of the earls and magnates being held over to Volume II.

---

[46] LRS Archive, RA correspondence.

The appearance of the *Registrum Antiquissimum* was greeted with enthusiasm. Canon Foster received many letters of congratulation, of which one from Lambeth Palace Library is a typical example:

> Dr Jenkins has asked me to write on his behalf to thank you for the beautiful edition of the Registrum Antiquissimum ... which has arrived to gladden his heart exceedingly and to enrich permanently this Library.[47]

The book was widely reviewed. Professor Nellie Neilson suggested that 'This important and beautiful volume should serve as an exemplar to editors of medieval texts.'[48] In a perceptive survey of the edition, Charles Johnson wrote:

> The archives of the Dean and Chapter of Lincoln are famous as the place of deposit of one of the two more legible copies of *Magna Charta*, but few historians can have realized, until Canon Foster produced this volume, what a wonderful collection of documents they contain ... The publication of the first volume of the oldest chartulary, after careful examination of the originals when they are to be found, is a shining example of the right use of an unbroken *fonds* or group of records.

Johnson made two criticisms: first, that it would have been useful to have given some details of the evidence used in assigning limits to the undated charters, and secondly, that the sparseness (for reasons of economy) of the annotations deprived the edition of some of its potential usefulness.[49] Canon Foster undertook to remedy the first of these defects but, so far as the second comment was concerned, he pointed out that the edition would run to six volumes even with the utmost economy of annotation, and that priority must be given to supplying an accurate edition of the texts. V. H. Galbraith applauded the work of both Foster and Stenton:

> This fortunate conjunction of scholars who were also enthusiasts has found its proper fulfilment in what, when it is finished, will be our first adequate history of a great secular Cathedral ... It would be a mistake to class this as a book for specialists only. For anyone with an elementary knowledge of Latin, the actual texts of the muniments form the best approach to ecclesiastical history ... These registers are the real stuff of Lincoln history.

Galbraith also suggested that the original charters of Henry II printed in the first volume were of such importance for the study of the royal chancery that

---

[47] LRS Archive, RA correspondence: Irene Churchill to Canon Foster, 27 October 1931.
[48] N. Neilson, review in *American Historical Review* 37 (1932), 534–5.
[49] C. Johnson, review in *EHR* 47 (1932), 486–8.

they should all be reproduced in facsimile, and not just a selection. Canon Foster was quick to agree.[50]

Although Canon Foster's health, which had never been robust, was beginning to deteriorate, he continued to work at the edition. In April 1933 he wrote to Doris Stenton, 'I have been rather better, and have begun to dally with charters again.' The following September he was able to report, 'Yesterday the last sheets of the text of R.A. II were passed for press, which leaves me with a comfortable feeling.'[51] The volume appeared at the beginning of 1934. Remarkably, the third volume of the edition, largely made up of charters relating to property outside Lincolnshire, appeared in September 1935, just a few weeks before Canon Foster's death. Paying tribute to its editor, Charles Johnson described it as 'a fitting memorial of his long and generous work for the history of the diocese of Lincoln, and of the unselfish assistance which he gave to all those whose work led them into the field which he had made his own'.[52]

---

[50] 'You have made a convert at a single stroke': LRS Archive, RA correspondence: CWF to V. H. Galbraith, 6 May 1933; V. H. Galbraith, review in *History* 18 (1934), 43.
[51] University of Reading, Stenton Papers: CWF to Doris Stenton, 21 April 1933 and 1 September 1933.
[52] Charles Johnson, review in *EHR* 51 (1936), 731.

FIVE

THE DEATH OF THE FOUNDER

By the early 1930s, the Society was well established. Between 1924 and 1931 membership was steady at just over 200; the accounts were healthy and six volumes were published. The financial crisis into which the world was plunged following the Wall Street Crash of 1929 seems to have affected the Society only slightly. In the year 1931–32 it was possible to publish three volumes – the first volume of the *Registrum Antiquissimum* and the two volumes of Kesteven Quarter Sessions records – at a cost of just over £750, while still leaving £1,500 in reserve. A demand by the Inland Revenue for the payment of income tax on the Society's investments was challenged, on the grounds that the Society existed for the advancement of knowledge. This appeal being rejected, Canon Foster and a young Lincoln solicitor, Francis Hill, met with the Chief Inspector of Taxes (Claims Branch), following which 'it is satisfactory to report that they were able to establish the Society's claim for exemption'.[1]

It would appear, nevertheless, that the work of the Society during the later 1920s was dangerously dependent on the single-handed efforts of its Founder. Canon Foster filled the positions of both Secretary and General Editor; since 1918 he had also been the Society's Treasurer. His closest supporters, the Stentons, continued to offer encouragement. It was Frank who found a suitable editor for an edition of early modern records in Sidney Peyton, the Librarian at Reading. Stenton had originally proposed Peyton for a projected volume of glebe terriers, writing enthusiastically to Foster in 1917:

> About those terriers. So far as I can see the only satisfactory way of dealing with them would be to print the lot in full. I should think that they might interest a considerable circle of members, after all they deal with glebe … As for the transcription, etc., I had a pupil who would be the very man for the purpose … He is now at the war, but when and if he comes back it would really be worth while considering whether he might not get to work. His industry is grim and passionate. You could lock him in the Exchequer Gate on Friday night with two loaves, seven herrings, and a can of water,

1 *Annual Reports 1924–31*, 7.

and next Friday you would find the terriers all copied and copied accu-
rately. His name is Peyton.[2]

In the event, the terriers were abandoned and Peyton edited the Kesteven
Quarter Sessions Rolls for the Society. The Stentons, however, could not
help with the day-to-day running of the Society. Not only did they live at a
distance, they were fully occupied with their own work. Frank was closely
involved in the development of Reading after its acquisition of university
status in 1926, while Doris was as closely involved in the affairs of the Pipe
Roll Society as Canon Foster was with those of the LRS.

Part of the problem lay in the fact that, throughout the 1920s, the Society
was effectively without a President. During the first ten years of the Society's existence, this office had been held by the Bishop of Lincoln, Edward
Lee Hicks, who not only hosted the inaugural meeting in October 1910
but continued to take the chair at Annual Meetings, and at the majority of
the meetings of Council, until his death in September 1919. Although his
successor, Bishop Swayne, was duly elected President of the Society in 1920
and remained in post thereafter, it is not on record that he ever attended
a single meeting. This may have reinforced the general feeling that Canon
Foster could be left to run the Society single-handed. The minute book indicates that no Annual Meeting was held between April 1926 and October
1931, and that only two meetings of Council were convened during that time.

Regular meetings were resumed in the summer and autumn of 1931. This
move may have been prompted in part by the demands of the Inland Revenue,
but there were also signs of willingness to become involved in the affairs of
the Society. Since 1929, a small sub-committee consisting of Francis Hill
and George Gibbons had been established to help with the accounts. Another
change came in September 1932. The announcement of Bishop Swayne's
forthcoming resignation of the see, made at the beginning of that month,
made it possible for the Council, meeting a fortnight later, to nominate Lord
Monson as his successor in the office of President of the Society.

Although he had been a member of the Society since its inception, Lord
Monson had not hitherto played a significant part in its affairs and had not
previously been a member of the Council. In 1932 he approached Canon
Foster with an offer to edit a volume of the Lincolnshire Church Notes made
by his grandfather, the sixth Lord Monson, during the 1830s. He had also
offered to pay for the printing of the volume himself. He was duly elected
President in October 1932 and began energetically to promote the Society and
its work to others. Canon Foster reported to Doris Stenton in the following
May:

---

[2] LRS Archive, Stenton correspondence: FMS to CWF, 16 September 1917.

Lord Monson bestirs himself about the Society, and he has brought in Lords Brownlow, Heneage and Liverpool, and Sir Berkeley Sheffield.[3]

The new President became increasingly friendly with Canon Foster, inviting him to lunch at Burton and arranging outings to inspect the archives of other Lincolnshire landed families. A memorable visit was made to Hainton in September 1934, to look at the Heneage family documents (Canon Foster, who shared with Doris Stenton an enthusiasm for motoring, reported with glee that 'The baronial car is a 20 Austin synchromesh'):

> He was most obliging and had got everything out. There was, however, no Legbourne cartulary, and only about 50 documents before Henry VIII.

From Hainton, Lord Monson took Foster to South Cadeby, where they

> got wet through for our pains in a thunder-storm. At Burton Lord M. lent me a pair of trousers, which a civil young footman helped me to change into: he did everything except put them on himself![4]

The friendship and support of Lord Monson was to prove crucial in securing the future of Canon Foster's work.

The acclaim with which the edition of the *Registrum Antiquissimum* was received in academic circles was reflected in the award by the University of Oxford to Canon Foster of the degree of Doctor of Letters *honoris causa*. The degree was conferred in Convocation on 28 November 1933, the Public Orator making the customary Latin introduction, greeting the Canon as *virum chartarum amantissimum*, sent by the Muse into *recessus horti sui secretiores*, to grow unsuspected flowers in carefully cultivated nooks. Frank and Doris Stenton travelled from Reading to witness the ceremony. Foster had written to Doris about the arrangements: 'I am sure that the new dress will be captivating. You have to thank me for giving you an excuse for buying it!' His new status proved somewhat problematic to one member of his flock at Timberland:

> One of my parishioners said that my being a doctor would make no difference to him, since he would not give up Dr Dyer.[5]

The Society expressed, through Lord Monson, its pleasure at this distinction, adding

---

3 University of Reading, Stenton Papers: CWF to Doris Stenton, 30 May 1933.
4 University of Reading, Stenton Papers: CWF to Doris Stenton, 6 September 1934.
5 *The Times*, 29 November 1933; University of Reading, Stenton Papers: CWF to Doris Stenton, 22 November, 20 December 1933.

its own appreciation of the labour and learning which [Dr Foster] has devoted to the Society's work during his tenure of the offices of Editor, treasurer and Secretary; it views with pride and gratitude the series of volumes published under his editorship, culminating in the monumental edition of the Registrum Antiquissimum now in course of publication; and it gladly recognises that the reputation which the Society enjoys among scholars is largely due to the high standard of his historical work.[6]

The following year, on 27 September 1934, the Society marked its Silver Jubilee with a luncheon at the White Hart Hotel in Lincoln. The driving force behind this was once again Lord Monson, who made all the arrangements, invited the Earl of Yarborough, as Lord Lieutenant, to take the Chair, and secured as the guest of honour Lord Hanworth, the Master of the Rolls. In doing this, Lord Monson's aim was that of 'bringing the members into friendly contact with himself as President, and with one another, and with the hope of promoting general interest in the Society and increasing its membership'. Ninety members and guests attended. As Master of the Rolls, Lord Hanworth had shown an active concern for the preservation of records, particularly those of manorial courts which had come under threat as a result of the changes introduced by the Law of Property Acts of 1922 and 1924. At Lincoln, he was shown round Exchequer Gate and the diocesan archives, and he commended the work of Canon Foster in putting them in order and making them available to students. He added that the work of the Record Society 'would make magnificent stores of historical treasures available to students'.[7]

Meanwhile, Canon Foster's health was noticeably deteriorating. Discussing the possibility of a visit to Reading to go through the charters in *Registrum Antiquissimum III* with Frank Stenton in October 1932, he commented:

Lately I have not felt up to a long journey, and it has sometimes been a labour to walk to the other end of the village; but I am improving.

Mrs Foster's health was also a cause for concern and he began to entertain thoughts of leaving Timberland for a less demanding benefice:

Constance did not get much good out of Sutton, and since she came home she has been more oppressed with the difficulties of life. She dislikes Timberland so much that she half wishes she had agreed to Thimbleby.[8]

---

6   *Annual Report 1933–34.*

7   Frederic Wrottesley (rev. Alec Samuels), 'Ernest Murray Pollock, first Viscount Hanworth', in *ODNB*.

8   University of Reading, Stenton Papers: CWF to Doris Stenton, 10 October 1932. The Fosters regularly holidayed at Sutton-on-Sea.

Following the death of his old college friend, Canon J. E. Standen, in August 1933, Foster was approached about the Wardenship of Browne's Hospital, Stamford.

> It is £325 and a house, and the duties are very light. In many ways it would suit me well, but 48 miles from Lincoln would make my work too difficult, I am afraid. I have made many sacrifices for the records, and I suppose I must make one more.[9]

Hubert Larken, a good friend of Canon Foster, had recently been appointed Archdeacon of Lincoln and a residentiary canon. Having served in the diocese throughout his ministry, he was in a good position to hear of possible vacancies in other parishes and from time to time he drew these to Foster's attention. In November 1933, he put forward a particularly tempting proposal:

> Yesterday the Archdeacon of Lincoln, Larken, told me that the Dean, the Chancellor, and he wished that I might be subdean, and might he tell the Bishop, whose is the appointment.[10]

The new Bishop, Nugent Hicks, took a much closer interest than his predecessor in Canon Foster's work on the archives and it is likely that, had such an offer come at an earlier stage, it would have been accepted. By this time it was too late; both Canon Foster and his wife felt overwhelmed by the thought of moving. Although the Stentons urged him to accept, he wrote back:

> I appreciate what you both said about the subdeanery. I have felt since more and more sure that my decision was right. Had it been possible, it would have been an ideal position. I have to pay now for working too hard: for besides Education, the Diocesan Trust and the documents, I had to earn between £1500 and £2000 per annum by making pedigrees for Americans and others in order to pay for the work on the records. Excuse me for troubling you with all this.

He went to see his local physician, Dr Dyer, who told him not to overwork.

> A second opinion would have been useless. My own knowledge reinforces Dyer's opinion. I can get on only if I take things very easily, and go very slowly... Timberland often seems rather a burden, but I shrink from the bother of moving, and the pain of parting from so many of my books and other things. Moreover, the people here are extraordinarily kind.[11]

---

9 University of Reading, Stenton Papers: CWF to Doris Stenton, 4 August 1933. Canon Standen had helped with the proofs of the first two volumes of the *Registrum Antiquissimum*.
10 University of Reading, Stenton Papers: CWF to Doris Stenton, 22 November 1933.
11 University of Reading, Stenton Papers: CWF to Doris Stenton, 20 December 1933.

A slight attack of influenza at the beginning of 1935 brought matters to a head, and Canon Foster began to consider the future of the Society after his death.

> They keep asking at Lincoln who is to take up my work for the Society when I can do it no longer. This last week this has seemed to me an urgent question, for my sight makes it rather difficult to carry on... Yesterday I came to the conclusion that the question ought to be considered by the council on the 31st. Before writing to Lord M[onson] I should like to know what you think.

Foster thought that Francis Hill would be a good choice for Treasurer, no doubt recognising in him those qualities of efficiency, hard work and willingness to delegate that he himself possessed. Lord Monson agreed:

> He seems to me a very clear headed young man and one on whose good judgment we can rely.[12]

The question of the editorship was not so clear-cut; Canon Foster told Doris:

> You would make the best possible editor – far better than I could ever be – but it is difficult to see how you could do it with all your work, and at the great distance.

There was only one other possibility, and that was Kathleen Major.[13]

Born in 1906, Kathleen Major first came to Lincolnshire when her family moved to Holbeach in the early 1920s. She studied history at St Hilda's College, Oxford, and went on to postgraduate research on the *acta* of Archbishop Stephen Langton, under the supervision of F. M. Powicke. In the course of her search for Langton charters, she naturally wrote to enquire at Lincoln and was invited to meet Canon Foster at Timberland.[14] She recalled their first meeting:

> the windows of the vicarage drawing room looking over a wide and rather featureless landscape of fertile fenland. He had been snoozing slightly after lunch when I was taken in to him and rose rather pink in the face and smiling.

Thereafter she used to visit Canon Foster every vacation, coming to realise that 'this elderly scholar ... welcomed every chance of talking about history'

---

[12] LRS Archive: Major correspondence: Lord Monson to CWF, 25 January 1935.
[13] University of Reading, Stenton Papers: CWF to Doris Stenton, 16 January 1933.
[14] G. W. S. Barrow, 'Kathleen Major', *Proceedings of the British Academy* 115 (2002), 319–329.

and in particular about the edition of the *Registrum Antiquissimum*, whose 'attractions are not apparent to everyone'.[15] In January 1931 she wrote to enquire about membership of the Record Society, reporting that she had completed her thesis on Langton and that one of the examiners was to be Professor Stenton. Foster replied:

> I think that you have done well to collect so many as 105 acta. You are fortunate in one, at least, of your examiners, Professor Stenton, for he is one of the most appreciative men I know ... I shall welcome you as a member of the Lincoln Record Society. Nothing is easier than to join it. All that is required is the payment of the annual subscription of a guinea. There is no election since the meetings are only business meetings connected with publications. We have the power to exclude, but a person would have to be almost inconceivably objectionable before we should use it.[16]

By 1935, Canon Foster had identified Miss Major as a potential successor as Editor:

> I think that she might do, and also that she might be willing. She is deeply interested in the county. She would probably be willing to act as assistant editor for the present, and that would certainly help me.[17]

Kathleen expressed her willingness to act, and at the Annual Meeting on 31 January 1935, she was duly appointed Assistant Editor.[18] Not long afterwards, Canon Foster wrote asking her to help with the edition of the *Registrum Antiquissimum*;

> she replied that she would gladly do so, and felt honoured at being asked. I also told her that Frank thought she was a good girl, which pleased her very much, for she values his opinion above that of all mankind.[19]

The other uncertainty about the future was the question of what was going to happen to the archives. The arrangements of storage and access to the records, which depended entirely on Canon Foster, had been praised at the Society's commemorative luncheon in September 1934, but it was becoming evident that something needed to be done about the long-term care of the archives. Lord Monson was ready to act. In May 1934, Canon Foster showed him round the various buildings:

---

15 LCL, Kathleen Major Papers: typescript of talk on Canon Foster and the *Registrum Antiquissimum*.
16 LRS Archive, Foster correspondence: CWF to KM, 19 January 1931.
17 University of Reading, Stenton Papers: CWF to Doris Stenton, 16 January 1933.
18 University of Reading, Stenton Papers: CWF to Doris Stenton, 30 January 1933; LRS Minute Book I, 152.
19 University of Reading, Stenton Papers: CWF to Doris Stenton, 16 April 1935.

On Monday I took Lord Monson over our depositories – Exch[equer Gate], Galilee, Aln[wick] T[ower]. He has been talking to the Bishop about their final custody; and he thought that a place ought to be found for Florence. The L[indsey] C[ounty] C[ouncil] also talked to me about having her some time. Lord M. said he could not understand 3 bishops having left me so far away as Timberland; and he wished he had known me when Burton was last vacant. It would have suited me rather well.[20]

Lord Monson succeeded in persuading Bishop Hicks of the need for action. At the Annual Meeting of the LRS on 17 August 1934, the Bishop spoke of his concern that Exchequer Gate 'should be re-conditioned and made into a thoroughly up-to-date Diocesan Record Office', although, he continued, 'It was not clear at present ... how the necessary funds were to be provided.'[21] A week later, as the commemorative luncheon drew nearer, Canon Foster reported:

Lord Monson thinks of a little conference before dinner on the 26th with Lord Hanworth about the housing of the records, and a talk afterwards with the Bishop there. The latter is certainly not going to let the matter drop.[22]

In October, however, Foster was less optimistic:

It does not seem that much will be done to the Exchequer Gate, for the Bishop finds that he must raise a fund of something between one and two hundred thousand for new parishes in the ironstone areas...[23]

Nevertheless, Lord Monson kept up the pressure, as Canon Foster reported the following January:

He was going to see the Bishop on his way home, to stir him up about the archives.[24]

The breakthrough came in May. Canon Foster described the sequence of events:

[20] University of Reading, Stenton Papers: CWF to Doris Stenton, 15 May 1934. The diocesan records were kept partly in Exchequer Gate and partly in the Alnwick Tower of the medieval bishops' palace. The records of the Dean and Chapter were kept above the Galilee Porch. Florence Thurlby, a native of Timberland, was Canon Foster's secretary; she had worked as one of his clerks for many years.

[21] LRS Minute Book I, 141.

[22] University of Reading, Stenton Papers: CWF to Doris Stenton, 24 August 1934.

[23] University of Reading, Stenton Papers: CWF to Doris Stenton, 23 October 1934.

[24] University of Reading, Stenton Papers: CWF to Doris Stenton, 30 January 1935.

One day the Bishop met Sir James Irvine, Principal of St Andrews, at the Athenaeum, who encouraged him to think that the Pilgrim Trust might make a grant… A few days later I heard that Lord Macmillan, Chairman of the P.T., was coming to look at the Cathedral, and I arranged with the Dean that we should ask him if he would care to see the documents. I felt that if he had seen them, it might help when the Bishop made an application. Lord Monson came in and joined me, and when we joined the Dean's party we found that he had mentioned the matter to Lord Macmillan, and that Lord Macmillan took much more interest in the documents than in the church. We spent a long time in the Gate, and he spoke of the Pilgrim Trust helping to adapt the building and to provide a salary. He said he wanted to do something more for the preservation of documents … Mr Baldwin, he said, was also interested in archives. In fact he was so encouraging that it is hard to think that he – a lawyer and a Scot – would raise our hopes only to dash them.

Encouraged by this, the Bishop appointed a small committee to fill in the details and make an application in his name. In addition, as Canon Foster was delighted to note,

he has got Jourdain [the Diocesan Registrar] to give up the custody of the ancient documents – a great stroke.[25]

A week later, Canon Foster was busy drafting the application and, on Lord Macmillan's advice, 'an alternative smaller one', involving the restoration of part of the Exchequer Gate only. He also reported that the Registrar, despite his surrender of custody, was being obstructive:

Jourdain is generally full of quibbles, and so I suggested to Lord M[onson] yesterday to invite him to lunch, and after a luscious luncheon and high society he simply oozed acquiescence. I mentioned this to Hill, and he thought that an action did not lie for bribery and corruption.

Canon Foster added in a postscript that 'Kathleen tells me she would like to be a candidate if there is to be a post at Lincoln.'[26]

The application was made and on 6 July 1935 Lord Macmillan informed the Bishop that the Pilgrim Trust would grant £1,700 for the restoration of Exchequer Gate and £500 per annum for three years for salary and other expenses.[27] On 17 August, Frank Stenton wrote a long letter to Canon Foster in support of Kathleen Major:

25 University of Reading, Stenton Papers: CWF to Doris Stenton, 21 May 1935.
26 University of Reading, Stenton Papers: CWF to Doris Stenton, 28 May 1935.
27 Sir Francis Hill, 'From Canon Foster to the Lincolnshire Archives Office', *LHA* 13 (1978), 71.

It seems to me that Miss Major has every qualification for the post. The Stephen Langton thesis on which she got her B.Litt. was based on record work, very well done. It showed that she has the makings of a good editor – she has a real sense of scholarship, and only needs wider knowledge and experience... I cannot bring to mind anyone of the same academic standing who would fit so well into the scheme. She knows the county, and I think she has the personality to make the Exchequer Gate a real centre to which students will refer... It is very pleasant to think of a scheme, so long debated, taking practical shape at last... It will give a permanent basis for the work of the L.R.S. The chances against getting someone who can make the scheme effective are really quite considerable, and Miss Major is a piece of sheer good luck.[28]

Kathleen was duly appointed Archivist to the Bishop of Lincoln. On 26 October, Canon Foster wrote to her father, George Major:

I send my best thanks for the brace of birds which you have so kindly sent me. I was very glad, when your daughter came over here, to learn that you had so far recovered from your serious operation; and I hope that the arrival of the birds means that you were able to shoot them yourself. We consider that we are very fortunate in securing Kathleen for the work at Lincoln, and her appointment is specially gratifying to myself. I do not suppose that any one ever had better testimonials. She will, I am sure, find the life at Lincoln socially pleasant, and she is already assured of a warm welcome from some of the people who are the best worth knowing, though she has not as yet met them all.[29]

Three days later, on 29 October 1935, Canon Foster was dead. Reporting his death, the *Lincolnshire Echo* recorded that

He had dealt with his letters and several other matters yesterday and went to bed, in accordance with his custom, at about 9.30, apparently in his usual state of health, but two hours later he had a heart attack and died at 11.45 p.m. before the arrival of Dr Dyer of Martin.[30]

His funeral, which took place at Timberland on Friday 1 November, was conducted (at his own request) by his great friend Hubert Larken, assisted by G. H. Chard, Vicar of Nocton, and Bishop Nugent Hicks who pronounced the blessing. Miss Thurlby was at the organ. There was present 'a large and distinguished assembly', as

Men and women prominent in the field of learning and particularly of history joined with the parishioners of Timberland today in paying tribute

[28] University of Reading, Stenton Papers: FMS to CWF, 17 August 1935.
[29] LCL, Kathleen Major Papers: CWF to George Major, 26 October 1935.
[30] *Lincolnshire Echo*, 30 October 1935.

to one who laboured, not only in his own country parish, but for the whole diocese and learning in general.

In Lincoln Cathedral, Chancellor Srawley referred to one who

> was known and loved as a devoted parish priest; known, too, in a wider circle as a patient scholar with a vast store of historical learning, who has done so much to make the local history of Lincolnshire a living story, and to render available to the world at large the treasures stored in the archives of this see and of this cathedral church. [31]

There were some who assumed that the death of its founder would inevitably mean the end of the Lincoln Record Society. To counter such an impression and to make it clear that the work of the Society would continue, a meeting of the Council was convened and held at the Jews' Court in Lincoln on 19 December 1935. The President, Lord Monson, took the chair; those present included Bishop Nugent Hicks, Chancellor Srawley, Professor and Mrs Stenton, and Professor Hamilton Thompson. Lord Monson paid tribute to the life and work of Canon Foster and all members stood in respect of his memory. Having acknowledged the debt of the Society to its founder, the Council then moved to secure its future by nominating, as its new officers, Miss Major to be Editor and Secretary, and Francis Hill to be Treasurer. An Editorial Sub-Committee of the President, Chancellor Srawley and Professors Stenton and Hamilton Thompson was appointed to assist Miss Major. It was agreed to establish a Foster Memorial Fund, to help with the printing of the next two volumes of the *Registrum Antiquissimum*.[32]

Although no one could have foreseen it at the time, the decisions of this Council meeting were to shape the future of the Society for the next thirty years, as the redoubtable team of Miss Major as Editor and Francis Hill as Treasurer built on the solid foundations laid by Canon Foster. What the Society owed to Canon Foster was expressed in a characteristically eloquent appreciation written by Hamilton Thompson:

> With the death of its founder and director the Lincoln Record Society enters upon a new phase of existence. For twenty-five years its labours were pursued under the guidance of the late Canon Foster, who inspired its counsels, edited many of its publications with his own hand while, as general editor of the whole series, he supervised the work of other contributors with unflagging attention to detail, and was in short its indispensable executive officer.

[31] *Lincolnshire Echo*, 1 November 1935.
[32] LRS Minute Book I, 155–161.

The life of Charles Wilmer Foster was devoted to the disinterested task of revealing the wealth of historical material contained in the collections of diocesan and other records preserved at Lincoln and of making it accessible to other students in the same field. Bringing to his work acute critical intelligence and a passion for tracing each detail to its ultimate source and cause, his mastery of English history, particularly in its legal and institutional aspects, was remarkable, and, while fully alive to the local and parochial importance of his material, his end and aim was to emphasise its value as illustrating and enriching the history of the nation in general. He combined in a very unusual degree the spirit of the antiquary to whom no fact is insignificant with the mind of the historian who assembles such facts with a proper sense of their connected meaning and relative value and employs them for purposes to which their local interest is entirely subordinate. As a pioneer in the work of demonstrating the dignity of local history and archaeology as a necessary part of historical study he must always take an honoured place; and apart from his other published writings, his thorough and concise account of the history of two small Lincolnshire parishes, conceived on these lines, furnished an impeccable model to all who undertake a similar task elsewhere from the enlightened point of view which he signally exemplified.[33]

---

[33] *Annual Report 1934–35*, 5.

SIX

THE IMPACT OF THE SECOND WORLD WAR

When Kathleen Major took over as General Editor at the end of 1935, the Society had just published the third volume of the *Registrum Antiquissimum*. As had been envisaged when she had agreed to assist Canon Foster with Volume IV, she now took over responsibility for the rest of the edition, which at that stage was expected to extend to three further volumes. There were two other works in progress. Lord Monson's edition of his grandfather's *Lincolnshire Church Notes* was almost ready to be issued to members, while a volume of the fourteenth-century proceedings of the Keepers of the Peace, edited by Miss Rosamond Sillem, was expected by the end of 1936.[1]

Monson's Church Notes duly appeared in February 1936. Like *Holles' Church Notes* earlier, it proved very popular with members, with a text in English (after three consecutive volumes of Latin charters) and plenty to interest both local historians and genealogists. As the *Church Times* noted

> The value of these notes, which deal with 227 churches, is that they show the old buildings as they were before Victorian 'restorers', often possessed of more zeal than knowledge, got to work upon them. 'I want to go down to Lincolnshire as early as I can,' wrote Monson in 1860, 'for they are pulling down an old church … and the incumbent is a violent Utilitarian, and wants to destroy a noble screen and possibly other dear old relics, which I must endeavour to rescue.'[2]

Much of the work of checking the text had been done by Canon Foster. He wrote in the summer of 1934 that it had been 'a troublesome job' and had impeded his progress with the *Registrum Antiquissimum*:

> Now there is the index of vol. III to be wrestled with. The present wrestling, however, is with the Church Notes: they take far more doing than I imagined they would. The learned George Gibbons has come to the rescue in identifying many of the arms. He is also helping with proof reading of

1   LRS Minute Book I, 160.
2   Review in *Church Times*, 27 March 1936.

the Notes, and also of R.A., a job at which he is good. I am rewarding him by putting him up for F.S.A.

An attempt to enlist the help of the diocesan clergy in checking the descriptions did not produce the intended results:

The clergy to whom we sent the M[onumental] I[nscription]s in manuscript failed us badly: I then sent proofs to them and they made many corrections which they might well have made before.[3]

The munificence of Lord Monson in presenting this volume to the Society did much to stabilise the financial position in the period after Canon Foster's death. Lord Monson's generosity went even further, as he arranged for the presentation of sixty further copies, free of charge, to American libraries, to bring the work of the Society to their notice and to encourage them to join. Some of these libraries did join, among them the Boston Athenaeum, the Public Libraries of Boston, Detroit and St Louis, the Peabody Institute of Baltimore and the University of St Louis.[4] Others followed their lead subsequently. The support of American libraries played a vital part, both in contributing to the financial stability of the Society and in upholding its international reputation.

It was an American scholar who played a major role in the next volume. *Some Sessions of the Peace in Lincolnshire 1360–1375* formed part of a series of fourteenth-century peace rolls whose publication was initiated by Professor Bertha Putnam. Her edition of *Kent Keepers of the Peace 1316–1317* had appeared in 1933, and volumes for Northamptonshire, Yorkshire and Warwickshire were also in preparation. In addition, Professor Putnam's monumental edition of *Proceedings Before the Justices of the Peace in the Fourteenth and Fifteenth Centuries* was published in 1938 by the Ames Foundation. The Lincolnshire volume was edited by Rosamond Sillem, a graduate of Somerville College, Oxford, who had gone on to postgraduate research at Mount Holyoke College, under the supervision of Professor Putnam herself. Miss Sillem had been recommended to Canon Foster by Maud Clarke of Somerville College. By the time of the Canon's death, the work was nearing completion. The indexes, however, took longer than anticipated, as Miss Sillem, now back in England and teaching in London, could only work on the book at weekends. Moreover, there was some urgency in completing the volume. She wrote in October 1936:

3   University of Reading, Stenton Papers: CWF to Doris Stenton, 15 May, 13 August, 29 November 1934.
4   *Annual Report 1936–7*, 5.

I am very anxious indeed to get it done as soon as possible ... as I am going out to a job in Singapore for two years in February.[5]

In the event, she sailed for Singapore before the index could be finished. Although she offered to take the proofs with her on the boat, it was decided that sending them back from the Far East would be too risky, and Miss Major completed the index herself, under the watchful eye of Doris Stenton:

Of course if you want me to I will have a look at R.S.'s indexes ... They are probably all right. Miss Putnam was looking after them and she – R.S. – is a careful person herself.[6]

The edition was published in June 1937. Miss Sillem wrote from Singapore:

The volume arrived yesterday, and looks very nice indeed ... I must thank you once more for all you have done for me in getting it through its final stages, and especially for helping with the Index. I do hope that you and the Society are pleased with it and that you feel it is what Canon Foster would have wished for, had he lived to see it.[7]

The volume included an introduction giving details of the procedure of the sessions and of the members of the local bench. There is much of social as well as legal interest in these records, including an incident of especial notoriety, the murder of Sir William Cantilupe in 1375 ('as good as a detective story', in the view of Miss Major).[8] The edition was given a warm review by Helen Cam, who concluded:

these rolls are worthy of the careful editing Miss Sillem has given them and of the admirable production on which we can count from the Lincoln Record Society.[9]

There were further Lincolnshire peace rolls still unedited. Thanking Miss Major for organising the sending out of review copies, Miss Sillem wrote:

---

[5]   LRS Archive, Major correspondence: Rosamond Sillem to KM, 14 October 1936.
[6]   LRS Archive, Major correspondence: Doris Stenton to KM, 1 February 1937. This was a change of plan, for a few days earlier she had written 'It is a relief to learn that I am to be spared the Index, for I have a large one of my own to check for my Selden Society volume, and I rather blench from the thought. However, the volume is, I hope, going to buy me a vacuum cleaner' (Doris Stenton to KM, 26 January 1937). The Selden Society was unique in paying its editors.
[7]   LRS Archive, Major correspondence: Rosamond Sillem to KM, 13 July 1937.
[8]   Personal knowledge. Miss Major was a connoisseur of detective fiction.
[9]   H. M. Cam, review in *EHR* 54 (1939), 721–3.

I am so glad that the Society is pleased with the book and feel very proud
that they had thought of asking me to do another. Of course I have no idea
what my plans will be when I come home, but if circumstances permit, and
the Society still wants it, I should love to do another then.[10]

These two volumes – *Lincolnshire Church Notes* and *Some Sessions of the
Peace* – had both been undertaken and largely completed during Canon
Foster's lifetime (he had read both the manuscript and the first proofs of *Some
Sessions of the Peace*). It was the issue in late 1937 of the fourth volume of
the *Registrum Antiquissimum* that inaugurated the new era in the publications
of the Society. Although Canon Foster had done much of the groundwork for
the volume, it was Kathleen Major who completed it, made the index and saw
it through the press. Thus, while the volume included an elegant tribute to the
Founder from the pen of Frank Stenton, together with a photographic portrait
of him (given by Lord Monson), it also signalled the resolve of the Society
both to carry on its work of publishing historical records and to complete the
monumental edition of the charters of Lincoln Cathedral.

This was, of course, Kathleen Major's first record society edition and she,
more than anyone else, felt the loss of Canon Foster's guidance. She therefore
relied for advice on the Editorial Sub-Committee, particularly the Stentons.
The help of Doris Stenton was especially valuable in making the index.[11] She
was always willing to discuss points of detail, even if this meant departing
from traditional practice:

> By the way, don't you think that [*sic*] might be inserted in the Antiquis-
> simum texts where the reading is obviously a clerical error. The Canon was
> all against too many [*sics*], but without them the reader may doubt.

She also gave Kathleen the sense of comradeship that only someone who was
engaged in similar work could provide:

> Ruddock is getting the 1936 Pipe Roll out this week, he says, and I have
> just sent him the text for the 1938 volume. He has the 1937 in galley proof.
> It's a treadmill running a society, but rather fun.[12]

She also acted as an intermediary over the completion of Stenton's memoir
of Canon Foster, writing to Kathleen:

> The sad thing is that by no means can you have the memoir by the 3rd
> week in August. Frank has settled down to A[nglo-] S[axon England] and

---

[10] LRS Archive, Rosamond Sillem to KM, 23 August 1937.
[11] *Reg. Ant. IV*, ix.
[12] LRS Archive, Major correspondence: Doris Stenton to KM, 26 January 1937. The
Lincoln firm of Ruddocks printed the volumes of the Pipe Roll Society for many years.

is immoveable and will be till the end of the vac. We are living cloistered lives that he may get a move on … It's very hot here now but pleasant. Frank is typing away in the garden. I will suggest the memoir when I can, but it's no good now. It can go in last all right.[13]

The memorial volume was published in February 1938; it was calculated that there would be a further three volumes to complete the edition. One other unfinished project initiated by Canon Foster as general editor was a proposed edition of seventeenth-century Quarter Sessions records for Lindsey, to follow up Peyton's two volumes for Kesteven. This work, first announced to the Society in October 1932, had been undertaken by Mrs Gladys Barrett of Newcastle upon Tyne. In 1936 Miss Major wrote to enquire whether the volume might be ready for the following Spring, so that it could go to press after Miss Sillem's book was published.

Unfortunately she replied that she would be unable to complete the work for some years, as she has a young son who takes up all her time. She has, however, offered to hand over the transcripts of the rolls to the Society, if we can find an editor.[14]

Mr Peyton, approached through Doris Stenton, expressed a willingness to write the introduction but, because of the pressures of his post as Reading University Librarian, said that he could not do anything about the text or the index. Miss Major then persuaded George Gibbons to undertake the work. However, the project was dropped not long afterwards.[15]

One of Canon Foster's own projects still listed in 1936 as one of the Society's forthcoming editions was a second volume of *The State of the Church*, but although many of the transcripts for this survived among his papers, it seemed unlikely that any other editor could be found to take it up. On Professor Stenton's recommendation, the Domesday project was officially abandoned, and the balance of the money in the Domesday Book Fund was transferred to the Registrum Antiquissimum Fund. The Society's annual reports continued to list among prospective publications chapter acts, Lincoln wills, marriage bonds and bishops' registers, but otherwise, when Miss Major took office, the editorial cupboard was bare.[16] At the meeting of Council held in December 1935 after Canon Foster's death, Hamilton Thompson

---

[13] LRS Archive, Major correspondence: Doris Stenton to KM, 3 August 1937.
[14] LRS Archive, Major correspondence: KM to Lord Monson, 16 October 1936.
[15] LRS Archive, Major correspondence: KM to George Gibbons, 18 October 1936.
[16] The list of prospective publications undoubtedly buoyed up some members with unrealistic hopes. At the Annual Meeting in October 1936, Professor Owen of Nottingham 'read a letter from Mr Wadsworth asking when the Society was going to publish the marriage bonds for which he had been waiting for 26 years. The President said … that the question could not be immediately settled.' (LRS Minute Book I, 177–8).

came to the rescue with an offer to edit three further volumes of Visitations of Religious Houses, this time for the period 1519–1536. Kathleen Major then set to work with characteristic thoroughness to establish, on this modest foundation, a list of forthcoming publications. At the Annual Meeting held in October 1936, members heard some of her plans for the future. These included two projected editions of episcopal registers – the first since the difficulties with Bishop Gravesend's rolls had led to the termination of the arrangement with the Canterbury and York Society a decade earlier. Miss Major's new role as Archivist to the Bishop of Lincoln put her in an ideal position to find suitable editors for the registers.

Miss Margaret Archer had first worked on the Lincoln records in the time of Canon Foster, in connection with her Oxford B.Litt. thesis.[17] Miss Major consulted Hamilton Thompson, who replied:

I think that the publication of Repingdon's Register would be extremely useful in view of what it may contain with regard to the councils of Pisa and Constance … Miss Archer has already made acquaintance with the administrative history of the diocese about this period, and knowing something of her work, I should strongly recommend that the work of editing Repingdon, which will certainly take some years, should be entrusted to her.[18]

Kathleen then approached Miss Archer herself:

This Society is considering the possibility of printing the Memoranda Book of Bishop Repingdon, and you have been suggested as a possible editor by Professor Jenkins and Professor Hamilton Thompson. I hope very much that you will be able to undertake the work.[19]

Miss Archer replied ('I feel very honoured indeed') that 'there is no work which would give me greater enjoyment' but went on:

I have obtained a teaching post, starting in September, at the County School for Girls, Bebington (near Birkenhead), which is just about as far as it could be from both Lincoln and Oxford.[20]

By October, however, Miss Major had persuaded the Bishop to agree to the temporary deposit of the register at Liverpool University Library for Miss

---

[17] Margaret Archer (ed.), *The Register of Bishop Philip Repingdon 1405–1419, Volume I* (Lincoln Record Society 57, 1963), v; Margaret Archer, 'The diocese of Lincoln under Bishops Repingdon and Fleming' (unpublished B.Litt. thesis, University of Oxford, 1936).
[18] LRS Archive, Major correspondence: Hamilton Thompson to KM, 22 April 1936.
[19] LRS Archive, Repingdon correspondence: KM to Margaret Archer, 13 July 1936.
[20] LRS Archive, Repingdon correspondence: Margaret Archer to KM, 18 July 1936.

Archer's use. The register was moved on 30 December ('The Surveyor to the Cathedral is packing it in a special box') and in early February Miss Archer was able to report:

> I am greatly enjoying my work on the Memoranda, and only wish that I had more free time. It is a pleasant change from teaching.[21]

The second register was that of Bishop Oliver Sutton (1280–1299). This was at that time the earliest unprinted register in the series, and previous proposals had been made for its publication (one of them, to the alarm of Canon Foster and Professor Hamilton Thompson, by the unrepentant F. N. Davis). In October 1936, Kathleen Major reported to Lord Monson that she had consulted her former supervisor at Oxford, Professor F. M. Powicke, who recommended

> Miss Rosalind Hill, a rather younger contemporary of mine at St Hilda's, who obtained a first class in history in 1931, and has since been working on Monastic Letter books for a doctorate of philosophy, on which she is being examined tomorrow. She is now assistant lecturer in Mediæval History at University College, Leicester. I think there is no doubt that … she would prove a very competent editor.[22]

Rosalind Hill was delighted at the suggestion ('It is a great privilege to be allowed to undertake it') and wrote back to Kathleen:

> I should be very pleased to do what I can to bring the good Bishop to the light of common day! Is there a time-limit or may I do it at my own speed?

It is doubtful whether either Miss Archer or Miss Hill foresaw just how long these projects were to take. The edition of Repingdon (in three volumes) was completed in 1982, while that of Sutton (in eight) was eventually finished in 1986.

Miss Major was also looking into the possibility of a volume of the Records of the Court of Sewers for Holland. Having herself lived in Holbeach, she was fully aware of the historical importance of drainage in the district.[23] In

---

[21] LRS Archive, Repingdon correspondence: KM to Margaret Archer, 30 December 1936; Margaret Archer to KM, 7 February 1937.

[22] LRS Archive, Major correspondence: KM to Lord Monson, 16 October 1936. Rosalind Hill's thesis was in fact awarded the degree of Bachelor of Letters: '[since] in the opinion of the Board I seem to have squeezed out all there is to squeeze, I have chosen the B.Litt.' (Rosalind Hill to KM, 29 August 1936).

[23] See her article, 'Conan son of Ellis, an early inhabitant of Holbeach', *AASRP* 42 (1934), 1–18.

October 1936 she went to look at the records in Boston, reporting to Lord Monson:

> there is no doubt that there is material for a very useful and interesting volume probably covering the period between the reigns of Henry VIII and the end of that of Elizabeth … Professor Stenton, with whom I discussed the matter in August, agreed that it would be best to approach Dr Darby with a view to finding an editor.[24]

Hamilton Thompson gave his support to the proposal:

> I agree thoroughly about the desirability of printing the Court of Sewers records. People like English volumes from time to time, and it would be good policy to print a Holland volume.[25]

It was decided to ask Dr Darby if he himself would edit the volume. H. C. Darby, a major figure in the study of historical geography in the twentieth century, had edited a major collection of papers on that theme in 1936. One of his own contributions to the volume was on the draining of the fens, and his classic study of that subject appeared in 1940.[26] After some correspondence, he came to the decision that because of his many other commitments he could not himself undertake the project:

> I cannot see that I shall be free to touch the Sewers Records for at least three years. To look beyond this is much too uncertain so that I think it only fair to you to say No. I think the Sewer Records ought to be done and must be done. If, in a remote future they still remain unedited, perhaps I can come back to them. But of course in the meantime you may find someone else to do them.[27]

In the event it was not until 1943 that Miss Major could report the finding of an editor for this volume; this was Miss Mary Kirkus, the Librarian of the University of Reading.[28]

It was one thing to produce a list of forthcoming volumes but quite another to bring them to fruition. The third volume of the *Registrum Antiquissimum*, published just before Canon Foster's death, was issued to members in respect of the subscription for 1931–32. The two volumes issued in 1937 and 1938 – *Some Sessions of the Peace* and *Registrum Antiquissimum IV* – were for the

---

[24] LRS Archive, Major correspondence: KM to Lord Monson, 16 October 1936.
[25] LRS Archive, Major correspondence: AHT to KM, 13 October 1936.
[26] H. C. Darby (ed.), *An Historical Geography of England before A.D.1800* (Cambridge, 1936); H. C. Darby, *The Draining of the Fens* (1940).
[27] LRS Archive, Major correspondence: H. C. Darby to KM, 26 October 1937.
[28] LRS Minute Book II: Annual Meeting, 24 September 1943.

years 1932–33 and 1934–35. This meant that, with no volume in prospect for 1938, the Society would fall further into arrears and it would become even harder to catch up with the deficit which had originally arisen during the First World War. Professor Hamilton Thompson was doing all he could to bring forward the first volume of the *Visitations* but he was hampered by the responsibilities of his position at the University of Leeds:

> I am sorry to have to keep you waiting like this, but University business, very much against my inclination, has to absorb a lot of my time this session, and I am constantly in the position of having to leave the word of God to serve tables.[29]

As a result of this, and the withdrawal of Mrs Barrett from the Lindsey Quarter Sessions edition, it was not possible to produce a volume in 1939. It was hoped that the early months of 1940 would see the publication not only of the first part of the *Visitations* but also the fifth volume of the *Registrum Antiquissimum*. External events, however, over which the Lincoln Record Society had no control, dictated otherwise. The disturbed nature of the times was perfectly summed up by the veteran H. E. Salter, to whom Miss Major had written for information about two early thirteenth-century subdeans of Lincoln, in connection with the dating of charters in the *Registrum Antiquissimum*:

> I can give you no help. I have no knowledge of the Subdeans Philip and John ... The years 1205 onwards until 1215 are not a good time. People were holding back, as they are now, uncertain about the future, and made few grants.[30]

Margaret Archer wrote in August 1939 to explain her lack of progress with Repingdon's register:

> with so many international crises I thought the register would be safer at Lincoln for a time. We seem to have spent the entire summer preparing for war, but it looks rather more hopeful at the moment, don't you think?[31]

She was not the only one hoping that the threat of war would just go away. Hamilton Thompson, who was looking forward to finishing off the first volume of his *Visitations* following his retirement from Leeds in July of that year, wrote:

---

[29] LRS Archive, Major correspondence: AHT to KM, 17 November 1937.
[30] LRS Archive, Major correspondence: H. E. Salter to KM, 4 February 1939.
[31] LRS Archive, Major correspondence: Margaret Archer to KM, 3 August 1939.

I am going to France from 22 August to 6 September inclusive, but shall hope to have the Lincolnshire part all done before I go.

He duly sent the Lincolnshire material on 14 August and promised the Bedfordshire and Hertfordshire portions before leaving. He wrote again on 30 August:

I sent you a parcel of MS just as I was going to France a little over a week ago … I had a rather strenuous time there and, owing to the crisis, had to return prematurely.

His next letter was dated 3 September:

I hope to send the remaining sheets of the present volume this week … It is most likely, considering the turn that things have taken, that we shall move from London to-morrow or Tuesday … We have already had warning of an air-raid here immediately after the news of the declaration of war came; but nothing seemed to happen, and I am not sure whether it was not a false alarm in order to try out the effect of the signals.[32]

The Annual Meeting of the Society was held on 20 October 1939. With members still waiting for the volume for 1935–36, it was inevitable that the subject of arrears should be raised. Miss Major reported that it was hoped to issue the first volume of *Diocesan Visitations* and the fifth volume of the *Registrum Antiquissimum* during the course of the following year, and further volumes would appear as and when this became possible. The first volume of Rosalind Hill's edition of Bishop Sutton's Register was nearing completion and in addition there was a new project which was almost ready. This was an edition of a Lincolnshire assize roll for 1298, which had been prepared in the first instance for a doctoral thesis at the University of Edinburgh. Miss Major asked for the patience of members during the difficult circumstances in which the Society was placed:

it had seemed, before war broke out, that the arrears in publication were at last to be overtaken. The Council therefore asks the indulgence of its members in this situation over which it has no control.[33]

There were three principal obstacles in the path of record publishing societies in wartime. In the case of those volumes which were ready to go to press, it might prove impossible for the printer to undertake the work. Many of the staff would be called up for military service or other war work, while the

---

[32] LRS Archive, Major correspondence: AHT to KM, 8 August, 30 August, 3 September 1939.
[33] *Annual Report 1938–39*, 5–6.

emergency powers assumed by the Government enabled it to commandeer printing presses at short notice, using stocks of paper that had been reserved for other jobs. However, the general uncertainty of the time could work either way. The Hereford Times, who had printed the volumes of the Lincoln Record Society since 1922, reported on 11 March 1940 that the proofs for the volume of *Diocesan Visitations* had come at an opportune moment:

> We are particularly glad to receive this from you, as owing to the disorgani-sation of things in general caused by the war we are very slack just now. All our men so far liable for Military Service have gone, but we are anxious, if possible, to find employment for those who remain, mostly old employees of the company, therefore if you should have any copy available it would be a very great help if you could let us have some.[34]

This window of opportunity undoubtedly contributed to the eventual appear-ance of both the *Diocesan Visitations* in October 1940 and of *Registrum Antiquissimum V* in December of that year. It did not last long, however, and attempts to continue with the Society's work were met with constant frustra-tions. In February 1942, the printers wrote:

> Unfortunately, the position here is almost hopeless at the moment, as in addition to our normal work we are under obligation to give priority to all printing for the Services and in connection with the war effort. On top of this a man experienced in the Record Society's work has been on the sick list for some weeks ... and unless he returns to work we fear it is useless to make any promises.[35]

The second obstacle to record publication was, as the Stentons had discovered in the First World War, the moving of valuable archives to places of safety to counter the risk of destruction. Kathleen Major was able to continue working on the *Registrum Antiquissimum* by using the transcripts made by Canon Foster and his clerks but she was unable to check these against the originals, as these were no longer accessible. In the case of Lincoln, it appears that the safest places were in the vicinity of the Cathedral and she prepared to resist suggestions that the records be moved further afield:

> Mr Jourdain and the Bishop of Grimsby have decided against sending any records out of Lincoln as the actual building offered by the P[ublic] R[ecord] O[ffice] is, as Mr Flower told me when I saw him on Saturday, not so strong as the Office itself and certainly not so strong as the places of deposit belonging to the Chapter. Mr Godfrey has agreed to take more in

---

34 LRS Archive, Major correspondence: Hereford Times to KM, 11 March 1940.
35 LRS Archive, Major correspondence: Hereford Times to KM, 14 February 1942.

from here and I am going to send them as soon as he has got men to move them. The Stentons, whom I saw on Saturday, thought that they were better here also. Mr Jourdain was totally opposed to their going and I have at any rate put all the arguments and possible places of reception before them.[36]

The third obstacle lay in the uncertainty that permeated the lives of all people at the time, from which those involved in the work of the Record Society were naturally not exempt. Hamilton Thompson, writing from London in August 1940 on matters connected with the *Visitations*, added:

I hope that Lincoln is more or less free from siren-voices and bombs: we have had a good deal of the former in the last few days, and on Friday my younger girl and I sat for an hour beneath a yew tree in Kew Gardens and heard the noise of war not far away. As the late Canon Sutton of Brant Broughton said in the last war, I wish the Germans would not make such a fuss. He would quite have agreed with Rose Graham, whom I saw on Saturday, and whose comment on a picture of a ruined sanctuary in a S.W. suburb was 'Only a Baptist chapel!'[37]

Writing again in October of the same year, just after the publication of the *Diocesan Visitations*, he reported:

I saw a copy of the volume to-day in the Leeds University Library and expect that my copies are waiting for me in London, where I am going for the night on Thursday. We are at Adel for some time to come, as our flat has been somewhat damaged by a bomb. We had left a few days earlier. Fortunately, the damage is not very serious as such things go, but the mess made was deplorable … I had taken away all valuable MSS with me, as the raiders had been very active in our neighbourhood, and I felt that it was quite unsafe to leave anything behind which could not be replaced.[38]

Even when there were no air raids, life could be uncomfortable. Margaret Archer reported from Birmingham in March 1943:

I am having to fire-watch every week in the centre of the city, under appalling conditions, and it makes life rather gloomy. It takes me the rest of the week to get over my night out![39]

Miss Major could report that Lincoln was relatively unscathed by the bombing:

[36] LRS Archive, Major correspondence: KM to JWFH, 19 May 1942.
[37] LRS Archive, Major correspondence: AHT to KM, 20 August 1940.
[38] LRS Archive, Major correspondence: AHT to KM, 7 October 1940.
[39] LRS Archive, Major correspondence: Margaret Archer to KM, 7 March 1943.

I am glad to say that Lincoln is at present very peaceful apart from an occasional siren and a few bombs on the outskirts.[40]

However, the city was at the hub of the RAF's counter-attack:

There is no question at all as to the numbers of aeroplanes we send over there, they make a continuous noise over our heads going out and returning from about eleven to three or four in the morning.[41]

In addition to the destruction from bombs and the noises of war overhead, the various displacements to everyday life caused by the state of emergency provided a constant disruption to any attempt to work on records. These distractions ranged from the minor – such as having to share one's house with a stranger (Miss Archer reported 'a rather irritating lodger'), or being short-staffed like Miss Major in Exchequer Gate:

We all seem to be in the state of being singlehanded so that if work calls elsewhere the office has to be shut up, but so long as I have a charwoman and don't have to clean the stone steps I feel I shall survive.[42]

– to the prospect of having to move to new work at short notice. In February 1942 Miss Major noted that

I shall have to register for National Service next month and am uncertain whether I shall be transferred from Lincoln in consequence.[43]

In these wartime circumstances, it is hardly surprising that it proved to be impossible to issue any volumes at all during the three years after 1940, pushing the Society even further into arrears. Such work as the printer could undertake during these years involved the second volume of *Diocesan Visitations* and the Assize Roll of 1298. The latter project was the work of a scholar from New Zealand, Walter Sinclair Thomson. After an earlier career in entomology, he had graduated in history at Edinburgh University and went on to work on the Assize Roll for his doctorate. In May 1938 he made contact with Kathleen Major:

As you know, Professor Stenton did me the great honour of suggesting that if my thesis for Ph.D. prove suitable it might be considered for publication, with modifications, by your Society.[44]

---

40 LRS Archive, Major correspondence: KM to Beatrice Hamilton Thompson, 9 October 1940.
41 LRS Archive, Major correspondence: KM to Margaret Archer, 27 June 1941.
42 LRS Archive, Major correspondence: KM to Margaret Archer, 18 November 1942.
43 LRS Archive, Major correspondence: KM to Hereford Times, 11 February 1942.
44 LRS Archive, Major correspondence: W. S. Thomson to KM, 25 May 1938.

The work was accepted for publication, subject to Stenton's approval, in the following October:

> I need hardly say how glad I am to hear of the Society's decision in regard to publishing the Assize Roll ... The work is pursuing its somewhat majestic course – or should I rather say ponderous? At any rate, I have begun to write my thesis for Ph.D. which is due for May 15th next.[45]

Thomson was awarded his doctorate the following year and in October he wrote optimistically to Miss Major:

> Your letter is one of the most cheering things I have received for quite a while – certainly since the war began: for I had quite made up my mind that the L.R.S. would find itself unable to complete its present plans until a problematical 'after the war', and was in consequence only working very leisurely at my MS and its appendages. Now, however, I can push ahead, though not full time, I'm afraid, because of other work.[46]

Although Miss Major's optimism proved to be misplaced, it was the encouragement she gave to Dr Thomson that enabled the volume to be completed. On 14 September 1940, not long after sending her the typescript of the edition, he died, suddenly and unexpectedly, of a rare form of diabetes. With the full agreement of his widow, the project was carried through by his former supervisor, Dr Harry Rothwell, with the assistance of Professor V. H. Galbraith. Kathleen Major completed the indexes.

The continuing difficulties in the printing industry meant that progress on this volume and *Diocesan Visitations II* was held up for long periods. Hamilton Thompson wrote sympathetically to Kathleen Major:

> It is of course rather vexatious that the Hereford Times shows so little disposition to move, but printers everywhere are in the same mood, with depleted staffs (or staves, but can one deplete a stave?) and, as in the case of Whitehead's of Leeds, with a superannuated and short-sighted compositor summoned out of retirement to fill several gaps.[47]

A few days after this letter was written, Miss Major made a personal visit to the Hereford works, following which she was assured:

> There is no doubt the personal touch goes a long way, and I am glad to say already plans are being made for an extra special effort to get one at least

---

[45] LRS Minute Book I, 193; LRS Archive, Major correspondence: W. S. Thomson to KM, 27 October 1938.

[46] LRS Archive, Major correspondence: W. S. Thomson to KM, 13 October 1939.

[47] LRS Archive, Major correspondence: AHT to KM, 2 September 1943.

of your volumes printed off. This will not be easy and may take some time but we will do our best.[48]

Whether it was the effect of Miss Major's visit, or due to the improving conditions as the war news began to change for the better, the following year saw the appearance of both of these long-awaited volumes. *Diocesan Visitations II* was issued in March 1944 and the *Assize Roll* at the end of the same year. The Society had now reduced its arrears up to September 1939.

Hamilton Thompson's *Diocesan Visitations* differed from his earlier series of volumes in that they included visitation material relating not just to religious houses but to parishes as well. The first volume included a lengthy introduction, based on the Birkbeck Lectures which he had delivered at Cambridge in 1934–5. Its advent was warmly welcomed by A. G. Dickens:

> The completed series should certainly rank as our most important source-collection for the state of the English church on the eve of the Reformation, this not only on account of the bulk and variety of the material presented, but also since the diocese of Lincoln, with its nine populous shires between Humber and Thames, constituted so vast and so widely representative a slice of medieval England.

The introduction in particular aroused his admiration, as

> combining judicious selection of examples from the text with literary qualities which one seldom associates with the learned editors of the Lincoln Record Society.[49]

Thomson's edition of the Assize Roll received high praise from F. M. Powicke who hailed it as 'a remarkable piece of work'. Noting that it originated in a suggestion of Frank Stenton, he continued:

> Few suggestions of this kind can have had more fruitful results. Mr Thomson's book, although it seems to owe nothing to local patriotism, is local history of a high order. He studied the life of Lincolnshire and the records of its obscure inhabitants with a microscopic intensity which the most ardent local antiquary might envy. He saw in a rather humdrum assize roll the opportunity to reveal 'a community much concerned with its own affairs but made aware, as a result of the war, of matters of national importance'. At the same time … he set himself to revise the history of our national administration in the later years of Edward I's reign in the light of his local investigations.[50]

---

[48] LRS Archive, Major correspondence: Hereford Times to KM, 11 September 1943.
[49] A. G. Dickens, review in *EHR* 56 (1941), 313–5.
[50] F. M. Powicke, review in *EHR* 61 (1946), 261–4.

Despite the manifold difficulties occasioned during the hostilities, the Society emerged from the Second World War in a remarkably healthy position. From a financial point of view this is unsurprising, given that it had proved impossible fully to maintain the regular issue of volumes. In 1939 there had been a balance of £1,555 to meet the cost of future publications; by 1945 this had increased to £2,097. What is particularly remarkable is that there had been no overall loss in membership. With the annual subscription remaining at one guinea, income from this source remained at the same figure – £156 – in both years. Only one institutional member had left the Society (unsurprisingly this was the Prussian State Library in Berlin) and while the ranks of the individual members had been depleted by death and resignation, new members had continued to join even during these inauspicious years. Some of these newcomers, such as Peter Binnall, Eric Kemp, Rosalind Hill, Harold Brace and Michael Sleight, went on to give many years of service to the Society as members of Council or the editors of volumes. A strong element of continuity was provided by the ten founder members of the Society who survived into the post-war years, men like Captain Cragg of Threckingham, Revd D. S. Davies, now retired to Llandrindod Wells, Colonel Grange, now residing in Cambridge, Mr Jourdain the veteran Diocesan Registrar, Hubert Larken, now Subdean, and J. H. Ruddock. It was Mr Ruddock who during the dark days of the war, in 1942, urged that the Society should do more to commemorate its Founder, pointing out that he was not mentioned as such in the Annual Report and urging the addition of the now-familiar words 'Founded in the year 1910 by the late Canon C. W. Foster for the Publication of Historical Manuscripts':

> The Society is so much his child that if he had not been so modest he might have called it the Foster Society.[51]

This addition was first made in the Annual Report for 1941–42.

Two significant alterations to the Society's activities were initiated during the war years. In 1938 Lord Monson had resigned the post of President which he had filled so energetically and capably during Canon Foster's last years and through the difficult period after his death. His successor, Lord Brownlow, had many other commitments which prevented him taking an active role in the Society. In 1942, therefore, the office of Patron of the Society was revived for him, leaving the Presidency vacant for a replacement who would, it was hoped, be more involved in the Society's affairs with his advice and support. A certain amount of backstairs intrigue appears to have ensued, inevitably leaving little trace in the records, although there seems to have been a clerical faction, perhaps putting forward the Bishop as a candidate. Francis Hill was firmly opposed to this, on the ground that Canon Foster (perhaps as a result of

---

[51] LRS Archive, Major correspondence: J. H. Ruddock to KM, 2 February 1942.

his unhappy experience with Bishop Swayne) had resolved that the President should always be a layman. Both he and Kathleen Major stood firm and the outcome was an offer to Frank Stenton that he should take the position. A few weeks before the Annual Meeting she reported:

> I have heard nothing from Lord Brownlow and am more glad than ever that we have asked Professor Stenton as Mrs Stenton said in a letter recently that she had not known him to be so pleased about anything for years.[52]

Stenton was duly elected, and a change in the rules was brought in, enabling the Annual Meeting to be held in September to make it easier for those like him who held academic positions to attend. He was scrupulous in his regular attendance at the Society's meetings, his presence at which was eagerly anticipated, not least by the archivists:

> Like other members of the Lincoln Record Society we came to look forward to the third weekend in September as to a series of special treats. Then we could show him our year's treasures (not always twelfth-century charters), ask our difficult questions and hear stories of Canon Foster's early activities, in which we soon felt, when asked if we remembered where the safe stood at Timberland, that we were part.[53]

At the Annual Meeting in 1942, Kathleen Major proposed another change:

> it was to be hoped that the Annual Meeting, at least after the War, could be made more than a merely business gathering and that it might include tea and an address as was the case with the Canterbury and York Society. This would provide an opportunity for people interested in Record Work to meet.[54]

It would appear that part of this proposal was carried into effect the following year. A few days after the Annual Meeting on 24 September, Hamilton Thompson (who had not been able to be present) wrote:

> I am so glad that the L.R.S. function went off so well and am a firm supporter of the combination of serious business with mild revelry. I well remember how, many years ago, the success of a ruridecanal meeting which I attended in a certain part of the diocese of Lincoln before the last war was greatly enhanced by the tea and supplements which followed and liberally

---

[52] LRS Archive, Major correspondence: KM to JWFH, 5 October 1942.
[53] Joan Varley and Dorothy M. Owen, 'Sir Frank Stenton', *Archives* 7 (1967–68), 146–7. Stenton became Vice-Chancellor of Reading University in 1946; he was knighted in 1948 (Doris M. Stenton, 'Frank Merry Stenton', 405).
[54] LRS Minute Book II (30 October 1942).

illustrated the main subject of discussion, which was the Forward Temperance Movement in the Church of England.[55]

The full effect of this change came into force in 1945, when the Annual
Meeting, which during the war years had been held at the Diocesan Offices
in Jews' Court, was moved to the imposing surroundings of the Guildhall
in Lincoln, with the Mayor entertaining members to tea afterwards. In
the following year, a pattern was established which remained essentially
unchanged for the next thirty years: a meeting of the Council in the morning,
after which members would take luncheon at the Saracen's Head or the White
Hart Hotel, and then the Annual Meeting at the Guildhall, culminating in an
address on an historical theme and ending with tea. The 1946 address was
given by Professor V. H. Galbraith, Director of the Institute of Historical
Research, on the appropriate subject of 'History from Originals'.

For the Lincoln Record Society, the autumn of 1945 heralded not only
the beginning of peacetime but a number of significant changes. Kathleen
Major was appointed Lecturer in Diplomatic at the University of Oxford and
consequently left her post as Archivist in Lincoln. Her successor, Mrs Joan
Varley, took over the task of transforming the Diocesan Record Office into
the Lincolnshire Archives Office, a pioneering co-operative venture between
the three Lincolnshire County Councils of Kesteven, Lindsey and Holland,
and the City of Lincoln. The new Lincolnshire Archives Committee came
into existence in September 1947 and Mrs Varley became County Archivist.
Her assistant, Miss Dorothy Williamson, was appointed the following year.[56]

Although Miss Major was now based in Oxford, she kept her house at 21
Queensway in Lincoln and returned there every vacation. She remained as
Secretary and General Editor of the Society, with willing support both from
Francis Hill as Treasurer and from the Archivists in Exchequer Gate. She
continued, too, the steady work on the *Registrum Antiquissimum* that had
been slowed, but never stopped, by the War. Reminders of the consequences
of the fighting, even to the pursuit of medieval history, were never far away.
A search of the archives in Normandy produced the following reply:

> J'ai bien reçu votre letter du 17 septembre dernier qui concernait le cartu-
> laire de Savigny. Il a malheureusement été détruit en 1944.[57]

Another letter concerning the Lincoln charters, however, shows that the spirit
of historical enquiry is in fact unquenchable. A Belgian scholar had written in
1937 in connection with his research on Gilbert, abbot of Swineshead. Miss

---

[55] LRS Archive, Major correspondence: AHT to KM, 4 October 1943.
[56] Hill, 'From Canon Foster to the Lincolnshire Archives Office', 72.
[57] LRS Archive, Major correspondence: L'Archiviste en Chef de la Manche to KM,
24 September 1951.

Major had replied that a relevant charter was to be published in the fourth volume of the *Registrum Antiquissimum*. No more was heard until August 1948 when she received the following:

> Ce jour-même, j'ai l'avantage de pouvoir reprendre en mains votre honorée lettre du 21 octobre 1937. Depuis 10½ ans en effet, il ne m'a plus été possible de m'occuper des etudes pour lesquelles j'étais entré en correspondence avec vous. Les terrible années que nous avons vécu, et dont j'espère vous n'avez subi aucun préjudice, ont retardé si longtemps la reprise d'un sujet d'étude, dont la maladie m'avait brusquement arraché.[58]

Ten days later, the writer of the letter was making arrangements to visit Lincoln and to acquire the relevant volume of the *Antiquissimum*.

Although by September 1945 the War was over, the economic difficulties facing the country showed every sign of becoming worse than ever and the outlook for producing volumes was little better than previously. The third volume of *Diocesan Visitations* was ready to go to press, as was the first volume of Rosalind Hill's edition of *Bishop Sutton's Register*. The proposed edition of *Sewers Records* had now found an editor in Miss Mary Kirkus, who was busily transcribing them from a microfilm. Margaret Archer was still working on *Bishop Repingdon's Register*. Three other proposals had been accepted during the war years, both of them resulting from Miss Major's wish to provide more post-medieval volumes in English (provided that they were 'competently edited'). Francis Hill had offered to produce a volume of papers of the Banks family, and Miss E. M. Hampson of Royal Holloway College had proposed a volume of Lincolnshire poor law records. Both of these were still at an early stage in 1945. The third proposal, put before the Council meeting in 1945, was for an edition of the records of the Gainsborough Monthly Meeting of the Society of Friends. This would be edited by Mr Harold Brace, Clerk of the Lincoln Monthly Meeting, who had already transcribed the material. It was reported that

> Mr Brace's knowledge would make him an excellent editor and the volume would be the first of its kind to be printed.[59]

The continuing years of austerity and in particular the difficulties being experienced in the printing industry meant that no volume appeared in 1945 or 1946. The Society was falling further into arrears and the Council expressed its gratitude to members for their patience. The logjam began to break in the following year with the publication of the third and last volume of Hamilton Thompson's *Diocesan Visitations*. This was issued in September 1947 and,

---

58 LRS Archive, Major correspondence: Jean de Laet to KM, 6 August 1948.
59 LRS Minute Book II (27 September 1945).

as was noted, represented the appearance of the thirty-seventh volume in the Society's thirty-seventh year. A year later in September 1948, the first part of Mr Brace's edition of the Gainsborough Monthly Meeting was published. The editor of the volume was untroubled by the length of time it had taken to get through the press:

> I can quite understand how irritating the printers' delays are to you, but to me, looking back, it seems only a short time since I found the Minute Book, with others, in a tin trunk up in the Women's Gallery of Brant Broughton Meeting House, and brought it back to Gainsborough.[60]

Kathleen Major could be uncompromising with amateur historians who had the temerity to submit material for publication without a thorough grounding in historical context, but Mr Brace at any rate was one who met with her approval. He was, she recalled, 'willing to be taught, and became very competent'.[61]

At the end of 1948 another volume was published. This was the first part of Rosalind Hill's edition of *Bishop Sutton's Register*, comprising the institutions to benefices in the archdeaconry of Lincoln. This brought the Society's publishing arrears down to 1942. The first fruits of what was clearly going to be a major project were welcomed by Dr J. R. H. Moorman:

> The medieval episcopal registers of the diocese of Lincoln are among the best in the country, but so far not much progress has been made with their publication. It is, therefore, with special delight that we welcome the first part of the *Rolls and Register of Bishop Oliver Sutton* … Miss Hill has done her work admirably. The more straightforward institutions, etc., she has been content to calendar, but any entry which presents interesting or unusual features is printed in full. The paper and type are excellent, the transcription and introduction scholarly; and we shall look forward to seeing the remaining parts of the Register in due course.[62]

By September 1950, Miss Major could report that the Society was 'beginning at last to overtake arrears'. The second volume of the *Gainsborough Friends' Minute Book* was published in December 1949 and the sixth volume of the *Registrum Antiquissimum,* together with a volume of facsimiles of some of the charters printed in Volumes 5 and 6, was about to be issued. These three volumes were swiftly followed by the second part of *Bishop Sutton's Register* which appeared in February 1951. The third and final volume of the *Friends' Minute Book* was published later in that year. The year 1952–53 saw the appearance of Francis Hill's edition of the *Banks Letters and Papers* (a

---

[60] LRS Archive, Major correspondence: Harold Brace to KM, 2 September 1948.
[61] Ex inf. Dr Alison McHardy.
[62] J. R. H. Moorman, review in *EHR* 64 (1949), 395–6.

double volume for two subscription years) and of *Registrum Antiquissimum VII*. These years of increased publishing activity were accompanied by a steady increase in the membership of the Society, which reached the 200 mark in 1950. In particular, a considerable number of libraries and other institutions joined during this period, the number rising from 83 in 1945 to 110 in 1953.

In 1954 the Society published an edition of *Papal Decretals relating to the Diocese of Lincoln in the Twelfth Century*. This volume had its origins in an offer made to Canon Foster by Dr Walther Holtzmann to supply an appendix of such documents for the edition of the *Registrum Antiquissimum*. At the Council meeting in 1948 it was decided that there was enough material for a separate volume, and that this would also include translations and an additional introduction on the administration of the canon law by Dr Eric Kemp.[63] Although the resulting book was small, it was hailed as a major contribution to the study of canon law:

> The importance of this short book (less than a hundred pages long) is out of all proportion to its size. For, valuable as has been the work of modern German scholarship on the decretal-collections of the twelfth century, they have hitherto appeared to the historian as they appeared to Stephen of Tournai: an *inextricabilis silva*. Now, at last, students have an adequately edited selection of canonistic texts, put in their historical setting; and this is the first edition of decretals to be supplied with an index of names and places.[64]

The publication of *Bishop Sutton's Register* continued in 1954 with the issue of the third volume, containing the first part of his memoranda register with an introduction dealing with the Bishop's life and administration of the diocese. The next volume to be issued returned to a series initiated before the war: the fourteenth-century peace rolls. Rosamond Sillem's stay in Singapore had culminated in her marriage to a Colonel in the Royal Engineers, and by 1940 she was back in England and preoccupied with a young daughter.[65] Fortunately there was another pupil of Professor Putnam who was willing to take up the work. This was Elisabeth Kimball who in 1939 had edited a similar volume of the Warwickshire rolls.[66] It was agreed that she should prepare for publication the remaining records for Lincolnshire, dealing with the reign of Richard II, but the outbreak of war prevented this from being taken any further for a time. In 1949 she reported that she was about to resume work and thereafter steady progress was made. At the Annual Meeting in 1954 it

---

[63] LRS Minute Book II (25 September 1948).
[64] C. R. Cheney, review in *EHR* 70 (1955), 314–5.
[65] LRS Archive, Major correspondence: Lady Sillem to KM, 6 April 1940.
[66] E. G. Kimball (ed.), *Rolls of the Warwickshire and Coventry Sessions of the Peace, 1377–1397* (Dugdale Society 16, 1939).

was reported that the first part, dealing with Kesteven, was in proof stage and the index was being prepared, 'but the transmission by parcel post across the Atlantic took some time'.[67] The volume appeared in the autumn of 1955.

Largely thanks to the work of Professor Putnam, fourteenth-century sessions rolls were by this time familiar material to users of the publications of local record societies. The volume issued by the Society in 1956, however, was another groundbreaking work. An edition of the seventeenth-century port books of Boston had been accepted for publication by the Council in September 1950. It was the work of R. W. K. Hinton, a graduate of Peter-house, Cambridge, who, like others among the Society's editors, was recommended for the task by Sir Frank Stenton.[68] He wrote to Kathleen Major:

> Mr Hinton has just obtained a Prince Consort Prize at Cambridge which really means that he will now be free to get to work seriously on the Port Books. I have discussed his plan with him and I think we are assured of a good and interesting volume. I have told him that he can have what elbow room he wants in the introduction (he is not a verbose writer), and also that from every point of view it is important that he should allow himself to be quite elementary at times. At any rate nothing resembling this projected volume has hitherto appeared, and indeed it could only be produced by one of the very few people who are specialists on Port Books.[69]

The significance of this edition was made clear in a laudatory review by J. D. Gould:

> The port books have been perhaps less explored than any other major source for the history of the overseas trade of Tudor and Stuart England. As such sources have been progressively worked through, this neglect has stood out more and more conspicuously, but some scholars are disposed to believe that the books' suspected defects justify it. This will not do. The time to assess the value of a historical source is after it has been subject to patient and scholarly scrutiny, not before. This is so obvious that it is hard to resist the suspicion that the ease with which the port books have been shrugged off is not unconnected with the fact that they are extremely tedious, dirty, and in some respects difficult sources on which to work ... The Lincoln Record Society has taken a welcome step towards repairing this notable omission. Dr R. W. K. Hinton brings to his editorial task exactly the qualities of patient and open-minded scholarship which are called for, and the result fully justifies the Society's enterprise.[70]

---

[67] LRS Minute Book II (25 September 1954).
[68] As were Sidney Peyton, W. S. Thomson and Mary Kirkus. In 1950 Hinton was a Lecturer at the University of Reading.
[69] LRS Archive, Major correspondence: FMS to KM, 16 March 1950.
[70] J. D. Gould, review in *EHR* 72 (1957), 541–2.

No work was published in 1957 but the two following years saw the appearance of a total of four volumes, finally enabling Miss Major to report that

> With the appearance of these volumes the Society has brought its publications up to date for the first time since the first world war.[71]

The first of these was *Registrum Antiquissimum VIII*, publication of which was assisted by a generous grant of £1,000, made by the Pilgrim Trust for the completion of the edition. It was followed later in the same year by *Bishop Sutton's Register IV*. In 1959 the Society issued G. A. J. Hodgett's edition of *The State of the Ex-Religious and Former Chantry Priests in the Diocese of Lincoln 1547–1574* and the first volume of Mary Kirkus's long-awaited *Records of the Commissioners of Sewers in the Parts of Holland 1547–1603*. Sadly Dr Kirkus died not long after the publication of her volume, and the remainder of the edition was passed to Mr Arthur Owen for completion.

The following year saw the publication of *The Building Accounts of Tattershall Castle 1438–71*, edited by Dr W. Douglas Simpson of the University of Aberdeen. This edition was originally proposed in October 1945:

> Shortly before the war I obtained access to these accounts by courtesy of the late Lord De L'Isle and Dudley and took a full transcription of them. I have now nearly completed a translation, with annotations and introduction. These building accounts are of great importance because they tell the whole story of the erection of one of the most remarkable castles in England and are not unworthy of being placed alongside the building accounts of Kirby Muxloe.[72]

It was accepted for publication in 1946 and was reported as being ready to go to press in October 1948. However, the project was repeatedly delayed, in the first place by a series of misfortunes befalling the editor – an attack of food poisoning, an accident resulting in chronic sciatica and a permanently crippled finger, and next

> an accident which I imagine must be unique in the history of such undertakings. My house was invaded by a vagrant monkey from a neighbouring circus and before he could be caught he had torn up or defaced a number of sheets of my typescript, so that I will have to do this work over again. I was extremely angry at the time but I can now look back on the incident with some amusement. The little beast did a good deal of damage but the circus people paid up very handsomely.[73]

---

[71] *Annual Report 1958–59*, 4.
[72] LRS Archive, Major correspondence: W. Douglas Simpson to KM, 26 October 1945.
[73] LRS Archive, Major correspondence: W. Douglas Simpson to KM, 1 September 1952.

A broken shoulder blade the following year delayed the volume still further. Then, when Miss Major received the text in 1953, it was found to need considerable revision and had to be returned to the editor. Further delays put back the volume from year to year until, in 1957, Miss Major took charge of the situation:

> I am trying to clear off Tattershall at present: I have had it typed as you know and am now checking with the Photostats and have done about three quarters. Once that is done I do not think it will take long to print as it is short, and the introduction and translation are straightforward ... I almost wish that Tattershall had never been built.

Finally, at the beginning of July 1960, she was able to report 'I am sending Tattershall to be printed off to-morrow – at long last – how thankful I am!' [74]

In 1960 the Society celebrated its Golden Jubilee. It was decided that the most appropriate way of marking this occasion, which coincided with the twenty-fifth anniversary of the death of the Founder, was to arrange for a tablet to be placed in Lincoln Cathedral commemorating Canon Foster and his work. Discussions with the Dean and Chapter were inaugurated by Sir Francis Hill as Secretary in October 1959. The Chapter's initial suggestion of a stall plate, to be placed in Canon Foster's prebendal stall of Leicester St Margaret, did not meet with the approval of Sir Frank Stenton who pointed out 'we are not just commemorating a canon'. Dean Dunlop then suggested that there was a suitable space for a memorial tablet in the Grosseteste Chapel near the door to the vestry. The matter was discussed with the Cathedral Architect, Lawrence Bond, as to the material to be used and the probable cost. Meanwhile, Stenton composed the inscription. The design and lettering of the tablet were entrusted to the sculptor and letter-cutter John Skelton. [75] An appeal was launched for contributions to the memorial. Among those who responded were Canon Foster's niece, Barbara Wilson ('I am sure my uncle would have been enormously pleased if he had ever thought that the work he cared about so much would be acknowledged in such a way') and his old friend Hubert Larken, one of the few surviving founder members of the Society. Sir Francis Hill wrote to thank him for his contribution:

> You were one of Canon Foster's closest friends and I well remember the instructions we found in his study that you should conduct the funeral service.

---

[74] LRS Archive, Hill correspondence: KM to JWFH, 10 August 1957; KM to JWFH, 3 July 1960.
[75] LRS Archive, Hill correspondence: KM to JWFH, 20 November 1959; Colin Dunlop to JWFH, 23 January 1960; KM to JWFH, 1 March 1960; Lawrence Bond to JWFH, 14 April 1960.

Larken, who was too old and infirm to attend the unveiling, also recalled that day in October 1935:

> I well remember the funeral of Charles Wilmer Foster: on that day Mrs Nugent Hicks, whom you and I have cause to remember, was more than usually tiresome![76]

The Jubilee was celebrated at the Society's Annual Meeting on 24 September 1960. A commemorative luncheon was held at the Eastgate Court Hotel in Lincoln. After the Annual Meeting, members of the Society attended Evensong in the Cathedral, at the conclusion of which the tablet placed in the south-east transept to the memory of Canon Foster was unveiled and dedicated by the Dean. After it was all over, Doris Stenton, who had been one of the Canon's closest friends since 1916, wrote to express her appreciation:

> it is most satisfactory to feel that everything went so well and that Wilmer is for ever commemorated as he would have wished to be.[77]

---

[76] LRS Archive, Hill correspondence: Barbara Wilson to JWFH, 14 July 1960; JWFH to Hubert Larken, 19 July 1960; Hubert Larken to JWFH, 27 July 1960. The eccentricities of Kathleen Nugent Hicks, the Bishop's wife, were well known: see E. W. Kemp, *Shy But Not Retiring* (London, 2006), 55.

[77] LRS Archive, Hill correspondence: Lady Stenton to JWFH, 26 September 1960.

9. Kathleen Major, c.1930.

·WHITLEY·PARK·FARM·
·READING·

13 February 1934.

My dear Foster,

The volume has come, and I send you my best congratulations on it. As to the dedication — it is more than kind, and much more than anything that I may have done deserves. It is very pleasant to be thus definitely associated with charters recalling early journeys from Southwell to the Exchequer Gate, and, in another sense, with what will be the model for all editions of English cathedral muniments. The terms of the dedication far exceed my merits; but I admire its lapidary spacing, and the subtle variation of its type. For myself, it will always be a record of a connexion which gave me

10. Letter from Frank Stenton to Canon Foster on publication
of *Registrum Antiquissimum* II, 1934.

11. Canon Charles Wilmer Foster, Founder of the Lincoln Record Society.

26 October, 1935.

Dear Mr Major,

I send my best thanks for the brace of birds which you have so kindly sent me. I was very glad, when your Daughter came over here, to learn that you had so far recovered from your serious operation; and I hope that the arrival of the birds means that you

12. Letter from Canon Foster to George Major, October 1935.

13. Sir Frank Merry Stenton.

IN MEMORY OF
CHARLES WILMER
FOSTER
1866 - 1935
M·A·Hon·D·Litt·Oxon
Founder of The Lincoln Record
Society · Vicar of Timberland
and Prebendary of Leicester
St·Margaret in this Cathedral
Church.through whose devoted
labours its muniments have
been made available to all
students of English history.

14. Memorial Tablet to Canon Foster in Lincoln Cathedral, 1960.

15. Canon Hubert Larken, Member of the Society from 1910 to 1964.

16. Kathleen Major, General Editor, Secretary, President and Benefactor.

SEVEN

CONTINUITY AND CHANGE:
THE SOCIETY FROM 1960 TO 2010

As the Society moved into its sixth decade, changes began to take place in the group who had administered its affairs since the death of Canon Foster. In 1956, after her appointment as Principal of St Hilda's, Kathleen Major decided that she should no longer continue to act as Secretary, as she would no longer be residing for part of the year in Lincoln. She continued as Editor and Frank Hill took over the duties of Secretary, combining this post with that of Treasurer, as Canon Foster had done. Ten years later, when Miss Major retired as Principal, she resumed the duties of Secretary, but at this point Hill gave up the office of Treasurer which he had filled with great efficiency for thirty years.[1] He was replaced, not by an active member of the Society, but by the Manager of Lloyds Bank in Lincoln, where the Society's account was kept. No doubt it was thought that the Society would gain financial expertise by this move. In the long run, however, the decision was to lead to the separation of the financial administration of the Society's affairs from the rest of its business, and this was to cause the accumulation of serious problems in the future.

Meanwhile, some of the Society's long-term publishing projects were bearing fruit. Elisabeth Kimball, who kept in regular contact with Miss Major (the two spent a holiday in Denmark together in 1959), produced a third volume in the series of fourteenth-century sessions of the peace in 1962. Covering the parts of Lindsey, this completed the edition of the rolls for the reign of Richard II. In the following year another project first mooted in the pre-war years made its first appearance. Margaret Archer's many years of labour on the memoranda register of Bishop Repingdon were rewarded by the publication of the first part of the edition. She used the same strategy employed by Rosalind Hill in her edition of Sutton's register, combining English summaries of routine business with the full transcription of more important or unusual entries. Despite this, the length of this first section of the edition made it necessary to break it up into two volumes. These were

---

[1] Frank Hill was knighted in 1958.

published together, enabling some economies to be made by printing the index to both of them in the second volume.

Hamilton Thompson, who had encouraged the Society to undertake Miss Archer's edition, had died in 1952 but Canon Foster's other staunch supporters, Sir Frank and Lady Stenton, were still there to provide counsel and encouragement. Sir Frank was above all concerned that Miss Major should allow herself space and time to complete the monumental edition of the *Registrum Antiquissimum*. He wrote to her in 1950:

> So far as I am concerned the Tattershall Accounts can remain on our programme as long as the Editor likes. What I am above all anxious for is the appearance of the remainder of Quissm. With the Quakers, Present-ments, and Port Books, we shall be doing quite well by those who can only read English ... But just as we have done very well for ourselves by completing H[amilton] T[hompson]'s unique series, I am sure that it is fundamental for us to finish within a measurable time the first edition on modern lines of the Charters of an English Cathedral. Still more personally I should add that I want to see that series complete while I am still in a condition to read Charters. It will be a great work when you have finished it, and it is urgently needed.[2]

Miss Major's appointment in 1955 as Principal of St Hilda's, however, meant that much of her time and energies had to be given to the College. Her achievements during the ten years she served as its Head were considerable:

> It has been said by a subsequent principal that KM's achievement at St Hilda's 'was to turn a small, inward-looking college, run from the outside, into a genuinely self-governing, self-confident organisation'. She was largely instrumental in bringing about the enlargement essential if St Hilda's was to play a proper part, as it clearly has, in the expansion of university education for women.[3]

All this meant that her work on the *Registrum Antiquissimum* had to take a back seat during these years. The eighth volume of the edition had appeared in 1958; this was the first of three which were to deal with the charters relating to the City of Lincoln. Its successor was not to appear until ten years later.

When Sir Frank Stenton died on 15 September 1967, he was hailed as 'one of the outstanding English medievalists of his generation'. Yet his great eminence was always at the service of others, and many paid tribute to the ease with which he communicated with historians of widely differing back-

---

2   LRS Archive, Major correspondence: FMS to KM, 16 March 1950.
3   G. W. S. Barrow, 'Kathleen Major', *Proceedings of the British Academy* 115 (2002), 325.

grounds. During the twenty-five years that he held the Presidency of the Society, he only missed the Annual Meeting on one occasion, so that these yearly gatherings

> thus afforded an opportunity for those interested in the history of the county or in the use of local records for general history to meet the most distinguished of English historians in this field. Those who came included not only the professional historian but even more the amateur, with whom Sir Frank, over tea, would readily discuss points of topography or place-name study. He had an astonishing capacity, not always found in those who pursue history in its most austere form, for speaking to a heterogeneous audience.[4]

He was succeeded in the office of President by Sir Francis Hill.

Stenton died before the completion of the edition of the *Registrum Antiquissimum*, which he had done so much to inaugurate and promote. This was a source of real regret, not least to Miss Major. Volume IX was issued in July 1968 and the final instalment in the autumn of 1973. What had started out as a plan for four volumes had expanded over the years to an outstanding series of ten volumes plus two separate volumes of facsimiles. It was, as Stenton had continually stressed, the first edition on modern scholarly lines of the charters of an English cathedral. In its structure, combining a cartulary with original charters, it had already begun to influence other editions, such as Christopher Holdsworth's Rufford Charters, the first volume of which was published by the Thoroton Society in 1972.

The conclusion of this monumental undertaking was celebrated by the Society at a luncheon held at the Eastgate Hotel in Lincoln on 29 September 1973 (egg mayonnaise to start, then roast saddle of lamb, followed by plum tart and fresh cream). Fittingly, among those present was Miss Barbara Wilson, Canon Foster's niece. The Suffolk Records Society sent a telegram of congratulations, consisting of just two words: *Admirabile contemplatu.* Professor J. C. Holt of Reading University, proposing the toast to the Society, paid tribute to those whose dedicated labours had brought the work to completion:

> Looking at the volumes of Registrum Antiquissimum arranged on a table confronting them, he asked how anyone could possibly have had the nerve to do all that. But perhaps it was not a question of nerve, but simply of vision: a testament of the vision, first of Canon Foster and their past president, Sir Frank Stenton. On that table stood more than forty years' work, in fact the practical planning went back to 1925 and the initial thinking to the years of the First World War. It represented, he said, the amalgamation

4   Kathleen Major, 'Sir Frank Merry Stenton', in *Registrum Antiquissimum IX* (LRS 62, 1968), xi.

of two scholarly traditions, that exemplified by Canon Foster … the man of genius who provided his own edition, and that exemplified by Sir Frank Stenton, the professional historian of vision. Both had been influenced by J. H. Round's Ancient Charters, published by the Pipe Roll Society in 1888. Round had the same vision of putting into print all charters before 1200. Men like Canon Foster were also drawing on an older tradition of study of local history. Such influences had produced a massive amount of other scholarly work in the present century … Without this scholarly groundwork, most of the history which his own generation had produced and was producing would be impossible. It was a monument to English scholarship in this century … At one end of this edition, he said, was the inspiration of Canon Foster, but from Volume Four they had to look to Kathleen Major, who had triumphantly finished it. Her achievement was the more remarkable in that at the same time she had been successively Diocesan Archivist at Lincoln, Reader in Diplomatic at the University of Oxford, Principal of St Hilda's College, Oxford, and then Professor of Diplomatic at Nottingham University. Nor had she only edited the *Registrum*. As General Editor of the Society, she had produced many volumes. He recalled how he himself had sat at her feet at Oxford in 1947–49 in her diplomatic classes. He had found tremendous learning, a wonderful grasp of her subject, but above all he had an impression of thoroughness, of someone who … would leave no stone unturned to get to the end of the argument. Now the Record Society was held together by her drive and magnetism and they were greatly in her debt.[5]

While the 1960s and 1970s saw the Society progressing with these significant projects – the *Registrum Antiquissimum*, the registers of Bishops Sutton and Repingdon, the *Sessions of the Peace* and the *Records of the Court of Sewers* – all of which had their origins in the pre-War years, space was also found for a handful of new editions. One of these, Margaret Bowker's edition of an early sixteenth-century court book, was in many ways an extension of Hamilton Thompson's three volumes of *Diocesan Visitations* for that period. It was the first time that the records of the court of audience of an English bishop had been printed in full. The remainder of these new works moved the Society's publications into new fields. The history of Lincolnshire in the nineteenth century, hitherto untouched by the Society, was visited in 1964 with the publication of *Letters and Papers of the Cholmeleys from Wainfleet 1813–1853*, edited by Guy Cholmeley from family archives in his own possession. A miscellany volume issued in 1973 included some letters of the Whichcot family of Harpswell, edited by Michael Lloyd, and some correspondence of the Deputy Registrar of the diocese, John Fardell, edited by Mary Finch, which illuminated the workings of ecclesiastical administration at the beginning of the nineteenth century.

---

[5]   LRS Archive, Major correspondence.

At the Council meeting in September 1969, Professor Bullough of Nottingham University urged that a volume relating to railways be considered, as a means of attracting new members. As a result, Miss Major discussed the matter with Dr Frank Henthorn, who undertook to produce a volume from material relating to a railway in north Lincolnshire contained in the Stubbs deposit in the Lincolnshire Archives Office. This edition appeared in late 1975 and more than justified Professor Bullough's advocacy when the entire stock sold out within a few years. The Society returned once more to the nineteenth century in 1979 with the publication of Dr Rod Ambler's edition of the Lincolnshire returns of the Religious Census of 1851, a source which was subsequently visited by nearly every other local record society in the country.

The Society continued to hold its Annual Meeting at the Guildhall until the late 1970s. The inclusion of this among the civic duties of the Mayor owed a great deal to the influence exercised by Sir Francis Hill in the affairs of the City. The arrangements followed a regular pattern, as noted by Mary Finch:

> The Mayor will give a word of civic welcome at the start of the A.G.M. and will then retire to his parlour, I think, but will reappear for tea, plus the (Lady?) Mayoress and the Sheriff's lady. The Mayor is keen on brass rubbing, but probably 12th c[entury] charters are beyond him.[6]

The meeting, as intended, gave members the opportunity to catch up with old friends; it also enabled newcomers to make themselves known. The depth of knowledge and experience represented on these occasions could be formidable. Attending his first meeting in 1977, the writer, then living in Collingham, was introduced to Dorothy Owen, who remarked: 'Ah, Collingham: that's where Canon Larken went to live on his retirement,' thus making a link right back to the foundation of the Society. Dorothy and Arthur Owen, Kathleen Major and Joan Varley were all regular in their attendance, as were such stalwarts of Lincolnshire history as Ron Drury, Terence Leach, Clifford Clubley and Reg Brocklesby. A customary feature of 'Any Other Business' was an enquiry from the Revd Cuthbert Casson, asking whether the date of the meeting might be before the end of British Summer Time.[7]

A number of changes took place among the officers of the Society during these years. In 1974 Miss Judith Cripps of the Lincolnshire Archives Office was appointed as Hon. Secretary. The following year Sir Francis Hill retired from the Presidency and Miss Major from the post of Hon. General Editor. In proposing her election as the new President, the Bishop of Chichester (Dr Eric Kemp) said that

---

6   LRS Archive, Major correspondence: Mary Finch to KM, 25 September 1968. Miss Major was due to speak on the *Registrum Antiquissimum* at the meeting.
7   LRS Minute Book IV (AGM, 31 October 1981).

[Miss Major] had been associated with the Society for forty years as Editor and thirty years as Secretary. Her devoted work, following on that of Canon Foster, had maintained the Society as the most important local publishing Society, with the possible exception of the Surtees Society. The Lincoln Record Society had had as Presidents and Editors persons of high standing in the world of scholarship, and it was fitting that Miss Major should succeed Sir Francis as President.[8]

Mrs Dorothy Owen was appointed as the new Hon. General Editor.

By the late 1950s, it had become evident that the Society could no longer keep the annual subscription at the sum of one guinea, at which it had remained since 1910. That it had been possible to continue for so long at the original rate was largely due to the highly efficient way in which the Society's finances were looked after for so many years by Sir Francis Hill and his staff.

Rising costs, however, had made it more and more difficult to pay for the programme of publications, and at the Annual Meeting in 1957 it was agreed to increase the subscription to two guineas, with effect from September 1958. During the 1960s, this produced a yearly subscription income in the region of £500. This in itself was insufficient to pay for the cost of printing and distributing a volume. Even the comparatively short *Cholmeley Letters* cost £569, while the sum paid for the fifth volume of Sutton's Register was £934. In 1969, therefore, another subscription increase was agreed, taking the annual rate to £3 with effect from 1970.

The new rate, however, was never realistic, and the hyperinflation of the 1970s rapidly took the cost of volumes to frightening levels. At the beginning of the decade, the slim volume of Whichcot and Fardell letters cost just under £1,000; by 1974 the seventh volume of Bishop Sutton was £2,700 and in the following year the outlay on Dr Henthorn's *Trent, Ancholme and Grimsby Railway* edition was more than £3,000. Prices continued to rise in an inexorable fashion and at the end of the 1970s the Religious Census of 1851 cost nearly £6,000 to produce, while at the beginning of the 1980s, the third volume of *Bishop Repingdon's Register*, despite all Miss Archer's efforts to cut it down in size, required the enormous sum of £7,738.

A comparison between Volume 56 (*Some Sessions of the Peace*) of 1962 and Volume 74 (*Bishop Repingdon III*) of 1982 – the two books being almost identical in size – indicates that the sum needed for the printing and distribution of a Record Society edition had increased almost ninefold. The annual subscription, which was two guineas at the start of this period, had risen to £3 in 1970 and again in 1974 to £4 for individuals and £5 for institutions. In 1980 it was found necessary to increase the rate once more, this time to £7 for individuals and £9 for institutions. However, not only did these increases lag behind the rise in prices but they were never enough to enable income to

8   LRS Minute Book III (27 September 1975).

match expenditure. A ninefold increase in the subscription during this period would have resulted in an annual rate of nearly £20, way beyond anything that was politically feasible.

The gap between subscription income and expenditure had to be met from other sources. In a good year, between £300 and £500 might be received from the sale of back volumes and from interest on investments. Another source was grants from outside bodies. The British Academy gave generously in this way throughout the 1960s and 1970s, until financial restrictions of its own made it impossible for it to continue this support. Institutions with which individual editors were associated also contributed: the University of Birmingham towards Repingdon's register and Westfield College towards Sutton's. In this way, the Society was able to cover its costs from year to year, assisted by generous donations from Miss Major in the early 1970s (she also contributed the entire cost of Volume 68, as a memorial to Canon Foster). Nevertheless, there were occasions when it looked as though there would not be enough money in the bank to cover impending costs. At the Council meeting in September 1968, it was reported that

> As the Society … would have to pay for the Sewers volume and Sutton VI in this financial year, it was possible that it might have an overdraft of perhaps £500 for the six months or so before next September.[9]

The editor of the Sewers volume, Arthur Owen (not yet a member of the Council), later came to the rescue with the offer of an interest-free loan of this amount, and in the event it proved not to be needed. But the incident served as a reminder of how precarious the finances of the Society had become.

One of the difficulties undoubtedly lay in the fact of there being, since 1964, an 'absentee' Treasurer, the Manager of Lloyds Bank, who could not be expected to have the same understanding of the Society and enthusiasm for its work that had been exemplified in the way that Canon Foster, Miss Major or Sir Francis Hill went about their duties as officers. The situation also produced an awkward separation between the administrative and publishing work on the one hand and the financial business on the other. At the Council meeting in September 1976, the Hon. Secretary, Judith Cripps, reported that

> the accounts had been received from the Treasurer's assistant only just in time to be duplicated for today's meetings, but cursory inspection revealed that there were serious discrepancies with the finances as understood by the Secretary. For instance she had been told that all save a few members had paid their subscriptions for the year, and the reprinted *Lincolnshire Domesday* had been distributed on this understanding, but even bearing in

---

[9] LRS Minute Book III, 17.

mind the subscriptions paid in advance, the subscription income of £1247 did not represent payment by a membership of 158 individual and 179 private members ... There were other omissions and discrepancies visible to the Secretary. The President commented on the unsatisfactory presentation of the account, and asked whether the Secretary received regular bank statements ... The Secretary admitted that she had never seen a bank statement, and Miss Major said that this was vital, citing the instance of her own cheque for £500 sent to the Treasurer but never paid in, which had ultimately to be cancelled. Several members of Council added their own comments on the delay in paying in cheques.[10]

In an attempt to resolve the situation, a Finance Committee was appointed, consisting of the officers and two other members of Council. A year later, the Treasurer resigned but as no one could be found to take on the post, it was decided that the work should be done by the Finance Committee. Shortly afterwards it was discovered that most of the Treasurer's records had been destroyed in a fire in the garage of the member of his staff to whom the work had been entrusted.

The financial difficulties of these years, undoubtedly exacerbated by the lack of a designated Treasurer, came to a head early in 1982 when it became apparent that there would not be enough money in the bank to pay for Volume 74 (*Repingdon III*).[11] Three steps were taken to remedy this situation. The immediate need was met by an interest-free loan advanced by Miss Major. The present writer was then recruited to undertake the office of Hon. Treasurer. As an inexperienced newcomer, he was greatly assisted by the advice of his counterpart in the Canterbury and York Society and by the guidance of a new Hon. Auditor, Nevile Camamile. By keeping a careful eye on subscriptions, and by promoting book sales (which exceeded £1,000 for several years during the 1980s), the Accumulated Fund for future publications grew to more than £30,000 by the end of the century. The third measure that was taken was the agreement which the Society entered into with Messrs Boydell & Brewer in 1985. Under this, Boydell & Brewer took responsibility for publishing and distributing the volumes under a joint imprint, and for dealing with sales and storage of back stock. The principal benefits for the Society were the ability to take advantage of new printing methods coming into use, and much wider publicity for the volumes, particularly overseas.

The Society continued to produce volumes, year by year, under the watchful eye of successive General Editors. Dorothy Owen was followed in 1995 by Professor David Smith, who in turn handed over in 2002 to the present writer. A number of these volumes continued themes which the Society had begun to explore in previous generations. Rosalind Hill's magnificent edition of

---

[10] LRS Minute Book III (25 September 1976).
[11] LRS Minute Book IV: Finance Committee, 19 February 1982.

Bishop Sutton's register was completed in 1986; ten years later, Dr Alison McHardy produced an edition of the writ register of Bishop John Buckingham, and shortly afterwards the first volume of another lengthy project, the registers of Bishop Henry Burghersh, was published.[12] The publication of early charters, so magnificently exemplified by the edition of the *Registrum Antiquissimum*, was taken in a new direction with the appearance of David Smith's collection of the *Acta of Bishop Hugh of Wells*, itself inspired both by Kathleen Major's work on the *acta* of Archbishop Stephen Langton and by the success of the British Academy's English Episcopal Acta series, of which Professor Smith was himself for many years the General Editor. The Society's interest in legal records, dating back to Doris Stenton's volume on the early assize rolls, was continued by an edition of the records of a royal inquest into official misconduct in 1341, the work of a young American scholar, Bernard McLane. Another subject to which the Society returned in these years was probate records, and, after a gap of more than seventy years, a fourth volume in the series of Lincoln Wills was published in 2001. Railway records, first visited for the Society by Dr Henthorn in 1975, were the focus of another publication. The remarkable survival of an album of photographs, showing the construction of the railway from Bourne to Saxby in the early 1890s, was the inspiration for *Building a Railway*, edited by Stewart Squires and Ken Hollamby in 2009. High-quality reproductions of the original photographs were interspersed with commentary and maps, with modern photographs showing the remains of the line since its closure to passenger traffic fifty years earlier.

Alongside the continuity with the past demonstrated by these volumes, the Society was exploring a number of new avenues of historical research during these years. A theme particularly encouraged by Dorothy Owen was the publication of municipal records, and in 1978–9 some preliminary ideas for a whole series of publications of borough records were discussed.[13] In the event, only two were published: the *Boston Assembly Minutes 1545–1575* and *The Hallbook of Grantham 1641–1649*. The overseas trade of Boston, previously examined in Dr Hinton's edition of the Jacobean port books, was the subject of Stephen Rigby's edition of its late fourteenth-century customs accounts. The city of Lincoln itself was the subject of several volumes. A bibliography of printed works relating to the city, compiled by Mary Short, was published in 1990; financed by the Francis Hill Commemoration Trust, it was prefaced by a memoir of Sir Francis and a photographic portrait. A year later, a volume of seventeenth-century probate inventories of Lincoln citizens appeared, edited by Dr Jim Johnston, Vice-Principal of Bishop

---

[12] The edition of Burghersh's registers evolved from a thesis of which Rosalind Hill had herself been one of the examiners.

[13] LRS Minute Book II (Council, 28 October 1978); Minute Book IV (Finance Committee, 12 October 1979).

Grosseteste College and subsequently a calm and unflappable Hon. Secretary of the Society. In 2004 the Society joined forces with the Survey of Lincoln to publish *Historic Town Plans of Lincoln*. The Survey had grown out of the earlier Survey of Ancient Houses of Lincoln, an organisation conceived, supported and encouraged throughout its existence by Kathleen Major. The magnificent volume, edited by Dennis Mills and Rob Wheeler, included beautifully reproduced plans of the city, notably those of J. S. Padley showing the development of Lincoln in the nineteenth century.

There were two other significant publications relating to maps of the county. In 1996, R. A. Carroll, formerly County Librarian of Lincolnshire, published a meticulously researched carto-bibliography, *Printed Maps of Lincolnshire 1576–1900*. The cartographic study of a notable area of the county was the subject of Rob Wheeler's *Maps of the Witham Fens*, tracing the course of drainage and navigation works in this area from the remarkable early thirteenth-century Kirkstead Map through to the end of the nineteenth century. Exploration and discovery provided a tangential theme to the publication of *Gratefull to Providence*, an edition of the diary and account books of Matthew Flinders, the eighteenth-century apothecary of Donington whose son, also Matthew, found lasting fame as the first man to circumnavigate Australia.

The nineteenth-century church in Lincolnshire was revisited by Dr Rod Ambler in his edition of the *Parish Correspondence of John Kaye, Bishop of Lincoln, 1827–53*. Nearly 500 pages in length, this volume represented only a sample of the voluminous correspondence of this indefatigable Bishop. It provided a mine of detailed information on the church and clergy during that period. The activities of a later Bishop of Lincoln gave the Society its first entry into the history of the twentieth century, with Graham Neville's edition of the *Diaries of Edward Lee Hicks*. The publication of the journal of the man who hosted the inaugural meeting of the Society in October 1910 serves to highlight the longevity of its existence.

Kathleen Major died on 19 December 2000. She had been a member of the Society for nearly seventy years, a member of its Council for sixty-five, and one of its officers for half a century. More than anyone else, she had taken up the work of Canon Foster and ensured that it would be continued, not least by her herculean labours in completing the edition of the *Registrum Antiquissimum*. Under the terms of her will, an appointment in favour of the Record Society gave it a large share in the sum of money resulting from the winding-up of the George Major Trust established by her father in 1944. This resulted in the Society receiving, during the financial year 2006–07, a sum in excess of £500,000. This generous endowment will enable the Society both to maintain and continue its existing work of publication and also to develop in new directions as it enters its second centenary. A Finance and Publications Committee was established in 2006 to manage the Society's affairs under the overall authority of the Council.

Several new initiatives have already been undertaken as a result of Miss Major's legacy. Under an agreement with Lincoln Cathedral, the work of the Cathedral Librarian has been supported financially to enable the release of a proportion of his time for his duties as General Editor. A programme has been inaugurated of making grants in support of external projects in line with the Society's objectives. By means of this, assistance has been given both to research work and publication. A major project is now in progress for the digitisation of the Society's back volumes, with the aim of making them accessible to members online. As the Society celebrates its Centenary, it can look back with satisfaction on the publication of one hundred volumes of records relating to the county and diocese of Lincoln, a rich resource for historians around the world and one that is truly 'wonderful to behold'. It can also look forward to the next hundred years with confidence, as it explores new ways of continuing to carry out the vision and enterprise of its Founder, Charles Wilmer Foster, and his worthy successor, Kathleen Major.

APPENDIX ONE

MEMBERS OF THE SOCIETY

1910 – 2010

OFFICERS OF THE SOCIETY

PRESIDENTS
1910   Rt Revd Edward Lee Hicks, Lord Bishop of Lincoln
1920   Rt Revd William Shuckburgh Swayne, Lord Bishop of Lincoln
1932   The Lord Monson
1938   The Lord Brownlow
1942   Professor F. M. (Sir Frank) Stenton
1967   Sir Francis Hill
1975   Miss Kathleen Major
1987   Professor J. C. Holt
1996   Mrs Dorothy Owen
2002   Professor David Smith
2007   Professor Michael Jones

GENERAL EDITORS
1910   Revd Canon C. W. Foster
1935   Miss Kathleen Major
1974   Miss Kathleen Major and Mrs Dorothy Owen
1975   Mrs Dorothy Owen
1995   Professor David Smith
2002   Canon Dr Nicholas Bennett

SECRETARIES
1910   Revd Canon James Bell
1911   Revd Canon C. W. Foster
1935   Miss Kathleen Major
1956   J. W. F. (Sir Francis) Hill
1965   Miss Kathleen Major
1967   Miss Kathleen Major and Miss Mary Finch
1974   Miss J. A. Cripps
1976   C. M. Lloyd
1982   Nicholas Bennett
1985   Dr G. A. Knight
1993   Dr J. A. Johnston
2002   Neville Birch
2006   Miss Lynn Godson
2009   Dr Paul Dryburgh

TREASURERS

1910	Gordon L. Simpson
1914	A. E. T. Jourdain
1914	Wilfrid Bond
1916	Revd C. Warren
1918	Revd C. W. Foster
1935	J. W. F. (Sir Francis) Hill
1965	R. G. Turner
1969	E. W. Millington
1977	[Finance Committee]
1982	Dr Nicholas Bennett
2002	Ken Hollamby

ALPHABETICAL LIST OF MEMBERS

INDIVIDUALS

[Each name is preceded by the year of joining the Society (shown in **bold** for current members), and followed by the address of the member at that time; any later addresses are added in square brackets. Any further details are given as appropriate, with the date of death (or if this is not known, the year (in square brackets) in which the member's name disappears from the Society's records). The names of Officers of the Society are given in capitals; those of members of Council are preceded by an asterisk.]

1923. Abbott, Revd Arthur. Corby Vicarage, Grantham. Died 19 May 1934.

2008. Acton, Mark. 37 Cromwell Street, Lincoln.

1976. Acton, R. Bishop Grosseteste College, Lincoln. [1980]

1975. Adams, Dr L. T. *See* Gilmour.

1910. Akenhead, Revd Canon E. St Martin's Vicarage, Lincoln. [1923]

2004. Albone, James. 11 Moorfield Road, Mattishall, Dereham, Norfolk.

1911. Allison, Revd H. F. Scothern Rectory, Lincoln. [1916]

1995. Allpress, Mrs P. A. 17 Ancaster Drive, Sleaford.

1968. *Ambler, Dr R. W. Morgan Hall, The Lawns, Cottingham, Yorkshire [323A Hainton Avenue, Grimsby; 182 Grimsby Road, Humberston; 37 Cumberland Avenue, Grimsby; 7 Heron Close, Grimsby].

1919. Ambrose, Revd W. C. Billinghay Vicarage, Lincoln ['Quy', The Avenue, Fareham, Hants]. [1938]

1925. Ancaster, The Earl of. Grimsthorpe, Bourne. Died 19 September 1951.

1950. Ancaster, The Earl of. Swinstead Hall, Grantham [Grimsthorpe Castle, Bourne]. [1977][1]

1979. Anderson, Charles L. 'Rooftree', Boston Road, Horncastle [26 West Street, Horncastle; 2 Rollestone Court, Bridge Street, Horncastle]. Died 1994.

1985. Anyan, Michael C. M. Belle Vue House, Springthorpe, Gainsborough.

1996. Appleby, John. 17 Meadow Drive, Healing, Grimsby. Died February 2008.

---

[1] Subscription transferred to Willoughby Memorial Library.

2002. Armstrong, Dennis L. Eresby Lodge, Spilsby.

1976. Armstrong, Mrs M. E. 4 Chandos Road, Scunthorpe. [1991]

1982. Arundale, R. L. The Precentory, Lincoln. Died April 1988.

1910. Ashby, Revd Canon P. O. The Rectory, Market Deeping [Hitchin, Herts.]. [1931]

1910. Askey, Revd Herbert. Ravendale Vicarage, Grimsby. Died 30 October 1917.

2007. Astley, Mrs Erica. 10 Reaper's Rise, Epworth.

1911. Astley-Corbett, Sir Francis, Bt. Elsham Hall. [1912]

2009. Atkin, Dr Wendy. 15 Castle Street, Sleaford.

2010. Atkinson, Mrs Anne. 4 Union Road, Lincoln.

1960. Atkinson, Capt. W. J. 2900 Halcyon Avenue, Baltimore [8506 Glenn Michael Lane, Randallstown, Maryland; 1659 Matheson Drive, Deltona, Florida; 181 Marine Oaks Drive, Baltimore, U.S.A.] [2005]

2009. Audis, Mrs Christine. 99 Station Road, Bardney.

1965. Avery, Mrs G. 24 Old Hertford Road, Hatfield, Herts. [1973]

1995. Ayris, Dr Paul. University College, Gower Street, London.

1910. Bacon, Sir Hickman Becket, Bt, F.S.A. Thonock, Gainsborough. Died 13 April 1945.

2005. Baile, Mrs Jane. The Prebendal Manor, Nassington, Northants.

2000. Bailey, Mrs H. J. Limepits Farmhouse, Greenfield Lane, South Thoresby, Alford.

1979. Bailey, Revd P. Holy Rood, King Street, Market Rasen. [1983]

1935. Baker, Mrs F. Fir Tree Cottage, Nettleham. Died 1967.

1964. *Baker, F. T., F.S.A. 210 Burton Road, Lincoln. Died 24 January 1998.

1958. Baker, R. Croft. 37 Bethlehem Street, Grimsby [Richmond Chambers, 71 Great George Street, Leeds; Department of Justice, Nairobi, Kenya]. [1976]

2010. Ball, Mrs A. 9 Wimberley Way, South Witham, Grantham.

2009. Ball, Peter. 9 Wimberley Way, South Witham, Grantham.

1968. Ballard, Mrs E. Abbey Farm, Holton Beckering, Lincoln. Died 20 December 1995.

1914. Banks, Lt-Col. Charles Edward, M.D., Senior Surgeon U.S.A. P.H.S. Milwaukee, Wisconsin, U.S.A. [2018 Prairie Avenue, Chicago, U.S.A.] Died 1931.

1941. Banwell, G. H. Deloraine Court West, James Street, Lincoln. [1944]

1954. Banwell, Sir Harold. 27 Prentis Road, Streatham, London [6 Queensway, Lincoln; 2 Vicars' Court, Lincoln]. Died 10 April 1982.

1992. Barker, T. R. Third Hill Farm, Heighington, Lincoln.

1952. Barley, M. W. The Old Hall, Muskham, Notts. [7 Salthouse Lane, Beeston; 66 Park Road, Chilwell, Notts.] [1975]

2005. Barnes, Stephen. 8 Dalmeny Road, Bexhill on Sea, East Sussex.

1976. Barrick, M. 319 Pelham Road, Immingham. [1983]

1985. Barton, Ifor. The Old Vicarage, Station Road, Grasby, Barnetby.

1924. Baskerville, G. H. Crowsley Park, Henley-on-Thames. Died 22 July 1944.

1918. Bates, Thomas. Nunsfield, Bargate, Grimsby. [1923]

1910. Bayly, H. Dennis. Lenton Abbey, Nottingham. [1918]

1923. Beavis, Miss M. W. 5 Duke Street, Sleaford. [1931]

1997. Beckett, Professor J. V. 44 Park Road, Chilwell, Nottingham.

1966. Beckwith, Ian S. 13 Thoresby Close, Hollywell Gardens, Brant Road, Lincoln [20 Curle Avenue, Lincoln]. [1975]

1984. Bee, Walter. 72 Newstead Road, Urmston, Manchester. Died September 2004.

1984. Beeby, Barry. Halstead Hall, Stixwould, Lincoln. [1986]

1995. Beevers, Mrs Ros. 4 Swinegate, Grantham [28 Altham Terrace, Lincoln]. [2006]

1912. Bell, Major Cecil. Bourne. [1931]

1910. *BELL, Revd Canon James. The Grove, Lincoln. Died 3 April 1918.

1976. Belsham, J. W. 19 Langwith Drive, Holbeach.

2001. Bennet, Mark. 13 Drury Lane, Lincoln.

1989. Bennett, Mrs Eleanor. Riverbank, Charles Street, Louth. [2006]

1910. Bennett, Major G. L. Westlands, Grimsby. [1937]

1910. Bennett, James. Fox Close, Grimsby. [1935]

1976. *BENNETT, [Canon Dr] Nicholas H., F.S.A. The Manse, Low Street, Collingham, Notts [Forge Cottage, Burton-by-Lincoln; 3 Vicars' Court, Lincoln; Hawthorn House, Nocton, Lincoln].

1910. Bennett, William. Bank House, Grimsby. [1912]

1910. Besant, Revd Frank. The Vicarage, Sibsey. [1914]

2007. Beswick, John. Eskham Farm, Seadyke Way, Eskham.

2009. Betteridge, Stephen. 35 Sudbrooke Road, Scothern, Lincoln.

1917. Billiat, Joseph. Junior Carlton Club, Pall Mall, London. Died 18 September 1955.

1941. *Binnall, Revd Canon P. B. G. The Vicarage, Holland Fen [The Rectory, West Barkwith, Lincoln; The Subdeanery, Lincoln; Elm Cottage, Church Street, Hemswell]. Died 29 November 1980.

1992. *BIRCH, N. C. 4 Broadway, Lincoln.

2007. Bird, Dean. 3 Rivermead, Lincoln.

1948. *Birkbeck, F. J. 3 Stonefield Avenue, Lincoln [White House, Riseholme, Lincoln; Lindsey Cottage, Fovant, Salisbury]. Died 1981.

1978. Bischoff, J. P. Oklahoma State University, Stillwater, Oklahoma U.S.A.

1925. Blackie, Rt Revd Ernest Morell. The Precentory, Lincoln [The
           Deanery, Rochester]. Died 5 March 1943.
1910. Blagg, T. M., F.S.A. 124 Chancery Lane, London; [Caldecote,
           Newport Pagnell]. [1918]
1950. Blow, J. E. County Offices, Sleaford. [1970]
1910. Bolam, Revd C. E. St Mary Magdalene's Rectory, Lincoln. [1923]
1910. Bond, Ven. John. Archdeacon of Stow. Died 14 May 1912.
1911. *BOND, Wilfrid, F.R.I.B.A.. Elmer Street, Grantham. Died 31
           October 1935.
1985. Booth, Mrs M. A. P. 2A Cornwall Street, Kirton-in-Lindsey. [1986]
1930. Boothby, R. E. Little Carlton, Louth [Burwell Hall, Louth]. [1948]
1984. Border, Michael G. 9 Connaught Avenue, Grimsby [10 Utterby
           Drive, Grimsby]. Died 2009.
1976. Boulton, David 45 Foundry Street, Horncastle [Redmill House,
           Kirkby on Bain, Woodhall Spa].
1969. Bowker, Mrs M. 5 Spens Avenue, Cambridge [4 Sylvester Road,
           Cambridge; The Cottage, Bailrigg, Lancaster; Sussex Street,
           Cambridge]. [2006]
1984. Bows, Miss B. J. 52 Lindum Avenue, Lincoln. [1994]
1990. Boyce, Douglas G. 29 Victoria Terrace, Market Rasen. Died
           October 2002.
1910. Boyd, W. K. 9 Archway Road, Highgate, London; [24 Bisham
           Gardens, Highgate, London]. [1915]
1933. Boys, Guy P. Thornhill, Stockton Avenue, Fleet, Hants. [1936]
1942. *Brace, H. W. Haltemprice, Lea Road, Gainsborough. Died 2
           October 1962.
1912   Brackenbury, Kenneth F. 5 Whittington Avenue, London [56
           Overstrand Mansions, Battersea Park, London; 5 Buckingham
           Vale, Clifton, Bristol; 12 Southfield Road, Cotham Brow, Bristol;
           St Beetha's, Steyning, Sussex; Crickets, Goring Road, Steyning,
           Sussex]. Died 26 March 1962.
1947. Bradley, K. Ash Villa, London Road, Frampton. [1961]
1932. Bramble, Percy O. Caister-on-Sea, Norfolk. [1937]
2009. Brammer, Mrs Betty. Bramlea, Station Road, Hubbert's Bridge,
           Boston.
2007. Breeden, Bill. Holmelea, Park Lane, Donington, Spalding. [2008]
1954. Briggs, Dr A. H. Birkindale Lodge, Church Lane, Lincoln. [1958]
1995. Bristow, S. J. 8 The Link, Wellingore, Lincoln.
2009. Britten, Clive. 35 Bonner Grove, Aldridge, Walsall.
1955. Brocklesby, R. The Elms, North Eastern Road, Thorne, Yorkshire.
2004. Brook, Dr Shirley. 10 Manor Road, Lincoln.
1924. Brooks, F. W. University College, Hull [The University, Hull; 14
           Wellesley Avenue, Beverley High Road, Hull]. Died 31 January
           1980.

1910. *Brotherton, Revd C. F. The Vicarage, Barnetby [Grayingham Rectory, Kirton in Lindsey]. Died 5 December 1929.

1952. Brown, [Professor] R. Allen. Public Record Office, Chancery Lane, London [King's College, Strand, London]. Died 1 February 1989.

1976. Brown, Miss Margery E. 36 Needham Road, Arnold, Nottingham [Cherry Cottage, North Muskham, Newark, Notts].

1979. Brown, Sandra. Derwent College, University of York. [1980]

1911. Brown, William, F.S.A. The Old House, Sowerby, Thirsk, Yorks. Died 22 July 1924.[2]

1910. Brownlow, The Earl. Belton Park, Grantham. Died 17 March 1921.

1932. Brownlow, The Lord. Belton House, Grantham. [1968]

1968. Brumby, H. The Rookery, Winteringham, Scunthorpe. [1976]

1917. Brumwell, Charles E. 10 Broad Street, Hereford. [1935]

1910. Bullock, Revd Canon R. The Parsonage, Spalding [Shurdington Vicarage, Cheltenham]. [1914]

1966. *Bullough, Professor D. A. The University, Nottingham [The University, St Andrew's]. [1976]

1911. Burchell-Herne, Miss M. D. Bushey Grange, Watford. [1913]

1990. Burger, Professor Michael. Constantine House, Bootham, York [Department of History, University of California, Santa Barbara, California; Division of Humanities, Mississippi University for Women, Columbus, Mississippi, U.S.A.] [1993]

1999. Burger, Professor Michael. Division of Humanities, Mississippi University for Women, Columbus, Mississippi, U.S.A.

1945. Burman, Revd R. Bishop's Hostel, Lincoln [96 Oswald Road, Scunthorpe; Barholme Vicarage, Stamford]. [1950]

2010. Burn, Nigel. 20 Egerton Road, Lincoln.

1974. Burton, D. Westlands, Meggitt Lane, Winteringham, Scunthorpe. [1978]

1944. Busby, J. H. Further Bowers, Harpenden, Herts [Flat 2, 27 Sandpit Lane, St Albans; 75 Lyndhurst Gardens, Finchley, London; 39 Castle Street, Eye, Suffolk]. [1979]

1949. Butcher, Miss E. Training College, Lincoln [Clare, Sudbury, Suffolk]. [1965]

2010. Caine, Mrs Jill. 18 Royal Arthur Close, Skegness.

2008. Callow, Rodney. 141 Wolsey Way, Lincoln.

1982. *Cameron, Professor Kenneth. 292 Queen's Road, Beeston, Nottingham [16 The Cloisters, Salthouse Lane, Beeston, Nottingham]. Died 10 March 2001.

1920. Capes, G. E. Woodlea, Ainslie Street, Great Grimsby. [1931]

---

2   William Brown (1854 1924): editor of archiepiscopal registers and other volumes for the Surtees Society and the Yorkshire Archaeological Society Record Series. See *YAJ* 28 (1924), 118 133.

1986. Carlisle, [Sir] Kenneth, M.P. Wyken Hall, Stanton, Bury St Edmunds, Suffolk.

1974. Carlton, Miss A. E. 11 Carlton Road, Boston [6 Ashlawn Drive, Boston].

1986. *Carroll, R. A. Spring Lodge, Churchgate, Gedney [Saxton House, 38 Town Drove, Quadring].

1925. Cave-Orme, George A. Chequergate House, Louth. Died December 1932.

2009. Carter, Mrs Beryl. 8 Hawthorn Road, Lincoln.

1946. Carter, Miss S. Mexborough House, Burton-by-Lincoln [6 King's Bench Walk, Temple]. [1956]

1945. Carter, His Honour [Sir] Walker K. Mexborough House, Burton-by-Lincoln [6 King's Bench Walk, Temple; Royal Courts of Justice, Strand, London]. [1975]

1946. Carter, Walter. The Grange, High Halden, Kent. Died 9 February 1975.

1995. Cassidy, P. J. 'Warren Lodge', Moulton Common, Spalding. [2006]

1964. Casson, Revd Cuthbert. The Vicarage, Twycross, Atherstone, Warwickshire [The Rectory, Alexton, Rutland; Birnam Cottage, 8 Stamford Road, Oakham]. Died 12 December 1985.

1952. Casson, Revd Canon Hugh. St Chad's House, 145 Coleman Street, Leicester [Twycross Vicarage, Atherstone, Warwick]. Died 9 June 1964.

2003. Casswell, M. R. 'Hill View', East Fen Lane, New Leake, Boston.

2008. Casterton, Michael. 9 Woodlands, Winthorpe, Newark, Notts.

1930. Cawley, Revd H. St John's Vicarage, Grantham. [1937]

1910. Chapman, Revd A. V. The Vicarage, Bottesford, Scunthorpe. Died 1 December 1912.

2009. Charlton, Tom. Charltons, Hallgate, Moulton, Spalding.

1910. Chase, Rt Revd Frederic Henry, Bishop of Ely. The Palace, Ely. Died 23 September 1925.

1910. Chatterton, Frank. Leicester House, Hull; [Belvedere, Newland Park, Hull]. [1931]

1910. Chatterton, Frank. Somerby Hall, Brigg. [1912]

1920. Cheales, Revd J. P. The Vicarage, Friskney. [1931]

1949. *Cheney, Professor C. R. 21 Rathen Road, Withington, Manchester [Corpus Christi College, Cambridge; 236 Hills Road, Cambridge]. Died 19 June 1987.

2007. Cherry, Mrs Anne. 57 Scawby Road, Scawby Brook, Brigg.

1927. Cheveley, R. D. 34 Stanley Road, Sutton, Surrey. [1935]

1933. Cholmeley, Sir Hugh, Bt. Easton Hall, Grantham. Died 1 February 1964.

1945. Christie, L. R. Lord's Waste, Breadfield, Woodbridge, Suffolk. [1947]

1983. Clark, Dr Alan. 38 Clarendon Street, Cambridge.

1910. Clarke, E. T., F.S.A. The Goddards, Snaith, Yorks. [1923]

1967. Clarke, J. N. 11 Dymoke Drive, Horncastle [Lindum, Iddesleigh
      Road, Woodhall Spa; 1 Southwold Close, Belchford, Horncastle;
      12 Stewart Court, Poclington, York]. Died 25 August 2006.

1978. Clarke, Mrs M. 4 Harpswell Road, Lincoln. Died 1985.

1985. Clarke, Norman. 4 Harpswell Road, Lincoln. Died 1990.

1910. Clements, Revd E. M. Barkstone Rectory, Grantham. [1923]

1962. Clubley, Revd C. Crowland, London Road, Bracebridge Heath,
      Lincoln [The Vicarage, Chapel St Leonards, Skegness; 203
      Rookery Lane, Lincoln]. Died September 1984.

2009. Cockayne, Dr E. Green Farm House, Woolpit, Bury St Edmunds,
      Suffolk. [2009]

1910. Cockburn, N. C. Harmston Hall, Lincoln. [1923]

2007. Cockerham, Dr Paul. Lezerea, Wendron, Helston, Cornwall.

2009. Codd, Mrs Stephanie. 3 Old Hall, Susworth, Scunthorpe.

1987. Coebergh-Traber, Mrs P. Zollerstr. 16, Erlenbach, Switzerland.
      [1991]

1910. *Cole, Revd Canon R. E. G. Pottergate, Lincoln. Died 9 January
      1921.

1932. Colegate, Arthur. Redbourne Hall, Kirton in Lindsey [Honington
      Hall, York]. [1943]

1941. Coles, Mrs S. 4 Chesterfield Road, Newbury, Berks. [1951]

1979. Collingwood, R. W. 73 Totteridge Lane, High Wycombe [Farley
      House, Farley, Much Wenlock, Shropshire]. [1991]

1972. Colyer, Miss C. Lincoln Archaeological Trust, 64 The Park, Lincoln
      [3 Drury Lane, Lincoln]. [1981]

1966. Constable, Professor Giles. 25 Mount Pleasant Road, Cambridge,
      Massachusetts, U.S.A. [1975]

1911. Cook, A. 16 Abbey Drive East, Grimsby. [1942]

1946. Cook, Revd Canon A. M., Subdean of Lincoln. Subdeanery,
      Lincoln. [1957]

1910. Cook, Mrs Henry L. 151 13th Street, Milwaukee, Wisconsin, U.S.A.
      [1916]

1925. Cooke, Revd A. H. Mapledurham Vicarage, Reading. Died 28
      November 1934.[3]

1925. Cooper, B. J. Clare Lodge, Market Rasen. Died 1956.

1951. Copland, H. County Offices, Newland, Lincoln [82 Yarborough
      Crescent, Lincoln]. [1960]

---

[3]   Alfred Hands Cooke (1854 1934): Fellow of King's College Cambridge;
Head Master of Aldenham School; Vicar of Mapledurham. Author: 'Molluscs' in
Cambridge Natural History, Vol. III; *The Early History of Mapledurham* (Oxfordshire
Record Society). [*Venn.*]

2008. Coppack, Glynn. The Limes, Howe Lane, Goxhill, Barrow-on-Humber.

1984. Copsey, Fr Richard. 216 London Road, Charlton Kings, Cheltenham [Aylesford Priory, Maidstone, Kent]. [1994]

1960. Cottam, Mrs R. E. 71 East 4th South, Provo, Utah. [1966]

2004. Coulson, Miss Brenda. 57 Lupin Road, Lincoln.

1968. Couth, W. 351 Harlaxton Road, Grantham. [1984]

2005. Coverley, Mrs J. 50 Welholme Road, Grimsby.

1965. Cowling, J. (Address unknown.) [1968]

1954. Cracroft-Amcotts, Sir Weston. Hackthorn Hall, Lincoln. [1956]

1910. *Cragg, Captain W. A.. Threckingham House, Folkingham [Billingborough]. Died 6 October 1950.

1952. Cragg, Major W. J. R. Threckingham House, Billingborough. [1956]

1910. Crathorne, Revd J. J. Creeton Rectory, Grantham [Swayfield Rectory, Grantham; Doddington Rectory, Lincoln]. Died 19 February 1952.

2008. Crees, Mrs Janet. 50 Eastfield Lane, Welton, Lincoln.

1967. *CRIPPS, Miss J. A. 48a Arboretum Avenue, Lincoln [Lincolnshire Archives Office, The Castle, Lincoln; 5 Olive Street, Lincoln; 28 Braehead Way, Bridge of Don, Aberdeen; 62 St Ronan's Drive, Peterculter, Aberdeen].

1916. Crispe, F. A. Grove Park Press, 270 Walwath Road, London. [1923]

1925. Croll, A. G. Diocesan Offices, 6A Guildhall Street, Lincoln [Jews' Court, Lincoln]. Died 27 October 1945.

1933. Cromwell, Revd R. H. Briarside, Howell Hill, Ewell, Surrey. [1948]

1990. *Crook, Dr David. 3 St Andrews, Belton Lane, Grantham.

1938. *Crookshank, H. F. C. [Rt Hon. The Viscount]. 51 Pont Street, London. Died 17 October 1961.

1915. Crowder, T. Bardney, Lincoln. [1931]

1910. Crowfoot, Revd Canon J. H., Chancellor of Lincoln. The Subdeanery, Lincoln [Colville, Worthing]. [1918]

1958. Cruser, Mrs C. Merrill. Monteview, Idaho, U.S.A. [849 K Street, Idaho Falls]. [1966]

1989. Crust, Mrs Linda M. The Coppers, Scothern Lane, Sudbrooke, Lincoln. [2000]

1961. Curlewis, M. 38 Via Luigi, Angeloni, Rome. [1965]

1910. Curtois, Revd Algernon. Monk's Leys Terrace, Lincoln. Died 13 September 1933.

2010. Curtis, Richard. 141A Doddington Road, Lincoln.

1912. Curzon of Kedleston, The Earl. Hachwood, Basingstoke. Died 20 March 1925.

1910. Cust, Very Revd A. P. Purey, Dean of York. The Deanery, York. Died 23 December 1916.

1910. Cust, The Lady Elizabeth. 13 Eccleston Square, London; [32 St George's Square, London]. Died 10 April 1914.

1910. Cust, Revd Canon W. A. Purey. St Margaret's Vicarage, Lincoln [Skendleby Rectory, Spilsby]. Died 28 September 1938.

1914. Cuthbert, Major General G. J. Bingfield, Corbridge, Northumberland [Sandhoe Garden Cottage, Hexham, Northumberland]. Died 1 February 1931.

1910. Dalby, Revd Canon F. H. The Vicarage, Cleethorpes. [1915]

1925. Dalby, Revd Canon F. H. Stoke Rectory, Grantham. Died 16 July 1933.

1976. Dales, R. W. 125 George Street, Mablethorpe. Died May 2003.

2009. Davey, Brian. 8 Midfield Way, Keelby, Grimsby.

1982. Davies, C. 4 King's Road, Stamford. [1984]

1910. Davies, Revd D. S. The Rectory, North Witham [Norwood, Montpellier Park, Llandrindod Wells, Radnorshire]. Died 10 December 1946.

1976. Dawson, Mrs C. M. 7 Sherwood Glen, Sheffield. [1984]

1961. Day, J. Owen. Southfield, Redbourne, Lincs. [1968]

1972. Day, Miss. 16 Towngate East, Market Deeping. [1978]

1910. Dean, A. W. Dowsby Hall, Bourne [The Hall, Carlton Scroop, Grantham]. Died 7 February 1929.

1931. Dean, Mrs A. W. 27 York House, Kensington. [1936]

1988. Dear, J. P. Devonport Cottages, Main Road, Stickney, Boston. [1991]

1984. Dennis, P. K. Stenigot House, Louth. [1984]

1979. De Ville, H. G. Bexton Mews, Bexton Lane, Knutsford. [1980]

1972. *De Waal, Revd Canon V. A. The Chancery, Lincoln. [1976]

1961. Dimock, Judge E. J. United States Courthouse, New York, U.S.A. [1971]

1916. Disney, Alfred N. Rutlish School, Merton, London [14 Wilton Crescent, Wimbledon]. Died 16 April 1929.

2000. Disney, Hugh A. F. 121 Cumnor Hill, Oxford [3 Parklands, Eynsham Road, Farmoor, Oxford]. Died 2 November 2009.

1925. Dixon, A. E. G. 62, St Martin's, Stamford. [1935]

1924. *Dixon, G. S., F.S.A. (formerly Gibbons). The Hall, Holton-le-Moor, Caistor. Died 30 July 1970.

1934. Dixon, Capt. Oscar. Kenwick Hall, Louth. [1942]

1910. *Dixon, Revd T. G. Holton Park, Caistor. Died 2 July 1937.

1976. Dixon, V. D. 4 Pipit Rise, Bedford [1A The Close, Great Barford, Bedford]. [1983]

1933. Dixon, Revd W. M. Timberland Vicarage, Lincoln. [1942]

1976. Dobson, E. 9 Park Avenue, Grimsby. Died February 1987.

1989. Dobson, John. 4 Cromer Bay, Winnipeg, Manitoba, Canada. [1992]

1990. Dobson, J. M. 6 Riseholme Road, Lincoln. [1994]

1928. Donington, R. S. 22 Welland Terrace, Spalding. [1935]

1925. Donson, J. A. Bridge Road, Gainsborough. [1935]

1923. Dorman, T. P. Fairfield, Billing Road, Northampton. [1931]

1962. Douie, Miss D. L. 123 Queensgate, Beverley, Yorks. [2a Charlbury Road, Oxford]. [1976]

2009. Dove, Geoff. 84 Hessle Avenue, Boston.

1982. Dowling, Mr A. 4 Howlett Road, Cleethorpes. [1996]

1976. Drewery, Miss M. M. West End, Conisholme, Louth. [1981]

1946. Drury, R. c/o Mrs Haw, 79 West End Avenue, Harrogate, Yorks [Aston Villa, King Street, Kirton, Boston; 27 Mayfair Avenue, Lincoln]. Died 7 December 2001.

2003. *DRYBURGH, Dr Paul. 7 Sandra Crescent, Heighington, Lincoln.

1936. Dudding, Surgeon Rear-Admiral J. S. Wintringham, Scunthorpe. Died 1951.

1953. *Dudding, J. [Sir John]. Scarborough House, Winteringham, Scunthorpe. Died 26 June 1986.

1910. *Dudding, Revd R. C., F.S.A. Saleby Vicarage, Alford. Died 16 December 1937.

1925. Duggins, Revd F. H. Aisthorpe Rectory, Lincoln. [1935]

1955. Duke, Miss D. Training College [Bishop Grosseteste College], Lincoln [Flat 14, Canwick Hall, Lincoln; 47 Nettleham Road, Lincoln]. [2001]

1910. Duke, Revd J. R. H. Thornhaugh Rectory, Wansford, Northants. [1923]

2008. Duncan, Ben. Oxbows, Kirkby Lane, Tattershall.

1957. Dunlap, Edward N. 3620 East First Street, Long Beach, California, U.S.A. Died 1973.

1950. *Dunlop, Rt. Revd D. C., Dean of Lincoln. The Deanery, Lincoln. [1965]

2007. Durrant, Ian. 10 Boultham Park Road, Lincoln.

2001. *Dyer, Professor C. C. Centre for Local History, University of Leicester, 5 Salisbury Road, Leicester.

1942. Dyson, Eric. 10 Morton Terrace, Gainsborough. Died 3 January 1961.

1971. Dyson, Mrs H. 2 Greestone Place, Lincoln. [1976]

1910. Dyson, T. A. Ivy Dene, Gainsborough. Died 1926.

1955. East, F. W. Brookside, Heighington, Lincoln. Died March 1985.

1968. Edgoose, Michael J. 16 West Close, Fernhurst, Haslemere [Black Fridays, Fridays Hill, Kingsley Green, Haslemere, Surrey]. [1982]

1984. Edwards, Revd Douglas. 7 Washway Road, Fleet, Spalding. Died September 2001.

1934. Ekwall, Professor E. The University, Lund, Sweden. Honorary Member. [1966]

1910. Eland, John. 40 Carey Street, Lincoln's Inn, London. [1916]

1977. Elford, D. G. Flat 1, Trentholme, Messingham, Scunthorpe. [1982]

1980. Ellis, J. C. 'Bouleville', Messingham Lane, Scawby, Brigg. [1982]

1967. Elvey, Mrs E. M. Stonewalls Farm [Stonewalls Cottage], Chalfont St Giles, Bucks. [1986]

1933. Elwes, Lt-Col. Geoffrey. Elsham Hall, Brigg. [1942]

2007. Eminson, Mrs Moira. Chancel Barn, Messingham, Scunthorpe.

1922. Eminson, Thomas B. F. Gonerby Cottage, Scotter, Gainsborough. Died 29 March 1940.

2008. Erskine-Crum, Simon. Glebe Barn, Wellingore, Lincoln.

2007. Evans, Ian. 21 Chestnut Avenue, Donington, Spalding.

1976. Everson, Paul. 5 Highfields, Nettleham, Lincoln. [1978]

2008. Everson, Paul. 6 Monks Lane, Nantwich, Cheshire.

2009. Fane, Julian. Fulbeck Manor, Grantham.

1910. *Fane [King-Fane], Colonel W. V. R. Fulbeck Hall, Grantham [George Hotel, Grantham]. Died 5 November 1943.

1910. Farrer, William. Hall Garth, Carnforth, Lancs. [Whitbarrow Lodge, Witherslick, Grange over Sands]. Died 17 August 1924.

2005. Feather, Mrs Anne. 10 Tinwell Road, Stamford.

2000. Ferrier, Brian H. 130 Mill Road, Cleethorpes.

2005. Field, Ms N. 25 West Parade, Lincoln.

1976. Fieldsend, D. 9 Horseshoe Close, Colehill, Wimborne, Dorset. [1983]

1961. Filby, P. W. Peabody Institute of Baltimore, Baltimore, Maryland, U.S.A. [307 Madison Street, Savage, Maryland, U.S.A.] [1968]

1960. *FINCH, Dr Mary E. 14 Drury Lane, Lincoln [Lincolnshire Archives Office, The Castle, Lincoln; 16 James Street, Lincoln]. Died 15 September 2007.

2008. Finch, Mrs Valerie. 6 Old School Lane, Billinghay.

1961. Fines, John. 18 Dryden Avenue, Lincoln [30 Salcombe Drive, Earley, Reading; 119 Parklands Road, Chichester.] Died 2 April 1999.

1981. Fines, R. 17 Queensway, Lincoln. [2006]

2008. Firman, Mrs Pat. 12 Elm Avenue, Beeston, Nottingham.

1953. Fisher, D. J. V. Jesus College, Cambridge. Died November 1993.

2008. Fisher, Dr Pam. 9 Slate Brook Close, Groby, Leicester.

1991. Fleming, D. P. Department of History, University of California, Santa Barbara, California, U.S.A. [1992]

2007. Flinders, John. 26 Clarkes Lane, Chiwell, Nottingham.

2007. Flinders, Terry. 50 Queensfield, Swindon.

1972. Flodman, K. J. 8 Cambridge Road West, Farnborough, Hants. Died October 1987.

1910. *Footman, M. H. Nocton House, Lincoln. Died 16 November 1923.

2001. *Forrest, Dr Ian. All Souls College, Oxford [Oriel College, Oxford].

1952. Foskett, Revd Canon [Very Revd; Rt Revd] Reginald. The Vicarage,

Ilkeston, Derbyshire [8 Lansdowne Crescent, Edinburgh; Bishop's House, Brathay, Ambleside, Westmorland; The Old Vicarage, Field Broughton, Grange-over-Sands, Lancashire]. Died 13 November 1973.

2009. Foster, Alan. 52 West Green Avenue, Derby.

1910. *FOSTER, Revd Canon Charles Wilmer, F.S.A. The Vicarage, Timberland. Died 29 October 1935.

1910. *Foster, Revd Canon J. The Vicarage, Tathwell. Died 18 December 1926.

1914. Foster, W. E., F.S.A. Lindum House, Aldershot. [1923]

1948. Foulkes, J. C. c/o The Grammar School, Brigg. [1953]

1922. Fowler, Dr G. H. The Old House, Aspley Guise, Beds. Died 15 August 1940.

1913 Fowler, Revd Canon J. T., F.S.A. Winterton, Scunthorpe. Died 23 March 1924.

1993. Fox, Mrs A. E. Manor Farm, Dry Doddington, Newark. [1997]

2009. Fox, Mrs Sally-Ann. 45 Bank Road, Matlock, Derbys.

1982. Foxell, Mrs Shirley. 4 Meades Lane, Chesham, Bucks.

1980. Franklin, Dr M. J. Gonville and Caius College, Cambridge [Wolfson College, Cambridge; 2 Beaulands Close, Cambridge; Hughes Hall, Cambridge].

1990. Franklin, Mrs S. 3 Queensway, Lincoln. [1998]

1967. French, Mrs. 43 Fleetgate, Barton-upon-Humber.

2010. Fridlington, Peter. Rose Cottage, Clint Lane, Navenby, Lincoln.

2009. Frost, Dr Judith. 9 St John Street, York.

1910. *Fry, Very Revd T. C., Dean of Lincoln. The Deanery, Lincoln. Died 10 February 1930.

1969. Fuggles, J. F. 963 Loughborough Road, Rothley, Leics. [St John's College, Oxford]. [1984]

1932. Fullalove, Alan Lindsey. Wantage. [1938]

1949. Fuller, A. R. B. Charterhouse, Godalming [5 Granville Road, Barnet, Herts.] Died 30 April 1981.

2004. Gadd, A. J. 45 Skellingthorpe Road, Lincoln. [2009]

1980. Galitzine, Prince Yuri. Quaintree House, Braunston, Oakham [Holywell Hall, Stamford]. Died 28 November 2002.

1934. Gamble, Henry G. 6 The Grove, Lincoln. [1944]

1910. Garbett, Miss H. L. East Keal Hall, Spilsby [25 Sandringham Gardens, Ealing]. [1931]

1980. Garghan, G. 16 Sherston Court, Monyhull, Birmingham. [1982]

1975. Garton, Professor Charles. 568 Seabrook Drive, Williamsville, New York, U.S.A.

2009. Genda, Ruth. Station House, Butt Lane, Wymondham, Leics.

1914. Genney, F. S., M.B. Marchmont House, Lincoln [The Manor House, West Malling, Kent]. [1931]

2010. George, Beryl. 3 Avocet Close, Lincoln.

1976. George, C. L. St James's School, Danesbury House, 18 Bargate, Grimsby. [1992]

1924. Gibbons, G. S. *See* Dixon.

1989. Gilder, Miss M. 22 Woodhurst Road, Canvey Island, Essex. [1990]

1910. Giles, Revd Edward. The Quarry, Lincoln. Died 19 January 1943.

1957. Gillett, Edward. 24 Crosscoates Road, Grimsby [3 St Anne's Avenue, Grimsby]. [1969]

1998. Gilliland, Mrs L. 9 Sudbrooke Lane, Nettleham, Lincoln [167 Low Street, Collingham, Newark, Notts.] [2006]

1975. Gilmour (née Adams), Mrs L. T. Lowthorpe Cottage, Southrey, Bardney [Lincolnshire Archaeological Trust, Sessions House, Lincoln]. [1985]

1942. Glazier, G. c/o Public Library, Harpur Street, Bedford. [1962]

1949. Godfrey, L. R. Denstone College, Uttoxeter, Staffs. Died 1957.

1921. Godfrey, R. S., F.S.A. Surveyor's Office, 26 Eastgate, Lincoln. Died 30 March 1953.

1910. Godson, E. H. Heckington, Lincs. [1912]

2008. Godson, Mrs Jean. 7 Nettleham Close, Lincoln. [2010]

2004. *GODSON, Miss Lynn. 4 Egerton Road, Lincoln [7 Spital Street, Lincoln]. [2009]

1910. Goodacre, Revd C. B. The Vicarage, Thornton Curtis. [1918]

1910. Goold, Revd W. Somerby, Highbury Road, Hitchin, Herts. [1912]

1976. Gordon, Miss J. L. 75 Monks Dyke Road, Louth. [1980]

1914. Gough, Revd E. P. The Parsonage, Spalding. [1923]

1910. Goulding, R. W. The Library, Welbeck Abbey, Notts. Died 8 November 1929.

1990. Gower, Trevor. 8 Irex Road, Pakefield, Lowestoft, Suffolk. [2000]

1985. Graham, Margaret. 132 Newland Street West, Lincoln [3 Durham Road, Lanchester, Durham]. [1987]

1910. Grange, Col. E. L., F.S.A. St Mary's Chambers, Grimsby [3 Bargate Grimsby; 37 Madingley Road, Cambridge]. Died 10 September 1947.

1998. Grant, David. 27 Chapel Road, Habrough, Immingham.

2004. Grantham, Mark. 91 Kathleen Crescent, Ottawa, Ontario, Canada. [2007]

1918. Grantham, Vincent A. 2 Warden Road, Bombay, India [Boughton Hall, Send, Surrey; Aldertons, Send, Surrey; St Clere's Hall, St Osyth, Essex]. Died 1 August 1968.

1915. Graves, Revd Canon Michael. Tilecotes, Marlow. Died 16 January 1934.

1973. Gray, T. B. 3 Occupation Road, Lincoln [Queen Elizabeth's Grammar School, Gainsborough; The Old Market Garden, 6 Sandy

Lane, Tealby, Lincoln, 256 Eastgate, Louth; The Bookshop, 3 Lodge Street, East Lothian, Scotland]. Died 1994.

1934. *Greaves, Rt Revd A. I., Bishop of Grantham [Grimsby]. The Subdeanery, Lincoln [The Precentory, Lincoln]. Died 29 November 1959.

1998. Greaves, A. S. 25 Alford Road, Sutton-on-Sea.

1910. Green, Everard, F.S.A., Somerset Herald. Heralds' College, London. [1923]

2009. Green, Miss Glynda. Walnut Tree Cottage, Main Street, Kneesall, Newark, Notts.

1998. Gregory, Mrs Pat. 37 Cliff Avenue, Nettleham, Lincoln.

1910. Griffith, E. C. Hacconby Hall, Bourne [9 Denmark Villas, Hove, Brighton; Ivy Nook, Steyning, Sussex]. [1938]

1949. Griffith, H. J. J. Northgate Lodge, Northgate, Lincoln [2 Bank Street, Lincoln; 12 James Street, Lincoln]. [1982]

1973. Griffiths, D. J. 25 Abbey Park Road, Grimsby.

1967. Griffiths, Revd D. N. The Cathedral Library, Lincoln [The Rectory, Park Street, Windsor]. [1977]

2004. Griffiths, Revd Canon D. N. 2 Middleton's Field, Lincoln.

1924. Grinter, Revd J. H. D. Mill House, Ingworth, Norwich. [1935]

1986. Hains, Mrs Grace C. 30 Curle Avenue, Lincoln [1 Middleton's Field, Lincoln]. Died 1994.

1910. Hall, Revd A. T. The Vicarage, Appleby, Brigg. [1913]

2001. Hall, Mrs Eleanor. Alderdean, Newlandrig, Gorebridge, Midlothian, Scotland. [2001]

1917. Hall, J. W. Minster Precincts, Peterborough. [1942]

1949. Hall, P. Stone House Farm, Burton Road, Lincoln. [1959]

1952. Hallam, [Professor] H. E. 13 Welland Terrace, Spalding [Holyrood House, Spalding; 41 Arthur Street, Loughborough; Department of History, University of Western Australia, Nedlands, Western Australia]. Died 8 July 1993.

2000. Hallgarth, Christopher. 98 Chichester Road, Cleethorpes.

1984. Halls, Henry. 61 Devon Road, Cheam, Surrey. [1990]

1992. Hamby, L. Grant. 2714 Cypress Street, Columbia, South Carolina, U.S.A. [1993]

2008. Hamilton, David. 26 Grainsby Avenue, Holton-le-Clay, Grimsby.

1999. Hamilton, Dr J. S. Department of History, Baylor University, Waco, Texas, U.S.A. [1547 Stillwater Drive, Waco, Texas, U.S.A.]

1996. Hammond, Michael G. Sunnydene, North Street, Middle Rasen [Chestnut House, Linwood, Market Rasen].

1925. Hancock, Revd Canon B. W. Algarkirk Rectory, Boston. [1944]

1934. Hanworth, The Viscount. 2 Lygon Place, London. Honorary Member. Died 22 October 1936.

1928. Harding, Revd N. S. All Saints' Vicarage, Lincoln. [1935]

1936. Harding, Revd Canon N. S. All Saints' Vicarage, Lincoln. Died 21 December 1952.

1988. Hardy, Rt Revd Robert M., Lord Bishop of Lincoln. Bishop's House, Eastgate, Lincoln. [2001]

1947. *Harland, Rt. Revd Maurice H., Lord Bishop of Lincoln. Bishop's House, Lincoln. [1957]

1954. Harmsworth, G. [Sir Geoffrey, Bt]. 8 Stratton Street, London. Died 23 October 1980.

1974. Harper-Bill, Christopher. St Mary's College of Education, Strawberry Hill, Twickenham [15 Cusack Close, Strawberry Hill, Twickenham]. [2006]

1910. Harries, Revd G. H. The Vicarage, Burgh [St Martin's Vicarage, Lincoln]. [1939]

1998. *Haseldine, Dr Julian. Department of History, University of Hull, Hull.

1920. Hastling, Revd A. H. L. Theddlethorpe All Saints Vicarage, Louth. [1935]

1976. Hawes, T. L. M. 8 Keswick Road, Cringleford, Norwich.

1968. Hawker, Revd P. C. Cherry Willingham Vicarage, Lincoln [St Botolph's Vicarage, South Park, Lincoln; 84 Little Bargate Street, Lincoln]. [1992]

1927. Hawley, Arthur. 4 Cadogan Place, London [The Top Hall, Lyndon, Oakham; Cranhill, Weston Road, Bath]. Died 17 March 1952.

1976. Hawley, Sir David, Bt. James Martin & Co, Bank Street, Lincoln [Tumby Lawn, Boston]. Died 19 March 1988.

1928. Hayes, Capt. J. W. Hereward House, Regent Street, Spalding. [1945]

1989. Hayward, J. 12 Preston Avenue, Higham's Park, London.

1952. Healey, The Ven. [Rt Revd] Kenneth, [Bishop of Grimsby]. Algarkirk Rectory, Boston [48 Lee Road, Lincoln]. [1966]

1972. Healey, The Rt Revd Kenneth, Little Needham, Gedney Dyke, Spalding. Died 12 February 1985.

1976. *Healey, Miss R. H. Friest Cottage, Drury Lane, Bicker, Boston.

2001. Heath, K. E. 7 St Chad, Barrow-upon-Humber.

1981. Helmholz, Professor R. H. University of Chicago Law School, Chicago, U.S.A.

1910. Hemmans, Revd Canon F. Died 24 January 1912.

1910. Hemmans, Miss. Kirke House, Devon Street, Cottingham, Yorks. [1915]

1910. Heneage, The Lord. Hainton Hall. Died 10 August 1922.

1932. Heneage, The Lord. Hainton Hall. Died 26 January 1954.

1910. Henniker-Gotley, Revd G. West Ashby Vicarage, Horncastle. [1913]

1946. *Henthorn, Dr Frank. Westrum Lane, Brigg. Died March 1995.

1998. Herber, Mark D. 117 Richmond Avenue, Islington, London.

1911. Hett, C. L. Springfield, Brigg. [1912]

1912 Hett, F. C. The Limes, Brigg. [1918]

1910. Heygate, Revd Canon R. T. The Vicarage, Boston. [1916]

1997. Hickman, Dr David J. 8 Gordon Square, Mohin Court, West Bridgford, Nottingham [Department of History, University of Sussex, Falmer, Brighton]. [2008]

1910. *HICKS, Rt Revd Edward Lee, Lord Bishop of Lincoln. The Old Palace, Lincoln. Died 14 August 1919.

1933. *Hicks, Rt Revd F. C. Nugent, Lord Bishop of Lincoln. The Old Palace, Lincoln. Died 10 February 1942.

1991. Higgins, R. Bracken Hill, North Road, Leigh Woods, Bristol. [1992]

1968. Higgs, Miss Phyllis Mary. 5 East Bight, Lincoln. Died 1 July 1971.

1990. Hildyard, Capt. A. J. C. Goxhill Hall, Goxhill, Barrow-upon-Humber. Died 20 March 1995.

1995. Hildyard, Hon. Mrs A. M. K. Goxhill Hall, Goxhill, Barrow-upon-Humber. Died 24 October 1998.

1961. Hill, Miss E. City Chambers, Lincoln [St Peter's Chambers, Silver Street, Lincoln; Thorpe House, Little Casterton, Stamford; 10 Homenene House, Bushfield, Orton Goldhay, Peterborough; 27 Torkington Gardens, Stamford]. [1993]

1923. *HILL, J. W. F. [Sir Francis], F.S.A. 2 Lindum Terrace, Lincoln [The Priory, Lincoln]. Died 6 January 1980.

1942. *Hill, Miss [Professor] R. M. T., F.S.A. Green Place, Stockbridge, Hants [Westfield College, London; 7 Loom Lane, Radlett, Herts.] Died 11 January 1997.

1911. Hill, Revd T. The Vicarage, North Somercotes. Died 1 April 1912.

1982. Hillier, R. W. E. 70 Vere Road, Peterborough [35 Prince's Gardens, Peterborough; 43 Oundle Road, Chesterton, Peterborough].

1998. Hillson, Mrs Elaine. 124 Thomas More House, Barbican, London. [2001]

1945. Hillyard, Mrs D. St Anselm's, Bakewell, Derbyshire. [1949]

2007. Hinde, K. G. S. Denny House, High Street, Waterbeach, Cambs.

1925. Hine, Rt Revd J. E., Bishop of Grantham. The Subdeanery, Lincoln. Died 9 April 1934.

1983. Hinkins, Mrs V. S. Moor Lodge, Roughton Lane, Woodhall Spa [63 Minster Drive, Cherry Willingham, Lincoln; Flat 17, Dilwin Court, Abercromby Avenue, High Wycombe; 55 Wordsworth Road, High Wycombe].

1990. Hoare, Douglas C. 34 Grantham Road, Sleaford.

1924. Hobday, S. R. 6 King's Bench Walk, Temple, London. [1952]

2008. Hodge, John. 23 Church Road, Branston, Lincoln.

1925. Hodge, Revd Canon Walter Fallows. Benington Rectory, Boston. Died 11 May 1938.

1951. Hodgett, G. A. J. King's College, Strand, London. [1980]

2009. Hodgkinson, Brian. 6 Walcot Court, Woodside Drive, Arnold, Nottingham.

1910. Hodgkinson, Lt-Col. R. F. B. Northgate House, Newark-on-Trent [Trent View House, Millgate, Newark-on-Trent]. [1931]

1910. Hodgson, Revd E. E. [1912]

2007. Hodson, Morrice B. 30 Malton Road, North Hykeham, Lincoln.

1957. Hogg, Gordon W. Grammar School, Brigg [Pegswood, Morpeth, Northumberland; 6 Beach Road, Tynemouth, Northumberland]. [1994]

1959. Hogg, J. Mount Craig Hotel, Ross on Wye, Herefordshire. [1963]

1986. Hohler, Christopher. Lyder Sagens Gate 23, Oslo, Norway. Died 15 February 1997.

1970. Holderness, B. A. 19 Rex Avenue, Millhouses, Sheffield [218 Dereham Road, Costessey, Norwich; University of East Anglia, Norwich]. [1995]

1931. Holderness, Col. H. United Service Club, Pall Mall, London [Over Costleys, Farnham, Surrey; The Old Rectory, Kirkby Underwood, Bourne; Hope Cottage, Cripple Corner, Pebmarsh, Halstead, Essex]. Died 1965.

1976. Hollamby, Ken. Ashbank, Old Balglove, Old Meldrum, Inverurie, Aberdeenshire. [1983]

2001. *HOLLAMBY, Ken. 2 Queensway, Lincoln.

2009. Hollingsworth, Richard. 144 Bottesford Lane, Bottesford, Scunthorpe.

1983. Hollinshead, Trevor. 20 Poplar Crescent, Bourne. [1985]

1963. *HOLT, Professor J. C. [Sir James] The University, Nottingham [The University, Reading; Faculty of History, West Road, Cambridge; Fitzwilliam College, Cambridge].

1986. Holton, I. L. 7 Stoney Lane, Thatcham, Newbury, Berks. [1998]

1934. Holtzmann, Professor W. Halle, Germany [Hindenburgstrasse 123, Bonn, Germany; Hausdorfstrasse 123, Bonn, Germany]. Honorary Member. Died 1965.

2003. Honeybone, Dr Michael. 11 Easthorpe Road, Bottesford, Grantham [99 Lincoln Street, Norwich; 36 The Close, Norwich].

1985. Hope, Dr A. M. Greenside House, 7 The Settlement, Ockbrook, Derbys.

1974. Hopper, P. 6 Canterbury Close, Westcliff, Scunthorpe. [1981]

2001. Hoskin, Dr Philippa M. 21 Heslington Road, York.

1954. Hotchin, H. E. Sycamore Lodge, Sutton-on-Sea. [1962]

1910. Houghton, Revd P. Haxey Vicarage. [1914]

1955. Howard, S. W. 179 Coombe Road, Croydon. [1981]

1964. Howden, D. G. B. Greenaway, London Road, Balcombe, Haywards Heath, Sussex [Harriman's Court, Old Knarr Fen Drove, Thorney, Peterborough]. [1983]

1991. Howden, D. B. G. Harriman's Court, Thorney, Peterborough. [1995]
1925. Howe, Revd W. Norton. The Vicarage, Sleaford [Withern Vicarage, Alford]. [1942]
1910. *Hudson, Revd J. Clare. Thornton Vicarage, Horncastle [The Briars, Tor o' Moor, Woodhall Spa]. [1931]
1977. Hudson, R. The Cottage, Cheapside, Waltham, Grimsby. [1978]
1988. Hudson, R. L. Hall Farm House, East Ravendale, Grimsby.
1985. Hulme, Revd Norman. Earl Shilton Vicarage, Leicester [9 Sunningdale, Luton; 9 Birch Grove, Spalding].
1980. Humphreys, Revd Canon B. B. The Vicarage, Middle Rasen [8 Barratt's Close, Lincoln]. Died 14 January 1987.
1996. Humphries, Alan. Rustics, Blacksmith's Lane, Harmston, Lincoln.
1910. *Hunt, Revd [Canon] Alfred. Welton Vicarage, Lincoln [Kirkby Laythorpe Rectory, Sleaford]. [1935]
1979. Hunt, C. C. 27 Bentley Street, Stamford [12 Reform Street, Stamford; 1A Woodcroft Road, Marholm, Peterborough].
1924. Husband-Clutton, F. Crowland. [1935]
1910. Hutton, Ven. William Holden, Archdeacon of Northampton. The Vineyard, Peterborough. [1912]
2003. Ille, Dr M. L. 19 Hill Road, Springthorpe, Gainsborough.
1976. Ingamells, J. R. 7 Waterfall Gully Road, Burnside, Adelaide [Room 41, 'Resthaven', 336 Kensington Road, Leabrook, Adelaide, South Australia]. [2006]
1990. Ingham, R. B. 138 Dowse Drive, Lower Hutt, New Zealand [80 Abilene Crescent, Churton Park, Wellington, New Zealand]. [2008]
1910. Ingle, Frederick. 24 Queen Anne's Gate, London. [1912]
1953. Ingram, N. Sir Robert Pattinson School, North Hykeham, Lincoln. [1964]
1954. Innes, Revd G. The South Manse, Skelmorlie, Ayrshire. Died 1972.
1969. Insley, J. 12 Isherwood Street, Preston, Lancs. [1975]
1976. Jacklin, Mrs G. Beaconhill Farm, Grainthorpe, Louth. [1980]
1910. Jackson, Theodore F. 260 Broadway, Brooklyn, New York, U. S. A. [1913]
1988. Jacob, Revd Canon [Ven.] W. M. Lincoln Theological College, Drury Lane, Lincoln [15A Gower Street, London].
1970. Jahn, R. A. 41 Richmond Road, Lincoln. [1978]
2007. James, Alan. 42 Church Street, Donington, Spalding.
1919. James, W. A. South Muskham Prebend, Southwell, Notts. Died 1949.
1975. Jarvis, A. G. Doddington Hall, Lincoln.
1934. Jarvis, Lt-Col. C. F. C. Doddington Hall, Lincoln. Died 18 January 1957.
1958. Jarvis, R. G. E. Doddington Hall, Lincoln. Died 28 February 1973.

1910. *Jebb, George S. W. Leintwardine House, Leintwardine. [1915]

1919. Jebb, G. S. W. The Manor House, Meldreth, Royston. [1931]

1995. Jebbett, Ian. 16 Ambleside Close, Sleaford.

2003. Jefferson, Miss Kathleen. 2 Wiseholme Road, Skellingthorpe, Lincoln.

2010. Jennings, Miss Louise. 12 Birch Close, North Hykeham, Lincoln.

1910. Jessopp, A. L. Leasingham, Sleaford [Lexham Hall, Swaffham, Norfolk]. [1915]

1947. Jeudwine, G. G. c/o Messrs Peake, Snow and Jeudwine, Sleaford. Died 1954.

1910. Jeudwine, Revd Canon G. W. The Archdeaconry, Lincoln. Died 18 October 1933.

1933. Jeudwine, J. G. Manor House, Northgate, Sleaford. [1942]

1910. Johnson, A. W. 12 Victoria Street, Westminster. [1916]

1971. *Johnson, C. P. C. Lincolnshire Archives Office, The Castle, Lincoln [24 Canterbury Drive, Washingborough, Lincoln].

2008. Johnson, Miss Kathleen. 12 Wake Street, Lincoln.

1910. Johnson, R. W. Messrs Lawrence, Johnson & Co., Philadelphia, U. S. A. [1912]

1971. *JOHNSTON, Dr J. A. 326 Burton Road, Lincoln. Died January 2007.

1912 *Johnston, Revd Canon J. O., Chancellor of Lincoln. The Subdeanery, Lincoln. [1931]

2002. Johnstone, Mrs Diane. 30 Daggett Road, Cleethorpes.

1976. Jones, D. S. Baxter's Cottage, North Carlton, Lincoln.

1982. *JONES, Professor M. C. E. Department of History, University of Nottingham, Nottingham [Parr's Cottage, Main Street, Norwell, Newark, Notts.].

2008. Jones, Dr M. J. 9 Queensway, Lincoln.

1910. Jones, W. H. 'Winnetka', Morland Avenue, Leicester. [1915]

1910. *JOURDAIN, A. E. T. Saltergate, Lincoln [35 Silver Street, Lincoln]. Died 4 December 1948.

1982. Kay, Mrs A. J. 49 Queen's Parade, Cleethorpes. [1991]

1976. Kaye, David. 40 Southlands Avenue, Louth [48 Queen Street, Louth]. [2000]

1910. Kaye, Ven. William Frederick John, Archdeacon of Lincoln. The Archdeaconry, Lincoln. Died 9 July 1913.

1941. *Kemp, Revd Canon [Very Revd; Rt Revd] E. W. Pusey House, Oxford [Exeter College, Oxford; The Deanery, Worcester; The Palace, Chichester; 5 Alexandra Road, Chichester]. Died 28 November 2009.

1976. Kennedy, M. J. Department of History, University of Glasgow, Glasgow. Died February 2004.

1985. Kerr, Mrs M. E. Manor Farm House, Spanby, Sleaford. [1985]

1998. Kershaw, R. R. 5 Smithfield, North Thoresby, Grimsby.

1911. Kesteven, The Lord. Casewick Hall, Uffington, Stamford. Died 23 July 1915.

1988. Ketteringham, [Dr] J. R. 27 Bunker's Hill, Lincoln.

1912. Key, R. E. Fulford Hall, York. [1915]

2001. King, Miss Dorothy. 25 Queen Street, Spilsby. [2007]

1968. *King, [Professor] Edmund. Department of History, The University, Sheffield.

1955. King, Revd E. C. Legbourne Vicarage, Louth. [1961]

2003. King, Professor James R. 9 Park Place Court, Wichita Falls, Texas, U.S.A.

1975. Kingdon, G. Oasby, Grantham. [1982]

1925. Kirk, G. E. 14 Carter Mount, Whitkirk, Leeds. Died 21 March 1960.

1974. Kirkham, Mrs B. High Street, Hogsthorpe, Skegness. [1997]

1943. *Kirkus, Miss Mary. 53 London Road, Reading [63 Hamilton Road, Reading]. Died 16 December 1959.

2001. Knapp, Mrs J. L. Spire View, 7 Swinegate, Grantham.

1910. Knapp, Revd T. Lloyd. Threckingham Vicarage, Folkingham. [1915]

1984. *KNIGHT, Dr G. A. Lincolnshire Archives Office, The Castle, Lincoln [17 Lady Frances Drive, Market Rasen].

1912 Lake, Revd E. T. West Keal Rectory, Spilsby. [1915]

1928. Lambert, Revd Lionel. The Rectory, Stafford. [1935]

1947. Lamplugh, The Ven. K. E. N., Archdeacon of Lincoln. Archdeaconry, Lincoln. [1951]

1916. Lancaster, Miss G. E. The Manor House, Keelby. [1923]

1958. Lane, W. E. Burton-by-Lincoln. Died February 2006.

1910. *Larken, Revd Canon Hubert. Irby-on-Humber Rectory; [Brocklesby Rectory; Limber Magna Vicarage; Theddlethorpe All Saints Vicarage; The Abbey Rectory, Croyland; Wilsford Rectory Grantham; The Archdeaconry, Lincoln; The Subdeanery, Lincoln; The Small House, Collingham]. Died 6 April 1964.

1998. Last, Geoffrey. 6 Chapel Lane, Ketton, Rutland.

1919. Lathrop, Kirke. 44 Bramham Gardens, South Kensington, London [Le Grand Hotel, Montreux- Territet, Switzerland]. [1937]

1983. Lavender, Mrs E. 9 Heathfield Court, Augusta Park, Grimsby. [2001]

1955. *Leach, T. R. Bridge View, Dunholme, Lincoln [The Green, Dunholme; 3 Merleswen, St Chad's Lea, Dunholme]. Died 16 April 1994.

2008. Leakey, Dr Colin. 15 Minster Yard, Lincoln.

1961. Le Cras, Alan. 81 Ashby Road, Spilsby. [1972]

1928. Lee, L. G. H. 3 Upper Avenue, Lincoln. [1935]

2008. Leggott, Mark. Rectory Farm, Sutton Road, Beckingham, Lincoln.

1966. Leveritt, Norman. Janlea, 148 Hawthorn Bank, Spalding. Died
    September 2001.
1966. *Lewis, His Honour Judge E. Daly. Kettlethorpe Hall, Lincoln.
    [1976]
1910. Lewty, Revd Walter. Rowston Vicarage, Digby, Lincoln. [1915]
1925. Lewty, Revd Walter. Rowston Vicarage, Digby, Lincoln. Died 21
    February 1949.
2007. Lidbetter, Ken. 11 Broadway, Lincoln.
1917. Lindsay, W. A., F.S.A., Windsor Herald [Clarenceux King of Arms].
    College of Arms, London. [1931]
1972. Litchfield, D. A. Beckingham, Lincoln. [1996]
1910. Little, Mrs. Heckington Hall, Lincs. [1912]
1941. Liverpool, The Ven. The Dean of. The Deanery, Liverpool. [1943]
1910. Liverpool, The Earl of. Hartsholme Hall, Skellingthorpe, Lincoln.
    [1923]
1960. *LLOYD, C. M. Lincolnshire Archives Office, Exchequer Gate,
    Lincoln [The Castle, Lincoln; 350 Sea Front, Hayling Island,
    Hants.]. Died July 1991.
2007. Lloyd, Mrs Wendy. Flat 2, 9 Minster Yard, Lincoln.
1986. Locking, M. 3 Boundary Road, Fairfield, Grimsby [67 Kenwick
    Road, Louth; 10 Stewton Lane, Louth].
2008. Lockwood, Mark. 25 St Catherine's Court, Lincoln.
1995. Lodge, Anthony A. E. The Old School House, Mareham-le-Fen,
    Boston. [2006]
1910. Loft, Revd E. W. B. St Paul's Vicarage, Grimsby [214 Herbert
    Road, Woolwich, London; Great Carlton Vicarage, Louth]. Died 1
    December 1928.
1910. Londesborough, The Earl of. Blankney Hall, Lincoln. Died 17 April
    1937.
1995. Long, Stephan. 24 Vine Street, Billingborough, Sleaford.
1910. *Longley, Revd Canon Thomas. Conisholme Rectory, North
    Somercotes. Died 24 November 1926.
2005. Lover, Mrs Sylvia. 'Ringinglow', King Street, Yarburgh, Louth
    [Freshfields, Main Street, Gayton- le-Marsh, Alford].
1938. Loyd, Lewis C. 25 Moore Street, London. Died 17 August 1947.
1923. Luard-Selby, Revd Canon R. B. The Vicarage, Ambleside [The
    Vicarage, Troutbeck, Windermere]. Died 1951.
2007. Lucas, Dr Mary. 14 James Street, Lincoln.
1968. Lunn, Revd [Rt Revd] David [Bishop of Sheffield]. The Bishop's
    Hostel, Lincoln [St George's Vicarage, Cullercoats, North Shields,
    Northumberland; Bishopscroft, Snaithing Lane, Sheffield; 28
    Southfield Road, Wetwang, Driffield]. [2000]
1983. Lunn, J. E. 23 Piper's Croft, Dunstable, Beds. [2001]

2009. Lyon, John C. M.J.L. Skipmaster Ltd, Branton's Bridge, Bourne
Road, Pode Hole, Spalding.

1968. Lyons, N. J. L. Nettleham Field, Nettleham, Lincoln [Pelham View,
Sturton Lane, Scawby, Brigg; 3 Carr Lane, Appleby, Scunthorpe;
12 Main Street, Saxby All Saints, Brigg].

1910. MacCarthy, Rt Revd Welbore, Bishop of Grantham. Stoke Rectory,
Grantham. [1918]

2004. McCartney, Mr and Mrs K. Pottergate Lodge, Lincoln.

2004. McConnell, Mrs Wendy. 4 Ewerby Road, Kirkby-la-Thorpe,
Sleaford.

1910. MacCormick, Revd F. Wrockwardine Wood Rectory, Wellington,
Salop. [1918]

1910. McDonald, J. A., M.D. Woolsthorpe, Grantham. [1931]

1954. McFarlane, K. B. Magdalen College, Oxford. Died 16 July 1966.

1969. *McHardy, Miss [Dr] A. K. 44 Davenant Road, Oxford [Department
of History, King's College, Old Aberdeen; 44 Bankfield Drive,
Bramcote Hills, Nottingham].

2001. McKenna, Mrs Caroline. 18 Halstead Road, London.

1970. Mackinder, N. H. 9 Grosvenor Road, Finchley, London. [1994]

1973. Macklin, D. D. Mexborough House, Burton-by-Lincoln. [1980]

2003. Mackman, Dr J. S. 26 Rowan Close, Ealing, London [59 Broadgate,
Whaplode Drove, Spalding].

1984. McLane, Dr Bernard. University of Rochester, Rochester, New
York, U.S.A. [Dartmouth College, Rochester, New York, U.S.A.]
[1990]

2006. McMath, Mrs Jayne. Fen Farm, Heckington Fen, Sleaford [5
Cowgate, Heckington, Sleaford].

1910. Maddison, Revd Canon Arthur Roland. Vicars' Court, Lincoln. Died
24 April 1912.

1976. Mahany, Miss C. M. Bath House, Bath Row, Stamford. [1981]

2001. Maile, Mrs Shirley. 13 Alexandra Terrace, Bourne. [2006]

2009. Maile, Mrs Shirley. 13 Alexandra Terrace, Bourne.

1930. *MAJOR, Miss Kathleen, F.S.A. Abbott's Manor, Holbeach [St
Hilda's College, Oxford; 21 Queensway, Lincoln]. Died 19
December 2000.

1938. Major, Mrs G. Abbott's Manor, Holbeach [15 Curle Avenue,
Lincoln; 6 Park Valley, Nottingham].   Died 1971.

1946. Mann, Miss J. de L. St Hilda's College, Oxford [The Cottage,
Bowerhill, Melksham, Wilts.] [1976]

1924. *Manning, Bernard Lord. Jesus College, Cambridge. Died 8
December 1941.

1975. Manterfield, Dr J. B. 9 Granta Crescent, Grantham [8 Grosvenor
Road, East Ham, London; 11 Rosina Close, Cowplain,
Portsmouth].

1910. *Maples, A. K. The Sycamores, Spalding [33 London Road,
Spalding; Navenby, Burnham Overy Staithe, Norfolk; 33 London
Road, Spalding]. Died 14 February 1950.
1997. *Marcombe, Dr David. 72 Millgate, Newark-on-Trent, Notts.
[2008][4]
1976. Marfleet, J. K. 4 Robotham Close, Huncote, Leicester.
1910. Marillier de Provence, J. H. c/o Miss Marillier, Essington House,
Rochfield Road, Hereford [Gloucester House, Exmouth]. [1923]
1910. Markham, Revd. Canon A. A. The Vicarage, Grimsby. [1918]
1924. Markham, Rt Revd. A. A., Bishop of Grantham. The Vicarage,
Grantham [Stoke Rochford Rectory, Grantham]. Died 27 June
1949.
1920. Markham, Major C. A. The Garth, Dallington, Northampton [Flore,
Northampton]. Died April 1937.
1967. Marlow, D. H. 22 Minster Yard, Lincoln. Died 2 March 1980.
1932. Marris, H. C. Burton Corner, Boston. Died 1966.
1938. Marsden, Revd Canon E. L. The Vicarage, Grimsby. [1947]
1952. Marsden, Ven. E. L. The Archdeaconry, Lincoln. [1958]
1925. Marshall, Major H. D. Pilham Hall, Gainsborough. [1935]
1969. *Martin, [Professor] Geoffrey. 21 Central Avenue, Leicester
[Public Record Office, Chancery Lane, London; Woodside
House, Wimbledon; Churchview Cottage, Finsthwaite, Ulverston,
Cumbria]. Died 20 December 2007.
1990. Martin, Mrs M. H. 74 Fort George, St Peter Port, Guernsey.
1923. Martin, Revd R. I. Moreton Pinkney Vicarage, Rugby. [1935]
1946. Matthews, N. C. The Grammar School, Brigg. [1948]
1953. Maude, E. W. Rose Cottage, Brant Broughton, Lincoln. Died 1957.
1911. Maw, Allan. 107 Windsor Road, Werneth, Oldham [31 York Road,
Birkdale]. [1935]
1965. Maxey, C. R. 22 Warescot Road, Brentwood [48 St Thomas's Road,
Brentwood, Essex].
2007. Maybury, Mrs Teresa. 4 Masson House, 58 Westgate, Louth.
1910. Mearns, Revd J. Rushden Vicarage, Herts. [1923]
1988. Medley, C. P. The Old Hall, High Street, Newton-on-Trent [6 Endell
Drive, Kirton-in-Lindsey].
2007. Mellows, Mrs Ros. 'Stackridge', 32 Lincoln Road, Dunholme,
Lincoln.
1925. Mellows, W. T. Scalford House, Thorpe Road, Peterborough [The
Vineyard, Vineyard Road, Peterborough]. Died 11 April 1950.
1910. Melville, A. H. Leslie. D'Isney Place, Lincoln. [1914]
1910. Melville, A. S. Leslie. Branston Hall, Lincoln. [1914]

---

4 Subscription transferred to Spital Chantry Trust of St Edmund.

1979. Michel, Peter. 71 Rasen Lane, Lincoln [Department of History, Washington University, St Louis, Missouri, U.S.A.] [1981]
1926. Midgley, E. C. St Swithin's Square, Lincoln. [1942]
1984. Midworth, Miss Joyce M. 42 Williamson Street, Lincoln. [1988]
1968. Milburn, G. W. 110 Old Lansdowne Road, Manchester [8 Ashbrooke Mount, Sunderland]. [1982]
1947. *Milford, Revd Canon T. R., Chancellor of Lincoln. The Chancery, Lincoln. [1958]
1966. *Miller, Professor Edward. 18 Rutland Park, Sheffield [36 Almoner's Avenue, Cambridge]. Died December 2000.
2009. Miller, Mrs Marjorie. 142A High Street, Belton, Doncaster.
1910. Milnes, Revd F. G. North Hykeham Vicarage, Lincoln. Died 2 October 1916.
1917. Milnes, Mrs. St Nicholas House, Newport, Lincoln. [1931]
1986. Mills, Dr D. R. 17 Rectory Lane, Branston, Lincoln.
2004. Mitchell, Mrs Denise. 22 Eleanor Close, Lincoln.
1933. *Mitchell, Very Revd R. A., Dean of Lincoln. The Deanery, Lincoln. Died 13 July 1949.
1969. Mold, Revd P. J. 6 Ardross Crescent, Mount Lawley, Western Australia. [1978]
1934. Monson, The Lady. Burton Hall, Lincoln. Died 1 January 1943.
1994. *Monson, The Lady. The Manor House, South Carlton, Lincoln.
1910. *MONSON, The Lord. Burton Hall, Lincoln. Died 10 October 1940.
1934. *Monson, The Lord. Burton Hall, Lincoln [South Carlton Hall, Lincoln]. Died 7 April 1958.
1960. *Monson, The Lord. South Carlton Hall, Lincoln. [1967]
1966. Montgomery Massingberd, J. Rondels, Cookham, Berks. [1972]
1978. Moon, Miss J. 27 Allington Garden, Boston. [1981]
1921. Moore, Revd Canon W. The Vicarage, Wragby [The Vicarage, Colsterworth]. Died 31 December 1943.
1968. Morgan, J. C. The Vicarage Flat, Loudwater, High Wycombe, Bucks. [5 Archway Road, Upper Holloway, London]. [1975]
1993. Morgan, J. C. Elia Street, Islington, London [St Andrew's, Hilder's Cliff, Rye, Sussex].
1974. Morioka, Professor K. 12 4-3 Sanno, Ota-Ku, Tokyo, Japan. [1997]
1910. Morkill, J. W. Newfield Hall, Bell Busk, Leeds. [1923]
1959. Morris, [Revd Professor] C. 12 Pembroke Street, St Aldate's, Oxford [Pembroke College, Oxford; Department of History, The University, Southampton]. [1993]
1910. Morse, Willard S. American Smelting and Refining Co., 165 Broadway, New York, U. S. A. [Seaford, Delaware, U. S. A.] [1923]
1975. Mortimer, R. 30 Myrtle Road, Hethersett, Norwich. [1982]

1910. Morton, W. K. The Elms, Horncastle. [1935]

2009. Moses, Dr Gary. 32 Grange Road, Woodthorpe, Nottingham.

1980. Mossop, P. J. 11 West End, Holbeach. [1987]

1918. Mountain, Thomas. Ashdell, Grimsby. [1935]

1978. Moyes, Miss G. T. Y. 5 Lintin Close, Heighington, Lincoln. [1984]

1958. Murray, Miss F. A. R. Exchequergate Lodge, Lincoln. [1965]

1977. Murray, Miss F. A. R. Exchequergate Lodge, Lincoln [Flat 7, Rasen House, Rasen Lane, Lincoln; 32 Rutland Court, Rutland Avenue, Lincoln]. Died 2 May 2009.

1925. Murray-Aynsley, C. M. 18 Grainger Street West, Newcastle-upon-Tyne. [1935]

2009. Musselwhite, John. 2 Cook's Lane, Great Coates, Grimsby.

2008. Musson, Mrs Janice. Stonepits Farm, The Saltway, Wartnaby, Melton Mowbray.

1990. Nannestad, Miss Eleanor. 20 Cranwell Street, Lincoln.

1962. Neale, Mrs V. Searby Manor [Searby Old Farmhouse], Barnetby. [1982]

1982. Neave, David R. J. 51 Whitecross Street, Barton-upon-Humber [5 The Beeches, Sidmouth Street, Hull; 29 Wood Lane, Beverley].

1983. Needham, J. R. Assistant Director's Bungalow, Crewe & Alsager College of Higher Education, Alsager, Staffs. [Oak Tree House, Dean's Lane, Balterley Green, Crewe].

2008. Nelson, Howard. 5 Rutland Close, South Witham, Grantham.

1910. Nevile, Mrs. 6 Lindum Terrace, Lincoln. [1915]

1910. Newsum, Arthur Crookes. Bracebridge Heath, Lincoln. Died 29 September 1934.

1926. Nicholas, Revd Canon B. G. The Parsonage, Spalding. [1936]

2007. Nicholson, Mrs Jean. York Cottage, 38 Green Lane, Lambley, Nottingham.

1934. Nixon, Revd Leigh H. Tydd St Mary Rectory, Wisbech. [1942]

1984. Noble, Miss Susan M. *See* Payne, Mrs.

1910. Noble, Revd W. M. Wistow Rectory, Huntingdon. [1915]

2004. Noon, Peter. North East Lincolnshire Archives, Town Hall Square, Grimsby.

1989. Norris, Andrew. 168 Kirkham Road, Freckleton, Preston. [2000]

1986. Norton, Miss Janet M. 24 Larkshall Crescent, Chingford, London. [1990] *See also* Thompson, Mrs J. M.

1910. Norwood, Revd R. P. Leverton Rectory, Boston [The Vicarage, Crowle; Withern Rectory, Alford]. [1931]

1976. Obelkevitch, Dr J. Department of History, Princeton University, Princeton, U.S.A. [64 Kensington Park Road, London; 29 Laurier Road, London; Department of English Social History, University of Warwick, Coventry]. [1982]

1920. Offer, Revd Canon Clifford J. Highmore Vicarage, Henley, Oxon [Ightham Rectory, Sevenoaks, Kent]. Died 14 June 1964.

1910. Oldfield, Revd Canon W. J. Culham Vicarage, Abingdon [Shipton under Wychwood Vicarage, Oxon; 93 Ermine Road, Lewisham]. [1931]

1968. Ollard, C. J. Scallows Hall, Binbrook. Died 1974.

2008. Ollard, John. Scallows Hall, Binbrook.

1970. *Olney, [Dr] Richard. Lincolnshire Archives Office, The Castle, Lincoln [26 Danby Street, Peckham Rye, London].

2010. O'Neill, Ms Judy. 26 Alexandra Terrace, Lincoln.

1910. Orwin, C. S. Panton House, Wragby; [7 Marston Ferry Road, Oxford]. [1931]

1948. Osborne, [Sir] Cyril, M.P. Welford House, Welford Place, Leicester. [1966]

1986. Osgerby, K. 9 Poplar Place, Lugarno, New South Wales, Australia. [1993]

1952. *Owen, Arthur Ernest Bion, F.S.A. 2 Fellows Road, London [Flat 4, 24 East Heath Road, London; 21 Whitwell Way, Cambridge; 79 Whitwell Way, Cambridge; 35 Whitwell Way, Coton, Cambridge; Old Manor House, Thimbleby, Horncastle]. Died 24 August 2008.

1948. *OWEN, Mrs D. M. (née Williamson), F.S.A. Lincolnshire Archives Office, Exchequer Gate, Lincoln [Flat 4, 24 East Heath Road, London; 21 Whitwell Way, Cambridge; 79 Whitwell Way, Cambridge; 35 Whitwell Way, Coton, Cambridge; Old Manor House, Thimbleby, Horncastle]. Died 13 February 2002.

1946. *Owen, Rt Revd Leslie, Lord Bishop of Lincoln. Bishop's House, Lincoln. Died 2 March 1947.

1920. *Owen, Professor L. V. D. University College, Nottingham [12 Derby Road, Beeston, Nottingham]. Died 16 February 1952.

1984. Pacey, Dr R. W. 3 Old Chapel Lane, Burgh-le-Marsh.

2009. Packer, Dr Ian. 19 Main Street, Eaton, Grantham.

2007. Page, Christopher. 13 Cherry Grove, Swanpool, Lincoln.

2007. Panton, Mrs Joan. 19 Carram Way, Lincoln.

1924. Parker, Col. J. W. R., F.S.A. Browsholme Hall, Clitheroe, Lancs. [1943]

2003. Parkin, Dr Kate. Sawyers House, 29 Main Street, South Rauceby, Sleaford.

1917. *Parkinson, William Gilliatt. The Hall, East Ravendale, Grimsby. Died 24 June 1945.

1999. Parratt, Graham. 11 Ormsby Close, Cleethorpes.

1917. Parsons, Miss Doris M. See Stenton, Mrs.

1990. *Pawley, Dr Simon. 25 Meadowfield, Sleaford [The Meadows, 7 Lafford Court, Sleaford].

1984. Payne (née Noble), Mrs Susan M. Lincolnshire Archives Office,

The Castle, Lincoln [Lincolnshire Archives, St Rumbold Street, Lincoln; 19 D'Aincourt Park, Branston, Lincoln]. [2006]

1910. Peacock, Frederick Arden. Cottesford Place, James Street, Lincoln. Died 10 May 1925.

1910. *Peake, Henry A. Westholme, Sleaford. Died 29 January 1923.

1981. Pearson, Mrs A. M. 'Silkby', School Lane, Silk Willoughby, Sleaford. [1982]

2009. Pearson, Adam. 14 Minter Court, Hangar Road, Tadley, Hants.

2009. Pearson, Alan. 39 Vicarage Wood Way, Tilehurst, Reading, Berks.

1965. *Peck, Very Revd Michael, Dean of Lincoln. The Deanery, Lincoln. Died 22 April 1968.

1992. Peeps, Brian. 1 Beretun Green, Barton-upon-Humber.

1954. Pemberton, Revd [Canon] Wilfred Austin. Breaston Rectory, Derby. Died April 1998.

1954. Perman, H. The Old Rectory, Tallington. [1966]

1968. Peterson, A. [Sir Arthur]. The House of Correction, Folkingham [The Greyhound, Folkingham]. Died 8 May 1986.

1986. Peterson, Lady. Norton Mill House, Nortonbury Lane, Baldock, Herts. [1992]

1994. Pettifer, B. W. B. Cob Hall, Priestgate, Barton-upon-Humber. [1996]

2001. Phillips, Gary. Cairns House, 46 Colegrave Street, Lincoln.

1923. Phipps, W. T., Barrister-at-Law. 38 Dudley Road, Grantham. [1949]

1966. Pick, John S. Woodside Farm, Newton, Sleaford [Welby Warren, Bridge End Road, Grantham].

1937. Pickwell, Miss Miriam. 77 Alexandra Road, Grimsby. [1942]

2007. Pinchbeck, Charles. 7 & 9 Cowgate, Heckington, Sleaford.

1992. Pinder, Bill. Tynygraig, Rhydycroesau, Oswestry. [1992]]

1968. Pink, Revd [Canon] D. The Vicarage, Kirton, Boston [St John's Vicarage, Spitalgate, Grantham; The Vicarage, Canwick, Lincoln; The Rectory, Church Hill, Washingborough; The Old School, Swarby, Sleaford].

2005. Plaskitt, Malcolm. New Darby House, 14 Tee Lane, Burton-upon-Stather, Scunthorpe.

1997. Platt, John G. The Glebe House, Church Lane, Withern, Alford. [2009]

1980. Platts, G. Groby Community College, Groby, Leicester [Flat 2, Enterprise House, Kirby Muxloe, Leicester; 52 Stadon Road, Anstey, Leicester; 166 Fircroft Road, Ipswich; 90 Woodbridge Road East, Ipswich; 22 Wavring Avenue, Kirby Cross, Essex].

1993. Plumb, Revd G. A. The Vicarage, Edinburgh Road, Grantham [The Rectory, Saxby All Saints; Ingham House, 45A Dams Road, Barton-upon-Humber].

1998. Pocock, Peter. 6 Station Road, Billingborough, Sleaford.

1968. Poole, M. D. W. 28 Washdyke Lane, Nettleham [141 Acre Lane, Cheadle Hulme, Cheshire; 17 Chamberlain Street, Wells].

1910. Portland, The Duke of. Welbeck Abbey, Notts. Died 26 April 1943.

1934. *Potter, Professor G. R. The University, Sheffield. [1964]

1910. Potts, Revd Joseph. Aubourn Vicarage, Lincoln. Died 2 October 1911.

1986. Powell, Dr Edward. 4 Corfe Close, Cambridge [23 Mulberry Hill, Shenfield, Essex]. [1988]

1912 Power, Professor Eileen. Girton College, Cambridge [20 Mecklenburgh Square, London]. Died 8 August 1940.

1929. *Powicke, Professor F. M. [Sir Maurice]   Oriel College, Oxford. [1947]

1911. Presgrave, Col. E. R. J. The Mount, Great Glen, Leicester [63 Gunterstone Road, West Kensington]. [1923]

1961. Presswell, A. J. Lincoln School, Lincoln. [1965]

1985. Prest, E. C. Rockery Cottage, Sutton-cum-Lound, Retford, Notts. [1989]

1910. Pym, Claude. Canwick House, Lincoln. [1939]

2002. Quinn, Mrs José. 125 Waltham Road, Scartho, Grimsby.

1910. Quirk, Revd Canon J. F. Great Coates Rectory, Grimsby. [1923]

1979. Raban, Mrs Sandra. Trinity Hall, Cambridge [191 Hills Road, Cambridge].

1910. Raithby, H. C. 18 The Fosse, Leicester. [1916]

1986. Raithby, Miss Victoria. Garthorpe Hall, Scunthorpe [The Sawrey Hotel, Far Sawrey, Ambleside, Cumbria; 36 High Street, Swinefleet, Goole, Yorkshire]. [1991]

1952. Rand, Major H. The Old Manor, Wye, Kent. [1960]

1912. Rawnsley, W. F. Shamley Green, Guildford. [1915]

1924. Rawnsley, Walter Hugh. Well Vale, Alford. Died 9 April 1936.

1972. Readman, Alan E. 23 St Ann's Avenue, Grimsby [West Sussex Record Office, Chichester]. [1981]

2006. Redford, Ms Jill. 26 Cromwell Street, Sheffield.

1996. Redmond, A. P. 25 High Street, Billingborough, Sleaford. Died December 2001.

2009. Redmore, Ken. 1 The Steepers, Nettleham, Lincoln.

2008. Reeds, Miss Catherine. 18 Holmfield, Fiskerton, Lincoln. [2009]

1968. Reedy, W. T. State University of New York, Albany, New York, U.S.A. Died 24 October 2008.

1986. Reeve, Dr J. L. 31 South Street, Bourne. [Died July 1986].

1910. Reeve, Capt. John Sherard. Leadenham House, Lincoln. Died 20 April 1955.

1955. Reeve, Colonel. Leadenham House, Lincoln. [1959]

1910. Reeve-King, Capt. Neville. Ashby-de-la-Launde Hall, Digby, Lincoln. Died 3 April 1920.

1978. Rich, Miss T. E. University Station, Baton Rouge, Louisiana [9411 Lee Highway, Fairfax, Virginia, U.S.A.] [1987]

1925. Richardson, H. G. High Barn, 14 Sheridan Road, Merton Park, London [The Grange, Goudhurst, Kent]. Died 3 September 1974.

1910. Richardson, Major-General J. H. Halton House, Spilsby. [1914]

2007. Richardson, Ms Jacqui. 12 Motherby Lane, Lincoln.

1957. *Riches, Rt. Revd Kenneth, Lord Bishop of Lincoln. Bishop's House, Lincoln. [1975]

1999. Rickard, John. Nye Glen, Lichfield Road, Hopwas, Tamworth, Staffs.

1910. Riggall, F. W. Heck House, Grimsby. [1918]

1914. Ring, Revd Canon T. P. 10 Lindum Terrace, Lincoln. [1918]

1960. Rissen-Kent, A. Stoke Hall, East Stoke, Notts. Died 13 July 1994.

2009. Roberts, Malcolm. 12 Victoria Place, Bourne.

1983. Robertson, Dr D. M. 'Field House', Braceby, Sleaford.

1977. Robinson, A. G. Flass Hall, Esh Winning, Durham [19 Miller's Court, Chiswick Mall, London]. [1981]

1980. Roffe, David. 11 Brazenose Lane, Stamford [68 Tower Street, Leicester; 72 Parkville Road, Withington, Manchester; 31 Moody Street, Congleton, Cheshire].

1976. Rogers, [Professor] Alan. 227 Plains Road, Mapperley, Nottingham [Institute for Continuing Education, University of Ulster, Northern Ireland; Ulph Cottage, Burnham Market, Norfolk; Adderley Street, Uppingham, Rutland; Hill House, Station Road, Reepham, Norfolk; Nash House, 37 Mill Road South, Bury St Edmunds, Suffolk].

2010. Rogers, Dr Mike. Gig Cottage, Gainsborough Road, Middle Rasen.

1965. Rooksby, R. L. Australian National University, Canberra [University of New England, Armidale, N.S.W.; University of Western Australia, Nedlands, Western Australia]. [1983]

1957. *Roskell, Professor J. S. The University, Nottingham [The University, Manchester; 42 Barchester Road, Cheadle, Cheshire]. Died May 1998.

1997. Rossington, John. 57 Minster Drive, Cherry Willingham, Lincoln.

1946. Rothwell, R. L. Baddeley Mount, Bowness-on-Windermere, Westmoreland. [1951]

2009. Rowlands, John. Brant House, 47 High Street, Brant Broughton, Lincoln.

2004. Rowson, R. I. Churchill Road, North Somercotes, Louth.

1986. Royce, T. W. 14 Windsor Drive, Spalding. Died January 2009.

1910. Royds, Sir Edmund. Holy Cross, Caythorpe, Grantham [Stubton Hall, Newark]. Died 31 March 1946.

1910. Rudd, S. Bentley. Welby Gate, Grantham. [1918]

1997. Ruddock, Henry. 287 High Street, Lincoln. [2000]

1974. *Ruddock, J. G. Boothby Graffoe Hall, Lincoln. Died March 1997.
1910. *Ruddock, J. H. 287 High Street, Lincoln. Died 6 July 1963.
2009. Rush, Andy. 6 Apple Grove, Eaton Ford, St Neots, Hunts.
1968. Russell, R. C. 11 Priestgate, Barton-upon-Humber.
1910. Ruston, Col. J. S. Aisthorpe Hall, Lincoln. [1915]
1910. Rutland, The Duke of. Belvoir Castle, Grantham. Died 8 May 1925.
1966. Rutter, Revd Canon D. C. The Precentory, Lincoln. [1982]
1912 Sanborn, Victor C. Kenilworth, Illinois, U.S.A. [1923]
1910. Sandall, Thomas. Rusholme Lodge, Stamford. [1923]
1976. Sardeson, Mrs S. M. A. Howell Manor, Sleaford [Hope Cottage, 22
    Church Street, Heckington, Sleaford].
2007. Sass, Jon. Flowerdew, 2a Cissplatt Lane, Keelby, Grimsby [4 Secret
    Gardens, Nettleton, Market Rasen].
1989. Saunders, Revd David. The Vicarage, Holmes Lane, Dunholme,
    Lincoln [2 Oundle Close, Washingborough, Lincoln].
1987. Scaman, H. N. 4 Etwall Road, Mickleover, Derby. [1994]
2004. Scarlett, Mrs Sarah. 58 Willis Close, Lincoln.
1984. Schmidt, Dr Albert J. 1446 Redding Road, Fairfield, Connecticut,
    U.S.A. [1992]
1985. Scoffin, Mrs Jean. 1 The Cloisters, Humberston, Grimsby. [1987]
1922. Scorer, Eric West. Mint Street, Lincoln [Lindsey County Offices,
    Newland, Lincoln; 1 Greetwell Road, Lincoln; 7 Sewell Road,
    Lincoln]. Died 11 August 1966.
1955. Scorer, Philip. Bank Chambers, Stonebow, Lincoln. [1972]
1931. Scorer, Reynolds. Bank Chambers, Stonebow, Lincoln. [1955]
1910. Scorer, William. Bank Street Chambers, Lincoln. [1913]
1910. Scott, Sir Robert Forsyth. Master of St John's College, Cambridge.
    Died 18 November 1933.
1911. Scott, Mrs. The Priory, Lincoln. [1912]
1912. Serjeantson, Revd R. M., F.S.A. St Peter's Rectory, Northampton.
    Died 15 November 1916.
2009. Shanks, Mrs Joyce. 24 Glenbank Close, North Hykeham, Lincoln.
2004. Sharpley, Neil. The Sycamores, 23 Westgate, Louth.
1956. Shaw, Peter J. 6 Westkirke Avenue, Scartho, Grimsby. [1959]
1932. Sheffield, Sir Berkeley, Bt. Normanby Park, Scunthorpe. [1939]
1951. Shepard, Charles. 45 Exchange Street, Rochester, New York [500
    Allen's Creek Road, Rochester, New York, U.S.A.] [1994]
1921. Sheppard, Revd J. W. Haxey Vicarage, Doncaster [Stones Place,
    Skellingthorpe]. [1937]
2007. Shields, Allan. 18 Church Lane, Hedon, Hull [4/744 Canning
    Highway, Applecross, Perth, Western Australia].
1914. Shipley, A. G. The Limes, Lincoln. [1935]
1951. Shove, His Honour Judge Ralph. The Old Hall, Washingborough,
    Lincoln. Died 2 February 1966.

1910. Shuttleworth, Alfred. Eastgate House, Lincoln. [1931]
1910. Sibthorp, C. C. Sudbrook Holme, Lincoln [Dower House, Canwick, Lincoln]. [1935]
1910. Sibthorp, Montagu R. Waldo. Canwick Hall, Lincoln. Died 1929.
1992. Sidebotham, Kenneth William. 27 Stewton Lane, Louth. Died December 1998.
1910. *SIMPSON, Gordon L. District Probate Registry, Lincoln [District Probate Registry, York]. [1916]
2008. Simpson, Raymond. The Moorings, Mill Lane, Donhead St Andrew, Shaftesbury, Dorset.
1924. Sinclair, Revd A. C. Beelsby Rectory, Grimsby. [1942]
1942. *Skelton, Rt Revd H., Lord Bishop of Lincoln. The Old Palace, Lincoln [Braid's Lea, Ditchling, Hassocks, Sussex; Stepping Stones, Maenporth Hill, Falmouth, Cornwall; 43 Wood Lane, Falmouth; 13 Cliff Lane, Falmouth; Carwinion Lodge, Mawnan, Falmouth]. Died 30 August 1959.
1970. Skinner, Miss J. Bishop Grosseteste College, Lincoln [10 Natal Road, Cambridge; 26 Rasen Lane, Lincoln].
1942. Slack, W. A. 17 Cornmarket, Louth. [1968]
1919. Sleight, Major Sir Ernest, Bt. The Crossways, Stallingborough. [1931]
1942. *Sleight, M. M. Weelsby Hall, Grimsby [Binbrook Hall, Lincoln]. Died August 1999.
1949. Sleight, Mrs. Binbrook Hall, Lincoln. Died 19 July 1963.
1971. Smith, The Ven. A. C. The Rectory, Algarkirk, Boston ['Farthings', Church End, Great Rollright, Chipping Norton, Oxon.] Died 3 April 2001.
1942. Smith, A. E. 43 South Street, Alford. [1944]
1965. *SMITH, [Professor] D. M. 52 Hunt Lea Avenue, Lincoln [Borthwick Institute of Historical Research, St Anthony's Hall, York; Crowham House, Market Plce, Masham, North Yorkshire; Cluj-Napoca, Romania].
1934. Smith, Eustace Abel. Longhills, Lincoln. Died 10 July 1938.
1918. Smith, George. Horbling, Folkingham. [1931]
1954. Smith, H. 38 Lee Road, Lincoln. [1958]
2004. Smith, Mrs Miriam. 2 Belgravia Close, Lincoln.
1920. Smith, Miss N. E. R. 42 Bell Road, Hounslow. [1931]
2002. Smith, Richard. 12 The Pippin, Calne, Wilts. [Cherry Trees, Spring Hill, Little Staughton, Beds.]
1910. Smith, Stephenson Percy. 'Matai-moana', New Plymouth, New Zealand. Died 19 April 1922.
1925. Smith, Canon W. H. Ingoldsby Rectory, Grantham. [1937]
1910. Smith-Carrington, H. H. Grangethorpe, Rusholme, Manchester. [1918]

1910. Smyth, Revd A. The Vicarage, Sutton-on-Sea. [1918]

2007. Snowdon, Mr and Mrs Michael. Hawkes House, 34 London Road, Spalding.

2008. Soderberg, Mrs Valerie. 8 Somerfield Drive, North Somercotes, Louth.

1910. Sowby, T. H. Grainthorpe, Lincs. [1912]

1910. Spalding John Tricks 22 Villa Road, Nottingham. Died 9 June 1924.

1910. Spawforth, Revd J. South Ferriby Rectory, Barton-on-Humber. Died 7 May 1923.

1982. Spurrell, Revd M. Stow Rectory, Lincoln. [1983]

1923. *Srawley, Revd Canon J. H., Chancellor of Lincoln. The Chancery, Lincoln [15 Minster Yard, Lincoln]. Died 6 January 1954.

2000. Standring, D. J. 24 Blenheim Road, Barnsley, South Yorks.

1912 Stanhope, Hon. R. P. Revesby Abbey, Boston. [1916]

1943. Stanhope Lovell, Revd W. Billinghay Vicarage, Lincoln. [1946]

1976. Staniforth, Mrs E. H. 68 Tetney Road, Humberston, Grimsby. [1979]

1982. Staniland, M. F. 4 St George's Street, Stamford. Died 14 January 1992.

2003. Staniland, Patrick W. East Keal Manor, Spilsby.

1946. Stanton, Lt-Col. H. M. A. 20 North Road, Bourne. [1970]

1964. Starkie, K. W. L. Parkstone [60 Fosseway], Upton Park, Chester. [1976]

1925. Statham, Revd S. O. W. Hill View, Cheddar, Somerset. [1935]

1927. Stedman, Revd W. D. Thimbleby Rectory, Horncastle [Cherry Burton Rectory, Beverley]. [1937]

1965. Steele, Miss Susan. Lincolnshire Archives Office, The Castle, Lincoln. [1968]

1954. Steer, Revd Canon Eric. Bierton Vicarage, Aylesbury, Bucks. [1960]

1915. *STENTON, Professor F. M. [Sir Frank]. 14 Morgan Road, Reading [University College, Reading; Whitley Park Farm, Reading]. Died 15 September 1967.

1917. *Stenton (née Parsons), Mrs D. M. [Lady] The Nook, Woodley, Reading [South Hill, Southwell, Notts; Whitley Park Farm, Reading]. Honorary Member 1934 1967. Died 29 December 1971.

2002. Stephenson, F. M. 40 Peachley Gardens, Lower Broadheath, Worcester.

1932. Stephenson, Miss M. E. The Hall, Burgh-le-Marsh. [1936]

1977. Stevenage, M. R. 31 Brooklyn Court, High Road, Loughton, Essex [49 Centre Drive, Epping, Essex]. [2009]

1999. Stevens, Mrs S. M. 3 Flaxwell Way, Leasingham, Sleaford.

1999. Stevenson, James. 10 Severn Street, Lincoln. [2008]

1925. *Stewart, Miss Constance. Training College, Lincoln [St Adrian's, Lancaster Road, St Albans; Stoneways, Weston Underwood, Olney; 1 The Mill Granary, Church Street, Olney; Tickford Abbey, Priory Street, Newport Pagnell, Bucks.] Died February 1990.

1988. *Stocker, David. 2 North Street, Osney Island, Oxford [Manor Farm House, Thorpe-on-the-Hill, Lincoln].

1910. Stocks, Canon J. E., Archdeacon of Leicester. Misterton Rectory, Lutterworth [Foston Rectory, Leicester; Minster Precincts, Peterborough]. Died 29 August 1926.

1921. Stone, F. Elsham, Brigg. [1931]

1910. Stoodley, Revd T. A. Dowsby Rectory, Bourne; [Albany Hotel, Hastings; Dowsby, Bournemouth]. Died 27 February 1915.

1966. *Storey, [Professor] Robin Lindsay. The University, Nottingham [The Old Station House, Scotby, Carlisle]. Died 4 July 2005.

1912 Strachan, John. District Probate Registry, Lincoln. [1918]

1958. Stubbs, A. A. F. 11 Bigby Street, Brigg. Died 1967.

1970. *Sturman, Christopher J. 30 Broadbank, Louth. Died 3 November 1997.

1910. Sumners, H. T. High Street, Heckington. [1923]

1918. Sutcliffe, Tom. Stallingborough Manor. Died 8 January 1931.

1910. *Sutton, Revd Canon A. F. Brant Broughton Rectory, Newark. Died 18 November 1925.

1969. Swaby, Revd Canon J. E. The Vicarage, Barton-upon-Humber [Uffington Rectory, Stamford; 'Farrendon', Southorpe, Stamford]. Died 26 February 2008.

1910. Swan, Col. C. A. Sausthorpe Hall, Spilsby. Died 9 January 1941.

1981. Swanson, R. N. School of History, University of Birmingham, Birmingham.

1921. *SWAYNE, Rt Revd W. S., Lord Bishop of Lincoln. The Old Palace, Lincoln. [1931]

1919. Swettenham, Sir Alexander. Bellevue, Gordon Town, Jamaica. Died 19 April 1933.

1953. Swinburn, W. R. Fernlea, Oak Road, Healing, Grimsby [Baysholme, 25 Cheapside, Waltham, Grimsby; 106 Clee Road, Grimsby]. Died 1980.

2009. Sykes, Dr Katherine. 129 Millgate, Selby, North Yorks.

2006. Sylvester, Tim. 10 St Paul Street, Islington, London [39 Northchurch Road, London].

1998. Taggart, M. F. 114 Tweedle Hill Road, Blackley, Manchester.

1910. Talbot, G. J. 36 Wilton Crescent, London. [1923]

2007. Tann, Geoff. 23 Spa Buildings, Lincoln.

2008. Tate, Mrs Enid. 8 Green Lane, North Hykeham, Lincoln.

1910. *Tatham, Revd Canon E. H. R., F.S.A. Claxby Rectory, Alford

[Jock's Lodge, Lodsworth, Petworth, Sussex]. Died 12 February 1938.

2004. Taylor, Hugh. 5 Nursery Grove, Lincoln.

2008. Taylor, Revd John. Sibsey Vicarage, Boston.

1976. Taylor, R. M. The Jolly Sailor, Fishtoft, Boston. [1980]

1910. Taylor, R. Wright. Baysgarth Park, Barton-upon-Humber. [1912]

1910. Tempest, Mrs. Broughton Hall, Skipton, Yorks. [Hobgreen, Markington, Harrogate]. Died 26 January 1928.

1993. Tennant, Maurice. 50 Hallgate, Holbeach.

1933. Tennyson D'Eyncourt, Mrs. Bayons Manor, Tealby. [1942]

1953. Thirsk, Mrs J. 36a Oppidans Road, London [St Hilda's College, Oxford]. [1982]

1969. Thomas, J. D. Atherstone Place, Eastgate, Lincoln [Corbett House, Castle Street, Stroud]. [1981]

1911. *Thompson, Professor Alexander Hamilton, F.S.A. Old Vicarage, Gretton, Kettering [De Grey Terrace, Leeds; Beck Cottage, Adel, Leeds; The Manor House, Adel, Leeds; 7 Beaufort Mansions, Beaufort Street, London]. Died 4 September 1952.

2008. Thompson, Miss Barbara. 9 Church Street, Castleton, Whitby, North Yorks.

1986. Thompson, Revd Edwin. 13 Ross Way, Gosforth, Newacstle-upon-Tyne. [1988]

1923. Thompson, H. V. Croft House, Garden Village, Stoke-on-Trent [Deanhurst, 32 Queen's Road, Hartshill, Stoke-on-Trent]. Died 1966.

1994. Thompson (née Norton), Mrs J. M. 44 Pittman Gardens, Ilford, Essex. [1995]

1985. Thornley, Mrs E. L. 74 Daggett Road, Cleethorpes [4 Jutland Court, New Waltham, Grimsby]. [2002]

1952. Thorold, Revd Henry. Marston Hall, Grantham. [1961]

1985. Timmins, E. W. 16 Vicarage Road, Rugby, Warwicks. Died January 1999.

1989. Tinley, Miss Ruth. 16 Lincoln Road, North Hykeham, Lincoln.

1924. Topham, Miss J. G. C. Middleham House, Middleham, Yorks. Died 24 July 1940.

1910. Townend, G. P. 39 Heidelberg Road, Bradford; [Sanquhar House, Logie Street, Oakleigh, Victoria, Australia]. [1918]

1976. Trevitt, E. H. 30 Aldrich Road, Cleethorpes. [1988]

1917. Trollope, Sir William Henry, Bt. 5 Montague Square, London. Died 24 August 1921.

1919. Trollope-Bellew, The Hon. Mrs. Casewick, Stamford. [1935]

2010. Trott, Dr Michael. 18 Wicklow Road, Doncaster.

1934. Trotter, Revd J. R. Freiston Priory, Boston [Spa Hotel, Woodhall Spa]. Died August 1954.

1956. Tunnard, Michael. 1a Vanbrugh Terrace, Blackheath, London [1 Locke Chase, Lee Park, Blackheath; 1 Marina Close, King Street, Emsworth, Hants; 69 Shooters Hill Road, Blackheath, London]. Died May 1995.

1933. Tupholme, Revd W. S. Steeple Langford Rectory, Salisbury. [1942]

2004. Turland, Michael. 1 Jonathan Gardens, Sleaford.

1989. Turner, A. S. 25 Rufford Green, Lincoln. Died May 1993.

1976. Turner, I. D. 'Warrendene', 222 Nottingham Road, Mansfield, Notts.

1973. Turner, J. 11 Merleswen, St Chad's Lea, Dunholme, Lincoln.

1980. Turner, W. B. 7 Burgess Road, Brigg [Nar Dee, Greetwell, Gainsborough; The Rowans, Dudley Road, Brigg; 18 St James's Road, Brigg; The Chestnuts, Old Rectory Lane, Kirmington].

1910. Turnor, Christopher Hatton. Panton Hall, Wragby [Stoke Rochford Hall, Grantham]. Died 19 August 1940.

1992. Twigg, D. J. 87 Blenheim Gardens, Kingston-upon-Thames, Surrey. [1998]

1910. Tyack, Revd G. S. The Rectory, North Cotes [The Vicarage, Caistor]. Died 19 January 1930.

1912. Tyrwhitt, Revd H. M. 19 The Glebe, Blackheath, London. Died 6 October 1937.

1998. Tyrwhitt, Lady. 51 Whitecross Street, Barton-upon-Humber.

2006. Ulyatt, Dr Donna. High Point House, Cambridge Crescent, Brookenby, Market Rasen.

1911. Uthwatt, William A. Great Linford, Newport Pagnell. [1916]

2009. Van der Kaaij, Dr Martyn. 1 Greeetwell Gate, Lincoln [Hillside House, Glentworth, Gainsborough].

1985. Varah, George Hugh. 4 Beck Hill, Barton-upon-Humber. Died July 1994.

1912. Varah, Revd W. E. The Vicarage, Barton-upon-Humber. [1936]

1949. Varah, W. O. 29 Butts, Barton-upon-Humber [14 Baskerville Road, London; 3 West Side, Wandsworth Common, London; 58 Central Avenue, Pinner, Middlesex; 76 Wattleton Road, Beaconsfield, Bucks.] [1985]

1945. *Varley, Mrs Joan. Diocesan Record Office, Exchequer Gate, Lincoln [Lincolnshire Archives Office, Exchequer Gate, Lincoln; The Castle, Lincoln; 164 Nettleham Road, Lincoln]. Died April 2002.

2009. Varlow, Mrs Barbara. 5 Coningsby Crescent, Bracebridge Heath, Lincoln.

1976. Venables, Miss K. D. The Old Vicarage, Burgh-le-Marsh. [1982]

2008. Ventham, Valentine. 20 Dunholme Road, Scothern, Lincoln.

1989. Vergette, P. W. 25 Church Road, Addlestone, Weybridge, Surrey. [1994]

1989. Vince, Dr Alan. City of Lincoln Archaeological Unit, Sessions House, Lindum Road, Lincoln [The Lawn, Union Road, Lincoln; 43 Beaumont Fee, Lincoln]. Died 23 February 2009.

1910. Vines, Revd Canon T. H. Fiskerton Rectory, Lincoln. [1915]

1943. Wade, Major F. R. Market Deeping, Lincs. [1970]

1910. Wadsworth, Frederic Arthur. 15 Weekday Cross, Nottingham [23 Cavendish Crescent South, The Park, Nottingham]. Died 15 April 1943.

1977. Wagstaffe, Miss E. T. 32 Baildon Crescent, North Hykeham, Lincoln.

1976. Wagstaffe, F. R. 32 Baildon Crescent, North Hykeham, Lincoln. Died March 1988.

1912. Wakeford, Revd Canon John, Precentor of Lincoln. The Precentory, Lincoln. [1923]

1981. Wales, C. J. 27 Fearnley Street, Watford [128 Mildred Avenue, Watford; Gaddesden Hall, Water End, Hemel Hempstead, Herts.]

1975. Wales, Derrick. Steeping Side, Vicarage Lane, Wainfleet.

1930. Walford Bros, Messrs. 6 New Oxford Street, London. [1951]

2002. *Walker, Dr Andrew. 14 Baker Crescent, Doddington Park, Lincoln.

1952. Walker, [Revd Canon] D. 48 St George's Terrace, Swansea [West Mount, Cockett Road, Swansea; 52 Eaton Crescent, Uplands, Swansea]. [2009]

1910. *Walker, Revd Canon G. G. Somerby Rectory, Grantham [Eastcliff Lodge, Lincoln]. Died 22 July 1935.

1980. Walker, J. A. 1 Sylvanus, Roman Wood, Bracknell, Berks. [1986]

1925. Walker, W. H. I. New Street, Heckington, Sleaford. [1935]

2009. Wall, Tony. 109 Bunkers Hill, Lincoln.

1946. Walshaw, Alderman G. R. Brumby Hall, Scunthorpe [29 Fairview Road, Oxton, Birkenhead]. [1954]

1957. Walter, H. A. H. County Hall, Boston. [1966]

1991. Waltham, C. E. 8191 Hudson Street, Vancouver, British Columbia, Canada. [1991]

1979. Walton, Professor R. C. Faculty of Theology, The University, Munster, Germany. [2001]

1976. Ward, Miss A. E. Flat 4, Canwick Hall, Lincoln [3 Lonsdale Court, Washingborough, Lincoln]. Died June 1988.

2009. Ward, Arthur. 25 Olive Street, Lincoln.

1910. Ward, Revd George, F.S.A. Mavis Enderby Rectory, Spilsby. Died 19 August 1929.

2000. Ward, Dr Jenny. La Haie Sainte, Watery Lane, Little Cawthorpe, Louth.

1918. Ward, Thomas. 70 Cromwell Road, Grimsby ['Patterdale', Welholme Avenue, Grimsby]. [1931]

1938. *Warner, Rt Revd K. C. H., Lord Bishop of Edinburgh. The

Archdeaconry, Lincoln [Bishop's House, Lansdowne Crescent, Edinburgh]. [1949]

1910. WARREN, Revd Charles. St Michael's Vicarage, Lincoln. Died 29 April 1919.

1976. Watkinson, L. 63 Highgate, Cleethorpes. Died December 1985.

1985. Watkinson, Mrs B. 63 Highgate, Cleethorpes. [1998]

1912. Watney, Revd H. J. Canwick Vicarage, Lincoln. [1923]

1958. Watson, G. R. 'Orillia', Brigsley Road, Waltham, Grimsby [40 Signhills Avenue, Cleethorpes]. [1967]

1912. Watson, G. W. 34 The Ridgeway, Golder's Green, London. [1931]

1998. Watson, Richard O. 3 Willow Field, Whittle-le-Woods, Chorley, Lancs.

2005. Watson, Dr Sethina. Balliol College, Oxford [Centre for Medieval Studies, University of York].

1982. Weale, Revd [Dr] C. A. Bengeo Rectory, Byde Street, Hertford [1 Diana Way, Caister-on-Sea, Norfolk].

1984. Webster, Mrs Brenda. 25 Fen Road, Heighington, Lincoln.

1911. Weigall, Mrs. Petwood, Woodhall Spa. [1915]

1935. *Welbourne, E. E. Granham, Great Shelford, Cambridge [Master's Lodge, Emmanuel College, Cambridge]. Died 28 January 1966.

1997. Welbourne, Mrs Kate. Manor Farm Barn, Little Humby, Grantham.

1979. Welby, Sir Bruno. Denton House, Grantham. [1993]

1910. Welby, Sir Charles G. E., Bt. Denton Manor, Grantham. Died 19 March 1938.

1910. Welby, Revd Canon G. E. White House, Barrowby, Grantham. [1912]

1910. *Welby, Col. Sir Alfred C. E. 26 Sloane Court, London [18 Chester Street, London; A8 Albany, Piccadilly, London]. Died 18 May 1937.

1937. Welby, R. A. E. 26 Caroline Place, London. [1945]

1910. Welby-Everard, E. E. 9 Eccleston Square, London [The Hall, Gosberton, Spalding]. Died 20 July 1951.

1910. Wells-Cole, Lt. Col. H. Naval and Military Club, 94 Piccadilly, London. [1913]

1983. Wells-Cole, Lt-Cdr C. P. N. 209 Yarborough Road, Lincoln [25 Upper Long Leys Road, Lincoln]. [1993]

1990. West, Alan. 19 Clevedon Gardens, Cranford, Middlesex. [1992]

1953. West, F. Westwood, Saunderton, High Wycombe, Bucks. [1964]

1910. Westbrooke, Revd Canon W. F. W. The Vicarage, Caistor. [1915]

2008. Wheatley, Miss Pearl. 8 Orchard Way, Nettleham, Lincoln.

2003. *Wheeler, Dr R. C. Sycamore Cottage, Chapel Lane, Harmston, Lincoln.

1960. Wheeler-Booth, M. A. J. House of Lords, London. [1963]

1945. Whitelock, Miss [Professor] Dorothy. St Hilda's College,

Oxford [Newnham College, Cambridge; 30 Thornton Close, Cambridge]. [1975]

1925. Whiting, Professor C. E., F.S.A. St Chad's College, Durham [Hickleton, Doncaster]. Died 24 March 1953.

2009. Whittaker, Adrian C. 19 Leith Park Road, Windmill Hill, Gravesend, Kent.

1947. Whitting, P. D. 9 Rivercourt Road [15A Rivercourt Road], London. Died 14 December 1988.

1988. Whittow, Mark. 1 The Pierhead, Wapping High Street, London [11 Holywell Street, Oxford].

1966. Wigan, Mrs M. Windrush, Blackness, Crowborough, Sussex [Kingsdown, Somerfield Road, Maidstone; 138 Upper Fant Road, Maidstone; 119 Western Road, Hurstpierpoint, Sussex]. [1981]

1976. Wilbie-Chalk, D. Well Close, Rothbury, Northumberland. [1985]

2009. Wildbore, Miss Julie. 35 Waterfields, Moorgate, Retford.

1998. Wilkinson, Dr Louise. 10 Wellington House, Exeter Close, Watford [60 London Road, Shenley, Radlett, Herts; 4 Barton Road, Canterbury].

1993. Wilkyn, Neil R. 48 Railway Street, Barnetby-le-Wold.

1973. Williams, Revd H. B. The Grammar School, Brigg [Mill House, Goulceby, Louth; 55 Upgate, Louth; 5 The Terrace, Stewton Lane, Louth].

1911. Williams, Col. J. G. Lindum Lodge, Sewell Road, Lincoln. [1931]

1982. Williams, Miss Joan. Flat 4, 22 Doddington Road, Lincoln [11 Waldeck Street, Lincoln]. [1987]

1948. *Williamson, Miss Dorothy. *See* Owen, Mrs.

1950. Willoughby d'Eresby, The Lord. *See* Ancaster.

1910. Wilson, E. T. Gilchrist. 7 Arkwright Road, Hampstead, London. [1914]

1925. Wilson, Mrs Gilchrist. Roxholme Hall, Sleaford [Newton House, Sturminster Newton, Dorset]. Died 1945.

1945. Wilson, Miss Barbara. Vine Cottage, Sixpenny Handley, Salisbury [Appletree Cottage, Woodcutts, Salisbury; 8 High Street, Toller Porcorum, Dorset; 4 Church Lane, Redenholt, Harleston; 7 Weavers Croft, Harleston, Norfolk]. Died March 1990.

2008. Wilson, Mrs Catherine. Penates, 5 Station Road, Reepham, Lincoln.

1968. Wilson, J. H. 27 Massey Road, Lincoln. Died November 1991.

1983. Wilson, John. 5 Gertrude Street, Grimsby. [1986]

2009. Wilson, Miss Marianne. 29 Albion Crescent, Lincoln.

1991. Wilson, Richard H. 85 Cherry Hinton Road, Cambridge [198 High Street, Chesterton, Cambridge; 4 Metclafe Road, Cambridge].

1938. Wimberley, Major-General D. 53 Fountainhall Road, Edinburgh [361 Perth Road, Dundee; Foxhall, Coupar Angus, Perthshire]. [1976]

1918. Winchilsea and Nottingham, Earl of. Haverholme Priory, Sleaford. Died 14 August 1927.

1911. Winckley, Revd A. R. Thorold. [1912]

1919. Winckley, Revd A. R. Thorold, Cadney Vicarage, Brigg. [1931]

1934. Wintringham, W. H. The Abbey, Grimsby [The Lodge, Bargate, Grimsby; 75 Abbey Road, Grimsby]. Died 1963.

2001. Withers, Malcolm. Greestone House, Greestone Terrace, Lincoln.

1952. Wood, Professor A. C. The University, Nottingham. [1961]

1974. Wood, Miss M. Holmelea, North Road, Sleaford. [1976]

1958. Wood, Mrs N. Rose Bank, Malvern Wells, Worcester. [1964]

1965. Woodbury, E. B. C. 7 Berkeley Court, Marylebone Circus, London [Glensyde, 253 Hawthorn Road, Aldwick, Bognor Regis, Sussex]. Died 1978.

1960. Woodhead, A. Geoffrey, F.S.A. Corpus Christi College, Cambridge. Died 6 November 2008.

1969. Woods, Mrs Marjorie. 32 Tytton Lane East, Wyberton, Boston. Died August 1990.

1965. *Woodward, S. W. Headmaster's House, The Grammar School, Spalding [Hares Form, Sparepenny Lane, Great Sampford, Saffron Walden, Essex]. Died 1981.

1916. *Woolley, Canon R. M. Minting Rectory, Horncastle. Died 5 September 1931.

1977. Wootton, W. E. J. Horbling Hall, Sleaford. [1978]

1910. Wordsworth, Revd Canon Christopher. St Nicholas Hospital, Salisbury. [1923]

1910. Wordsworth, Rt Revd John, Lord Bishop of Salisbury. The Palace, Salisbury. Died 16 August 1911.

1910. Wormal, R. O. Capital and Counties Bank, Lincoln [Ganstead, Wragby Road, Lincoln]. [1935]

1925. Worsley, Revd F. S. Dowsby Rectory, Bourne. [1937]

1983. Worth, Mrs G. R. Carlton Scroop Hall, Grantham.

1935. Wright, Mrs. Kirkby Green, Lincoln. [1959]

1975. Wright, N. R. Yarborough Lodge, 32 Yarborough Road, Lincoln. [2000]

2009. Wright, N. R. Yarborough Lodge, 32 Yarborough Road, Lincoln.

1918. Wright, R. C. Ivy Dene, North Thoresby. [1923]

1910. *Wright, William Maurice, F.S.A. Wold Newton Manor, North Thoresby. Died 17 October 1956.

1910. Yarborough, The Earl of, F.S.A. Brocklesby Park, Lincs. Died 12 July 1936.

1936. Yarborough, The Earl of. Brocklesby Park, Lincs. Died 7 February 1948.

1948. Yarborough, The Earl of. Brocklesby Park, Lincs. Died 2 December 1966.

1966. Yarborough, The Earl of. Brocklesby Park, Lincs. Died 21 March 1991.

1916. Yates, Revd W. E. Welton Manor, Louth [Westgate, Louth]. Died 17 December 1935.

1911. Yerburgh, Revd E. R. Wrentham Rectory, Wangford, Suffolk [10 Royal Crescent, Bath]. [1931]

1910. Yerburgh, Robert. 25 Kensington Gore, London. Died 18 December 1916.

1959. Young, A. J. Meadowhill, Saltergate Lane, Bamford, Sheffield. [1965]

INSTITUTIONS

UNITED KINGDOM

1948. Aberdeen University Library. [1996]

1930. Aberystwyth: National Library of Wales. [Copyright from 1942]

1946. Aberystwyth: University College, Wales [Hugh Owen Library, University of Wales].

1942. Bedford County Library. [2003]

1927. Birmingham: Public Libraries.

1941. Birmingham: University Library.

1932. Boston: Parochial Church Council. [1978]

1948. Boston Public Library. [Transferred to Lincolnshire County Library, 1976]

1966. Boston Spa: National Central Library [British Library Lending Division]. [2009]

1924. Bristol: University Library.

1956. Buckinghamshire Archaeological Society, The Museum, Aylesbury. [1996]

1917. Cambridge: University Library. [Copyright from 1942]

1955. Durham University Library, Palace Green, Durham.

1925. Edinburgh: University Library.

1979. Essex University Library, Colchester. [1993]

1943. Exeter University Library.

1948. Gainsborough: Public Library. [Transferred to Lincolnshire County Library, 1976]

1974. Glasgow University Library.

1927. Grantham: Public Library. [Transferred to Lincolnshire County Library, 1976]

2003. Grimsby: North East Lincolnshire Archives, Town Hall Square.

1910. Grimsby: Public Library [North East Lincolnshire Council, Central Library].

2007. Heritage Trust of Lincolnshire, Heckington, Sleaford.

1952. Hertfordshire Record Office, Hertford. [2006]
1910. Hull Public Libraries, Albion Street, Hull. [1997]
1929. Hull University College [Hull University, Brynmor Jones Library].
1971. Hull University Department of Adult Education. [2000]
1974. Huntingdonshire Record Office, Grammar School Walk, Huntingdon. [2009]
1966. Kent University Library, Canterbury. [1976]
1948. Kesteven County Library, Sleaford. [1974]
1950. Kesteven Training College, Stoke Rochford. [1957]
1966. Kesteven College of Education, Stoke Rochford. [1976]
1925. Leeds: University Library [Brotherton Library].
1946. Leicester Corporation Museum [Leicestershire Record Office], New Walk, Leicester [Long Street, Wigston Magna, Leicester].
1910. Leicester: Leicestershire Architectural and Archaeological Society.
1964. Leicester: Leicestershire County Library, Clarence Street. [1976]
1949. Leicester: Leicestershire County Record Office, Greyfriars [57 New Walk]. [1975]
1937. Leicester: Public Library [Leicestershire Libraries]. [1992].
1928. Leicester: University College [University Library].
1910. Lincoln: Cathedral Library.
1989. Lincoln: City of Lincoln Archaeological Unit, The Lawn, Union Road. [1999]
1936. Lincoln: Diocesan Training College [Bishop Grosseteste College].
1955. Lincoln: Foster Library, Lincolnshire Archives Office.
2010. Lincoln: LCM Digital Media Ltd, Bailgate.
1910. Lincoln: Lincolnshire Architectural Society [Lincolnshire Local History Society; Jews Court Trust]. [1971]
2008. Lincoln: Lincolnshire County Council, Historic Environment Record.
1976. Lincoln: Lincolnshire County Library.
1925. Lincoln: Lindsey County Council Education Committee Library [Lindsey and Holland County Library]. [1974]
1911. Lincoln: Public Library. [Transferred to Lincolnshire County Library, 1976]
1942. Lincoln: Scholae Cancellarii [Theological College]. [1957]
2004. Lincoln: Society for Lincolnshire History and Archaeology, Jews' Court, Steep Hill.
1969. Lincoln: Theological College. [1973]
2004. Lincoln University Library, Brayford Pool, Lincoln.
1926. Liverpool: Public Library, William Brown Street. [1991]
1923. Liverpool University, Sydney Jones Library.
1927. London: Bedford College for Women [Bedford College]. [1982]
1950. London: Birkbeck College. [1976]
1914. London: British Museum Library. [Copyright from 1942]
1912. London: College of Arms.

1910. London: George Harding Antiquarian Bookseller, Great Russell Street. [1995]

1943. London: Guildhall Library.

1934. London: Institute of Historical Research.

1953. London: Lambeth Palace Library.

1946. London Library, St James Square, London.

1971. London: Merton Borough Library, Merton Park. [1976]

1966. London: National Central Library, Store Street. *See* Boston Spa.

1910. London: Public Record Office Library [National Archives, Kew].

1955. London: Queen Mary College, Mile End Road. [1982]

1935. London: Royal Historical Society.

1910. London: Sion College Library, Victoria Embankkment. [1983]

1910. London: Society of Antiquaries, Burlington House, Piccadilly.

1924. London: Society of Genealogists.

1952. London: University College, Gower Street. [1980]

1934. London: University Library. [2006]

1956. London: Westminster Public Library, St Martin's Street. [1984]

1964. Loughborough College of Further Education [Loughborough Technical College], Library School. [1986]

1924. Louth: Antiquarian, Naturalist and Literary Society. [1937]

1991. Louth: Antiquarian, Naturalist and Literary Society, The Museum, Broadbank.

1923. Manchester: Chetham's Library. [1981]

1910. Manchester: Public Libraries. [2005]

1910. Manchester: The John Rylands Library. [Amalgamated with University Library 1973.]

1926. Manchester: University Library.

1957. Newark: Gilstrap Public Library. [1975]

1964. Newcastle University, Newcastle-upon-Tyne. [1998]

1984. Norfolk and Norwich Archaeological Society, Norwich.

1921. Northamptonshire Record Society, Lamport Hall [Delapré Abbey, Northampton; Wootton Hall Park, Northampton].

1963. Norwich: University of East Anglia, Earlham Hall [University Plain, Norwich].

1920. Nottingham: Central Public Library [Nottinghamshire County Library]. [1988]

1969. Nottingham University Department of Adult Education. [1998]

1925. Nottingham University Library.

1924. Oxford: Balliol College Library.

1910. Oxford: Bodleian Library. [Copyright from 1942]

1961. Oxford: History Faculty Library, Merton Street.

1955. Oxford: Lincoln College. [2004]

1925. Oxford: Magdalen College Library.

1937. Oxford: St John's College Library.

1929. Peterborough: Dean and Chapter Library.
2009. Peterborough Regional College, Park Crescent, Peterborough.
1925. Reading University Library.
1972. Reading University, Stenton Library. [1998]
1965. St Andrew's University Library, St Andrew's, Scotland.
1950. Scunthorpe Public Library. [1983]
1998. Scunthorpe: North Lincolnshire Council, Central Library, Carlton
    Street.
1917. Sheffield: City Library [Central Library, Surrey Street].
1933. Sheffield University Library.
1923. Sleaford Study Circle, c/o Miss M. Wood, Sleaford. [1974]
1948. Southampton University Library.
1928. Spalding Gentlemen's Society. [1994]
2002. Spalding Gentlemen's Society, The Museum, Broad Street.
2008. Spital Chantry Trust of St Edmund, Millgate, Newark.
1928. Stamford: Historical Association Branch. [1935]
1974. Stamford Public Library. [Transferred to Lincolnshire County
    Library, 1976]
1974. Swansea: University College of Wales.
2003. Swets Blackwell Ltd, Abingdon.
1970. Warwick University Library, Coventry.
1977. Willoughby Memorial Library, Corby Glen.
1966. York: Borthwick Institute of Historical Research, St Anthony's
    Hall. [2003]
1984. York Minster Library.
1962. York University Library [J. B. Morrell Library], Heslington, York.
1960. Yorkshire Archaeological Society, Leeds.

EUROPE
1968. Belgium: Ghent University Library. [1992]
1955. Belgium: Louvain University Library. [1981]
1966. Denmark: Royal Library, Copenhagen. [2002]
1930. Denmark: Stednavneudvalget [Institut for Navneforskning],
    Copenhagen.
1957. Germany: Auffarth Neumannsche Buchandlung, Frankfurt Main
    [Ursellis Buchhandlung]. [1975]
1925. Germany: Bavarian State Library, Munich. [1936]
1974. Germany: Bavarian State Library, Munich. [2001]
1983. Germany: Free University of Berlin. [1991]
1925. Germany: Prussian State Library, Berlin. [1942]
1923. Sweden: Lund University Library. [2005]
1923. Sweden: Uppsala University Library. [1998]

UNITED STATES OF AMERICA

1980. Arizona University Library, Tucson, Arizona. [2004]
1937. Baltimore: Peabody Institute [Enoch Pratt Library]. [1986]
1949. Biddle Law Library, University of Pennsylvania. [2000]
1937. Boston: Library of Boston Athenaeum. [1991]
1910. Boston: New England Historic Genealogical Society.
1937. Boston: Public Library. [2010]
1948. Brown University, Providence, Rhode Island. [1992]
1958. Cache Genealogical Library, Logan, Utah. [1972]
1940. California University Library, Berkeley, California. [1989]
1957. California University Research Library, Los Angeles, California. [2001]
1915. Chicago: Newberry Library.
1927. Chicago: University Libraries.
1969. Clemson University Library, Clemson, South Carolina. [1976]
1928. Cleveland: Public Library, Cleveland, Ohio. [1985]
1913. Cornell University Library, Ithaca, New York.
1978. Dallas Public Library, Dallas, Texas. [1993]
1937. Detroit Public Library. [2003]
1952. Duke University, Durham, North Carolina.
1984. Emory University, Robert Woodruff Library, Atlanta, Georgia.
1972. Fort Wayne and Allen County Public Library, Fort Wayne, Indiana. [1982]
1968. Georgia University Libraries, Athens, Georgia. [2004]
1930. Hamilton College Library, Clinton, New York.
1920. Harvard University Law School, Cambridge, Massachusetts.
1910. Harvard College Library, Cambridge, Massachusetts.
1925. Haverford College Library, Pennsylvania. [1995]
1973. Illinois University Library, Chicago Circle. [1988]
1948. Illinois University Library, Urbana.
1952. Indiana University, Bloomington, Indiana.
1949. Iowa State University Library, Iowa City.
1963. Kansas University Libraries, Lawrence, Kansas.
1937. Los Angeles Public Library, California.
1966. Michigan State University, East Lansing, Michigan.
1931. Michigan University Library, Ann Arbor.
1930. Minnesota University Library, Minneapolis. [1994]
1970. Missouri University Library, Columbia, Missouri. [1981]
1952. Mount Holyoke College, South Hadley, Massachusetts. [1997]
1966. Nashville Joint University Library [Vanderbilt University Library], Nashville, Tennessee.
1919. New York: Columbia University. [1996]
1927. New York: General Theological Seminary Library. [1976]
1910. New York Public Library.
1969. New York State University, Albany.

1966. New York State University, Buffalo. [1976]
1965. New York State University, Stony Brook, Long Island. [1993]
1944. New York University Library, University Heights, New York. [1973]
1969. North Carolina University, Greenboro, North Carolina. [1976]
1966. Northwestern University Library, Evanston, Illinois. [2000]
1992. Ohio State University Libraries, Columbus, Ohio.
1973. Oregon University Library, Eugene, Oregon. [1994]
1939. Philadelphia: Yarnall Library of Theology, St Clement's Church.
[University of Pennsylvania, Van Pelt Library, from 1974].
1946. Princeton University Library. [2000]
1966. Rochester University Library, Rochester, New York.
1961. Rutgers University Library, New Brunswick, New Jersey. [1990]
1937. St Louis Public Library, Olive Street, St Louis, Missouri. [1985]
1937. St Louis University, Pius XII Memorial Library, St Louis, Missouri.
1925. San Francisco Law Library. [1976]
1929. San Marino: Henry E. Huntington Library, San Marino, California.
1966. Seabury-Western Seminary [Garrett/Evangelical Seabury Western],
Evanston, Illinois.
1984. South Carolina University, Thomas Cooper Library, Columbia, South
Carolina. [1994]
1966. Stanford University, Stanford, California.
1966. Stanford University in England, Harlaxton Manor, Grantham. [1969]
1958. Texas University Library, Austin, Texas.
1910. Utah: The Genealogical Society of Utah, Salt Lake City. [1997]
1952. Virginia State Library, Richmond, Virginia. [1987]
1984. Virginia University, Alderman Library, Charlottesville, Virginia.
1966. Wake Forest College Library, Reynolda Station, Winston-Salem,
North Carolina. [2000]
2006. Wake Forest University, Z. Smith Reynolds Library, Winston-Salem,
North Carolina.
1910. Washington D.C.: Library of Congress. [2003]
1980. Washington University Library, Seattle.
1949. Washington University Law Library, St Louis, Missouri. [2000]
1918. Wisconsin State Historical Society, Madison. [1945]
1945. Wisconsin University Library, Madison. [1996]
1968. Wyoming University Library, Laramie, Wyoming. [1992]
1917. Yale University Library [Sterling Memorial Library], New Haven,
Connecticut.

CANADA
1974. Calgary University Library, Calgary.
1974. Lakehead University, Thunder Bay, Ontario. [1992]
1961. North American Genealogical Society, Calgary, Alberta. [1975]

1951. Queen's University, Douglas Library, Kingston, Ontario. [1992]

1946. Toronto University Library.

AUSTRALIA

1973. Adelaide University, Barr Smith Library.

1925. Melbourne: Victoria State Library.

1967. National Library of Australia, Canberra. [1995]

1979. Queensland University Library, St Lucia, Queensland. [1994]

1949. Sydney University Law School [Fisher Library, University of
     Sydney].

1962. Western Australia University, Reid Library, Nedlands, Western
     Australia.

NEW ZEALAND

1958. Alexander Turnbull Library [National Library of New Zealand],
     Wellington.

JAPAN

1956. Yushodo Company, 92 Omotemachi, Bunkyoku, Tokyo [Shiujuku-ku,
     Tokyo]. [1982]

APPENDIX TWO

PUBLICATIONS OF THE SOCIETY

1910 – 2010

PUBLICATIONS OF THE SOCIETY

1

LINCOLNSHIRE | CHURCH NOTES | MADE BY | GERVASE HOLLES | A.D. 1634 TO A.D. 1642 | AND EDITED FROM HARLEIAN MANU-SCRIPT 6829, IN THE BRITISH | MUSEUM.

Edited by R. E. G. Cole, M.A. Pp. xiii + 281. Printed by W. K. Morton & Sons Ltd., 290 High Street, Lincoln. Issued in 1911. For the year ending 30 September 1911.

Content
Frontispiece: Plate, facsimile of page 239 of Harleian Manuscript 6829 in the British Museum. Introduction (Lincoln, 29 September 1911), 9 pp. (with repro-duction of the signature of Gervase Holles from British Museum Additional Manuscript 6118). Pedigree of the Holles family, 1 foldout page. The text, 249 pp. Index of names and places, 22 pp. Index of coats of arms, 5 pp.

Description
Gervase Holles, M.A. & M.P., royalist Colonel of Foot, and above all 'a learned and judicious Antiquary,' to whom we are indebted for the following Notes on our Lincolnshire Churches as they were before the Great Rebellion, was born at Great Grimsby on 9 March 1606/7. This volume commences with a full account of Grimsby and the adjoining parishes of Little Cotes and Humberstone. Following this description there comes the *Chronicon de Allerdale post Conquest Anglia,* relating to Cumberland. Holles next gives a long series of documents illustrating the history of the ancient family of Clifton, of Clifton, Notts. The remainder of the volume records the monuments and coats of arms in some 200 of our Lincolnshire churches. He only diverges from the county to include Mansfield, Haughton and Tuxford in Nottinghamshire and Staveley in Derbyshire.
[Adapted from the Introduction to the Volume.]

2

LINCOLN | EPISCOPAL RECORDS | IN THE TIME OF | THOMAS COOPER, S.T.P. | BISHOP OF LINCOLN | A.D. 1571 TO A.D. 1584.

Edited by C. W. Foster, M.A., F.S.A., Vicar of Timberland and Canon of Lincoln. Pp. xxiv + 447. Printed by W. K. Morton & Sons Ltd., Saltergate, Lincoln. Issued in 1912. For the year ending 30 September 1911.

Content

Frontispiece: Plate, Buckden, the principal residence of the Bishops of Lincoln prior to 1838. From a drawing by B. Rudge. Contents, 3 pp. Introduction, 12 pp. Abbreviations, 2 pp. Additions and Corrections, 2 pp. Plate: Facsimile of Bishop Cooper's signature, 19 January 1581/2, from Clerical Subsidy Roll 40/835 in the Public Record Office, London. Bishop Thomas Cooper's *Act Book*, 101 pp. Bishop Thomas Cooper's *Register*, 54 pp. *Liber Cleri*, A.D. 1576, 83 pp. Plate, Seal of Bishop Cooper. Grants of Advowson, 16 pp. Presentation Deeds, 18 pp. Crown Presentations, 8 pp. Institution Bonds, 4 pp. Resignations, 17 pp. Register of Archbishop Parker at Lambeth, 3 pp. Additional Admissions to Benefices, 22 pp. Additional Ordinations, 2 pp. Appendix I: Statistics from the *Liber Cleri* 1576, 3 pp. Appendix II: Itinerary of Bishop Cooper, 3 pp. Appendix III: Bishop Cooper's Last Will and Testament, 4 pp. Appendix IV: Abstract of the Wills of Dr John Belley LL.D. and of Mrs Elizabeth Belley, 1 p. Appendix V: Suffragan Bishops in the Diocese of Lincoln in the Sixteenth Century, 4 pp. General Index, 81 pp. Index of Counties, 10 pp. Index of Subjects, 7 pp.

Description

This volume was part of an endeavour to calendar the episcopal records at Lincoln for the period 1545 to 1660. Unfortunately the act books of the bishops during the greater part of that time have been lost and the chronicle of events which they recorded has had to be reconstructed from other sources. A volume dealing with the years 1547 to 1570 had been intended to be the first of a series, but it was found impossible to collect the necessary materials. The sources from which this volume has been compiled are listed above. The original intention was to print no more that the bishop's *Act Book* and *Register*, with the *Libri Cleri* of 1576 and 1580, but it soon became clear that the Act Book was by no means complete, and other records were included with a view to supplement its deficiencies.
[Adapted from the Introduction to the Volume.]

3

ROTULI | HUGONIS DE WELLES, | EPISCOPI LINCOLNIENSIS, | A.D. MCCIX–MCCXXXV.| VOLUME I.

Edited by W. P. W. Phillimore, M.A., B.C.L. Pp. xxvii + 304. Printed by W. K. Morton & Sons, Saltergate, Lincoln. Issued in 1912. For the year ending 30 September 1912.

Content

Contents, 1 p. Introduction (124 Chancery Lane, Whitsuntide, 1909), 27 pp. Roll relating to all the archdeaconries previous to the tenth year of the episcopate, 130 pp. Roll relating to all the archdeaconries in the tenth year of the episcopate, 46 pp. Vicarages ordained in the archdeaconry of Oxford, 8 pp. Vicarages ordained in the archdeaconry of Bedford, 4 pp. Vicarages ordained in the archdeaconry of Huntingdon, 6 pp. Vicarages ordained in the archdeaconry of Buckingham, 4 pp. Vicarages ordained in the archdeaconry of Stow, 3 pp. Vicarages ordained in the archdeaconry of Northampton, 9 pp. Institutions in the archdeaconry of Stow, 27 pp. Matriculus of the archdeaconry of Leicester, 35 pp. Rotulus Taxationis of the archdeaconry of Leicester, 7 pp. Index to Volume I, 20 pp. Corrigenda for Volume I, 5 pp.

Description
The rolls of Bishop Hugh of Lincoln are perhaps the earliest known episcopal record. No other diocese is known to possess any earlier continuous series of Bishop's registers. Bishop Hugh was also called *Secundus* to distinguish him from his predecessor, Saint Hugh of Lincoln, who was Bishop of the diocese from 1186 to 1203. The text is printed is given in the original Latin, with a brief English summary at the beginning of each entry.
[Adapted from the Introduction to the Volume.]

4

SPECULUM | DIŒCESEOS LINCOLNIENSIS | SUB EPISCOPIS | GUL: WAKE ET EDM: GIBSON | A.D. 1705–1723 | PART I | ARCHDEACON-RIES OF LINCOLN AND STOW.

Edited by R. E. G. Cole, M.A., Canon of Lincoln. Pp. xxiv + 210. Printed by W. K. Morton & Sons, Saltergate, Lincoln. Issued in 1913. For the year ending 30 September 1912.

Content
Frontispiece: Plate, facsimile of page 15 of the Speculum. Abbreviations, 1 p. Introduction, 24 pp. Archdeaconry of Lincoln, 149 pp. Archdeaconry of Stow, 25 pp. Appendix I: List of Bishops Mentioned, 1 p. Appendix II: Bishop Gibson's Visitation Returns June 1718, 8 pp. Index, 24 pp.

Description
Dr William Wake was consecrated Bishop of Lincoln in 1705 and was succeeded by Dr Edmund Gibson in 1716. Bishop Wake's primary Visitation of his diocese took place in May and June 1706 and in preparation for it he addressed, in April 1706, a Letter of Advertisement to the Clergy of the Diocese. In the letter he requested details of each parish in seven questions. Subsequent visitations took place in 1709, 1712 and 1715. Bishop Gibson held his primary Visitation in 1718. His letter included twelve questions. The results of these enquiries were summarised in the Speculum under five headings. The source document is a manuscript book sometimes in English, but mostly in much abbreviated Latin. This material has been translated into English and laid out in a logical manner to enable the information contained therein to be easily accessible.
[Adapted from the Introduction to the Volume.]

5

LINCOLN WILLS | REGISTERED IN THE | DISTRICT PROBATE REGISTRY AT LINCOLN | VOLUME I | A.D. 1271 TO A.D. 1526.

Edited by C. W. Foster, M.A., F.S.A., Canon of Lincoln and Vicar of Timberland. Pp. xv + 264. Printed by J. W. Ruddock & Sons, High Street, Lincoln. Issued in 1914. For the year ending 30 September 1912.

Content
Contents, 1 p. Preface (Timberland, 17 September 1914), 3 pp. Abbreviations and Explanations, 1 p. Additions to the Indices, 1 p. Lincoln Wills, 188 pp. Index of Persons and Places, 44 pp. Index of Counties, 4 pp. Index of Subjects, 6 pp. Glossary, 20 pp. List of Authorities, 2 pp.

Description
This is the first of a series of volumes that the Society planned to issue containing abstracts of wills relating to the diocese and county of Lincoln. These ancient testamentary documents are of value because they throw much light upon the language, the religious customs and observances, and the manners and social life of our forefathers. Moreover, they are of very great service for genealogical purposes since, in the period prior to the institution of parish registers, they are often the only available source of information relating to families which did not hold land or use armorial bearings; and even when they relate to the same period as extant parish registers, they are no less important to the genealogist. Every will in the District Probate Registry from 1271 to 1526 has been included, with the exception of three wills which were found too late to be included.
[Adapted from the Preface to the Volume.]

6

ROTULI | HUGONIS DE WELLES, | EPISCOPI LINCOLNIENSIS, | A.D. MCCIX–MCCXXXV. | VOLUME II.

Edited by W. P. W. Phillimore, M.A., B.C.L. Pp. [viii] + 347. Printed by W. K. Morton & Sons, Saltergate, Lincoln. Issued in 1913. For the year ending 30 September 1913.

Content
Preface, 1 p. Contents, 1 p. Corrigenda and Addenda, 1 p. Institutions in the archdeaconry of Oxford, 47 pp. Institutions in the archdeaconry of Buckingham, 50 pp. Institutions in the archdeaconry of Northampton, 85 pp. Charter roll of the Archdeaconry of Northampton, 90 pp. Institutions in the archdeaconry of Leicester, 55 pp. Index to Volume II, 20 pp.

Description
See LRS Volume 3 (Rotuli Hugonis de Welles, Volume I).

7

VISITATIONS | OF | RELIGIOUS HOUSES | IN THE | DIOCESE OF LINCOLN | VOLUME I | INJUNCTIONS | AND OTHER | DOCUMENTS FROM THE REGISTERS | OF | RICHARD FLEMYNG AND WILLIAM GRAY | BISHOPS OF LINCOLN | A.D. 1420 TO A.D. 1436.

Edited by A. Hamilton Thompson, M.A., F.S.A. Pp. xxxi + [463]. Printed by W. K. Morton & Sons, Ltd., 27 High Street, Horncastle. Issued in 1914. For the year ending 30 September 1913.

Content
Preface (Gretton, Northants, July 1914), 1 p. Corrigenda, 1 p. Contents, 4 pp. Introduction, 23 pp. Visitations and Injunctions, 145 pp (Latin) and 145 pp (English). Appendix I: List of Houses of Monks, Canons and Nuns in the Diocese of Lincoln, 25 pp. Appendix II: The Dean and Chapter of Lincoln in 1432, 43 pp. Appendix III: Addenda and Corrigenda, 5 pp. Glossary, 32 pp. Index of Persons and Places, 46 pp. Index of Counties, 9 pp. Index of Subjects, 10 pp.

Description
This is the first of a three volume series dealing with the history of the diocese of Lincoln during the first half of the fifteenth century. Episcopal registers during this period are as a rule not rich in material. Bishop's clerks had the precedents which they wanted in earlier registers, and, while they still recorded such formal business of the see as was necessary for the purposes of future reference, there was no longer the same need to leave casual letters as epistolary models for their predecessors. This aspect of an episcopal register is often forgotten. Such a volume is not a journal or material for a biography; it is a collection of common forms and useful memoranda. This accounts for the omission from a register of much which would certainly have been included had the compilers done their work with a view to the researches of future historians. The volumes embrace every document of importance which deals with the affairs of religious houses in the registers of Bishops Flemyng and Gray. One or two specimens of formal documents have been printed, and at the end of the volume the full and valuable account of Gray's visitation of his cathedral church in 1432 has been added. The Latin text is printed in full, with an English translation on the facing page.
[Adapted from the Introduction to the Volume.]

8

THE | VISITATION | OF THE | COUNTY OF LINCOLN | MADE BY | SIR EDWARD BYSSHE, KNIGHT | CLARENCEUX KING OF ARMS | IN THE YEAR OF OUR LORD | 1666.

Edited by Everard Green, F.S.A., Somerset Herald-of-Arms, with an Introduction by W. Harry Rylands, F.S.A. Pp. xiv + 99. Printed by W. K. Morton & Sons, 27 High Street, Horncastle. Issued in 1917. For the year ending 30 September 1913.

Content
Contents, 1 p. Preface (Herald's College, London, 19 December 1916), 1 p. Introduction, 6 pp. Pedigrees, 79 pp. Disclaimers, 1 p. General Index, 17 pp.

Description
The Visitation of Lincolnshire was made in 1666 by Sir Edward Bysshe, Clarenceux King of Arms. This volume is based on a copy of the edition held in Herald's College Library. It records for each family, four generations in the direct line. For many there are also heraldic details of the families' coats of arms and crests.

9

ROTULI | HUGONIS DE WELLES, | EPISCOPI LINCOLNIENSIS, | A.D. MCCIX–MCCXXXV. | VOLUME III.

Edited by F. N. Davis, B.A., Rector of Crowell, Oxon. Pp. [viii] + 235. Printed by W. K. Morton & Sons, Saltergate, Lincoln. Issued in 1914. For the year ending 30 September 1914.

Content
Preface, 1 p. Contents, 1 p. Institutions in the archdeaconry of Bedford, 32 pp. Institutions in the archdeaconry of Huntingdon, 22 pp. Vicarages ordained in the archdeaconry of Lincoln, 37 pp. Pensions, etc., granted by Bishop Hugh to the Regular Clergy, 5 pp. Institutions in the archdeaconry of Lincoln, 122 pp. Index to Volume III, 17 pp.

Description
See LRS Volume 3 (*Rotuli Hugonis de Welles*, Volume I).

10

LINCOLN WILLS | REGISTERED IN THE | DISTRICT PROBATE REGISTRY AT LINCOLN | VOLUME II | A.D. 1505 TO MAY, 1530.

Edited by C. W. Foster, M.A., F.S.A., Canon of Lincoln and Vicar of Timberland. Pp. xxviii + 300. Printed by W. K. Morton & Sons, 27 High Street, Horncastle. Issued in 1918. For the year ending 30 September 1914.

Content
Preface (Timberland, 1 August 1918), 1 p. Contents, 1 p. Introduction, 17 pp. Abbreviations and Explanations, 1 p. Judges and Officials of the Ecclesiastical Courts before whom the Wills were Proved, 1 p. Additions and Corrections, Errata in Volume I, 1 p. Lincoln Wills, 214 pp. Appendix: The Testament of Henry de Colebi of Lincoln, 4 pp. Index of Persons and Places, 56 pp. Index of Counties, 5 pp. Index of Subjects, 12 pp. Glossary, 8 pp.

Description
In 1914 the Society issued Volume I of Lincoln Wills (LRS Vol. 5). This volume continues the same series of wills from the beginning of 1527 (Old Style), where Volume I stopped. A few earlier wills found since Volume I was issued are included at the beginning and a few others while this volume was in the press have been added at the end. The Introduction includes a detailed account of testamentary practice.
[Adapted from the Introduction to the Volume.]

11

ROTULI | ROBERTI GROSSETESTE | EPISCOPI LINCOLNIENSIS | A.D. MCCXXXV–MCCLIII | NECNON | ROTULUS | HENRICI DE LEXINGTON | EPISCOPI LINCOLNIENSIS | A.D. MCCLIV-MCCLIX.

Edited by F. N. Davis, B.A., B.Litt., Rector of Crowell and Chaplain of Thame Park, Oxfordshire. Pp. xii + 557. Printed by W. K. Morton & Sons Ltd, 27 High Street, Horncastle. Issued in 1914. For the year ending 30 September 1915.

Content
Contents, 1 p. Corrigenda, 1 p. Introduction (Crowell Rectory, June 1913), 9 pp. Itinerary of Robert Grosseteste, 3 pp. Institutions by Robert Grosseteste: Archdeaconry of Lincoln, 132 pp. Archdeaconry of Stow, 25 pp. Archdeaconry of Northampton, 92 pp. Archdeaconry of Huntingdon, 51 pp. Archdeaconry of Bedford, 39 pp. Archdeaconry of Buckingham, 45 pp. Archdeaconry of Leicester, 58 pp. Archdeaconry of Oxford, 66 pp. Institutions by Henry de Lexington in the Archdeaconry of Huntingdon, 5 pp. Privileges of the Cathedral Church of Lincoln, 5 pp. Index, 39 pp.

Description

The rolls relate almost entirely to the routine work which went on in the diocese. They are primarily records of institutions to benefices, and in this lies their chief interest, but incidentally other useful and important information can be gleaned. In the record of an institution the parish is named, its patron, and the person instituted together with the official by whom a previous "inquisition" had been made. At this time the diocese extended from the Thames to the Humber, and it comprised eight counties – a sixth of the kingdom. Today five Bishops rule where the early Bishops of Lincoln were supreme. The archdeaconries of Leicester and Northampton (this latter including also the county of Rutland) are now the diocese of Peterborough, which on its foundation in 1541 received Northampton, Leicester being transferred to it in 1837. Oxford became a bishop's see in 1543, at first for Oxfordshire only, Buckinghamshire and Berkshire were added in 1837; while Bedfordshire and Huntingdonshire were joined to Ely also in 1837. That part of Hertfordshire which appears in Grossteste's Roll as in the archdeaconry of Huntingdon is part of the modern diocese of St Albans. The Latin text is given in full, with a brief English summary at the beginning of each entry.
[Adapted from the Introduction to the Volume.]

12

CHAPTER ACTS | OF THE | CATHEDRAL CHURCH | OF | ST MARY OF LINCOLN | A.D. 1520–1536.

Edited by R. E. G. Cole, M.A., Canon of Lincoln. Pp. xxii + 238. Printed by W. K. Morton & Sons Ltd, 27 High Street, Horncastle. Issued in 1915. For the year ending 30 September 1915.

Content

Contents, 1 p. Introduction, 16 pp. Chapter Acts, 200 pp. Appendix I: Dignitaries & Prebendaries of Lincoln Cathedral, A.D. 1520–1536, 6 pp. Appendix II: Subsidy of 1526, 5 pp. Appendix III: Signatures to Royal Supremacy, 1534, 3 pp. Addenda et Corrigenda, 1 p. General Index, 22 pp.

Description

This is the first of three volumes of the Act Books containing the minutes of the proceedings of the Dean and Chapter of Lincoln. Volume I contains the entries from October 1520 to the end of the Chapter year in September 1536. Originally the 464 folios were bound in one volume but they were rebound in two volumes in 1878. Ten folios are missing from the beginning of Volume 1 which now commences with the probate of a will on folio 11. At this time the diocese stretched from Oxford to the Humber and there is much it of interest to local historians, accessible through the comprehensive index. The acts, which are mostly in Latin, have been calendared in English, on the model of the publications of the Public Record Office; documents in English such as wills and leases have been transcribcd verbatim.
[Adapted from the Introduction to the Volume.]

13

CHAPTER ACTS | OF THE | CATHEDRAL CHURCH | OF | ST MARY OF LINCOLN | A.D. 1536–1547.

Edited by R. E. G. Cole, M.A., Canon of Lincoln. Pp. xxv + 223. Printed by W. K. Morton & Sons, 27 High Street, Horncastle. Issued in 1917. For the year ending 30 September 1915.

Content
Contents, 1 p. Erratum, 1 p. Introduction, 19 pp. Chapter Acts, 153 pp. Appendix I: Notes on the Feasts & Services according to the Use of Lincoln, 5 pp. Appendix II: Dignitaries & Prebendaries of Lincoln Cathedral, A.D. 1536–1547, 6 pp. Appendix III: Revenues of the Dean & Chapter of Lincoln, from the *Valor Ecclesiasticus*, 27 Henry VIII [3 September 1535], 34 pp. General Index, 23 pp.

Description
This volume is a continuation of LRS Volume 12 and contains folios 150–277 of Act Book, comprising the minutes of the Chapter from 18 September 1536 to 18 September 1547. This period covers the later years and death of Henry VIII (28 January 1547) and the confiscation of the Cathedral treasures by the King's commissioners, although there is scant coverage in the Chapter Acts. More is recorded of the further spoliation in 1540 when Cromwell ordered the Cathedral Chapter to transfer the gold, silver and jewels from the shrine of St. Hugh to the Tower of London.
[Adapted from the Introduction to the Volume.]

14

VISITATIONS | OF | RELIGIOUS HOUSES | IN THE | DIOCESE OF LINCOLN | VOLUME II | RECORDS OF VISITATIONS | HELD BY | WILLIAM ALNWICK | BISHOP OF LINCOLN | A.D. 1436 TO A.D. 1449 | PART I.

Edited by A. Hamilton Thompson, M.A., F.S.A. Pp. lxix + [436]. Printed by W. K. Morton & Sons, 27 High Street, Horncastle. Issued in 1918. For the year ending 30 September 1916.

Content
Preface (Gretton, Northants, 8 July 1917), 2 pp. Contents, 2 pp. Introduction, 61 pp. Bishop Alnwick's Visitations: Ankerwycke Priory to Littlemore Priory, 218 pp in Latin, 218 pp in English.

Description
The manuscript of Bishop Alnwick's Visitation Book consisted of seventeen unbound folio quires of paper, containing 135 leaves. Kept with other diocesan

records in the Alnwick Tower at the Old Palace in Lincoln, they have suffered from damp and decay. The introduction gives a detailed account of the manuscript, an outline of Alnwick's career and an English translation of his will. An itinerary of his activities as Bishop of Lincoln is constructed from the evidence of his episcopal register and the Visitation manuscript. The relationship between the documents in the manuscript and visitation procedure is examined, and the effect of the visitations on the life of the religious houses is considered. The Latin text is printed in full, with an English translation on the facing page. See also LRS Volume 7 (*Visitations of Religious Houses*, Vol. I).

[Adapted from the Introduction to the Volume.]

15

CHAPTER ACTS | OF THE | CATHEDRAL CHURCH | OF | ST MARY OF LINCOLN | A.D. 1547–1559.

Edited by R. E. G. Cole, M.A., Canon of Lincoln. Pp. xxxv + 206. Printed by W. K. Morton & Sons, 27 High Street, Horncastle. Issued in 1920. For the year ending 30 September 1917.

Content
Erratum, 1 p. Contents, 1 p. Preface (Timberland Vicarage, 17 August 1920), 1 p. Introduction, 26 pp. Plate: Sketch by Samuel H. Grimm, dated 1786, showing 'a lot of Persons crawling on a Ladder from a gallery in Great Tom's Tower in Lincoln Minster on the West to an opening in the South side of [the] Tower, which could no otherwise be entered. It has since been discovered to belong to what was in times past the common Prison, 'vocat le Wynde,' belonging to the dean and chapter's jurisdiction in the Close.' Note on Le Wynde in Lincoln Cathedral, 3 pp. Chapter Acts, 170 pp. Addendum, 1 p. Appendix I: Dignitaries & Prebendaries of Lincoln Cathedral, A.D. 1547–1559, 6 pp. Appendix II: Displacements (mostly Deprivations for Marriage) in the Dignities and Prebends, and in the Patronage of Lincoln Cathedral Chapter, as shown by the Chapter Acts, 1 Mary (6 July 1553) to 1 Elizabeth (17 November 1559), 8 pp. General Index, 20 pp.

Description
This is the third and last volume of the great minute book of the Chapter Acts of Lincoln Cathedral which from its bulk and weight had gained itself the name of the *Liber Crassus*. It contains folios 277–464d, covering the period from 19 September 1547 to 19 September 1559. As in the previous two volumes there is a long and informative introduction which sets the historical scene both nationally and locally.

[Adapted from the Introduction to the Volume.]

16

CALENDARS | OF | ADMINISTRATIONS | IN THE CONSISTORY COURT OF LINCOLN | A.D. 1540–1659.

Edited by C. W. Foster, M.A., F.S.A., Canon of Lincoln and Vicar of Timberland. Pp. xi + 410. Printed by W. K. Morton & Sons, 27 High Street, Horncastle. Issued in 1921. For the year ending 30 September 1918.

Content
Contents, 1 p. Introduction (Timberland, 23 April 1921), 2 pp. Explanation of the Calendars, 1 p. Additions and Corrections, 1 p. Administrations Granted in the Consistory Court of Lincoln A.D. 1540–1600, 159 pp. Administrations Granted in the Consistory Court of Lincoln A.D. 1601–1659, 218 pp. Index of Places I: In the County of Lincoln, 26 pp. Index of Places II: Other Counties, 5 pp.

Description
This volume, containing more than 40,000 references, is an alphabetical index to the individuals named in Grants of Administration from the Consistory Court in Lincoln from 1540 to 1659. The term Consistory Court includes the Consistory Court of the Bishop of Lincoln, and the Court of the Archdeacon of Lincoln within his Archdeaconry. A considerable number of administration documents which properly belong to other courts are now incorporated in the records of the Consistory Court. The documents indexed in this volume are the administration bonds with their accompanying inventories, and the probate and administration act-books in so far as they relate to the business of granting administrations. These documents had, until the publication of this volume, been practically inaccessible to students.
[Adapted from the Introduction to the Volume.]

17

FINAL CONCORDS | OF THE | COUNTY OF LINCOLN | FROM THE FEET OF FINES PRESERVED IN | THE PUBLIC RECORD OFFICE | A.D. 1244–1272 | WITH ADDITIONS FROM VARIOUS SOURCES | A.D. 1176–1250. | VOLUME II.

Edited by C. W. Foster, M.A., F.S.A., Canon of Lincoln and Vicar of Timberland. Pp. lxxxi + 448. Printed by W. K. Morton & Sons, 27 High Street, Horncastle. Issued in 1920. For the year ending 30 September 1919.

Content
Frontispiece: The two parts of a Chirograph with the Foot of Fine. Contents, 4 pp. Preface (Timberland, 1 May 1920), 1 p. Abbreviations, 2 pp. Introduction, 63 pp. Formulary, 10 pp. Final Concords, 294 pp. Appendix I: Additions to Volume I, 12 pp. Appendix II: Additions to Volumes I and II from sources outside

the Public Record Office, 9 pp. Appendix III: Table shewing the present references to the Concords contained in *Final Concords* Volume I, 4 pp. Appendix IV: Errata in *Final Concords* Volume I, 5 pp. Appendix V: Additional Concords, 9 pp. Appendix VI: Errata in Pipe Roll Society's Volumes, 1 p. Appendix VII: [Library of the Dean and Chapter of Peterborough: from the Goxhill Leiger, ff. 5d and 6, No 25], 2 pp. Corrections and Additions, 2 pp. Index of Persons and Places, 84 p. Index of Counties, 5 pp. Index of Subjects, 14 pp.

Description
In 1896 Revd W. O. Massingberd, rector of South Ormsby, edited a volume of *Abstracts of Final Concords* relating to the county of Lincoln and covering the period from 1193 to 1244. This volume is a continuation of that work to the end of Henry III's reign (1272), with the addition of appendixes containing some earlier concords from various sources. The index includes references to places mentioned in Volume 1. Most of the concords are cast in a common mould and it has been found possible to omit, without loss, a good deal of the common form. In some cases unusual particulars are recorded and a full translation is given. The property that was dealt with in final concords was land, or some right or interest of a transferable nature connected with land. Final concords help to identify places mentioned in other records and furnish information about parishes, vills, hamlets and manors which have become depopulated, or of which few traces remain. The Introduction includes a detailed account of the procedure involved, and a pioneering survey of 'Lost vills and other Forgotten Places'.
[Adapted from the Introduction to the Volume.]

18

TRANSCRIPTS | OF | CHARTERS | RELATING TO THE GILBERTINE HOUSES | OF | SIXLE, ORMSBY, CATLEY, BULLINGTON, | AND ALVINGHAM | EDITED, WITH A TRANSLATION, FROM THE | KING'S REMEMBRANCER'S MEMORANDA ROLLS | NOS 183, 185, AND 187.

Edited by F. M. Stenton, M.A., Professor of Modern History, University College, Reading. Pp. xxxvi + [279]. Printed by W. K. Morton & Sons, 27 High Street, Horncastle. Issued in 1922. For the year ending 30 September 1920.

Content
Contents, 1 p. Preface (University College, Reading, 2 May 1922), 1 p. Errata, 1 p. Introduction, 28 pp. Sixle Priory Series, 38 pp in Latin and 38 pp in English. Ormsby Priory Series, 33 pp in Latin and 33 pp in English. Catley Priory Series, 19 pp in Latin and 19 pp in English. Bullington Priory Series, 11 pp in Latin and 11 pp in English. Alvingham Priory Series, 12 pp in Latin and 12 pp in English. Index I: Persons and Places, 45 pp. Index II: Counties and Countries, 3 pp. Index III: Subjects, 5 pp.

Description

Increasing expenses and a falling revenue compelled Henry IV, eight times in his short reign, to obtain extraordinary grants of money from Parliament and Convocation. The charters of which copies are printed in this book were shown to the barons of the Exchequer by the attorney of five Lincolnshire monasteries of the Gilbertine order, the priories of Catley, Ormsby, Alvingham, Sixle and Bullington, which claimed that their possessions were exempt from such taxation. The exchequer allowed the claim. The charters which had been submitted as evidence were enrolled upon the Memoranda Roll of the King's Remembrancer with a record of the circumstances which had led to their production. The full Latin text of the charters is printed, with an English translation on the facing page.

[Adapted from the Introduction to the Volume.]

19

THE | LINCOLNSHIRE DOMESDAY | AND THE | LINDSEY SURVEY.

Translated and edited by C. W. Foster, M.A., F.S.A., Canon of Lincoln and Vicar of Timberland, and Thomas Longley, M.A., Canon of Lincoln and Rector of Conisholme, with an Introduction by F. M. Stenton, M.A., Professor of Modern History, University College, Reading, and Appendixes of Extinct Villages by C. W. Foster, M.A., F.S.A. Pp. xc + 315. Printed by W. K. Morton & Sons, Horncastle. Issued in 1924. For the year ending 30 September 1921.

Content

Frontispiece: Two-colour reproduction in black and red of Domesday Book (folio 344, part of column I), containing the first seven entries of the Bishop of Lincoln's Land. Preface (12 April 1924), 3 pp. Contents, 2 pp. Abbreviations and Explanations, 3 pp. Introduction, 38 pp. Appendix I: Extinct Villages and Other Forgotten Places, 25 pp. Appendix II: Boroughs, Wapentakes, Villages, and other Places, 12 pp. Appendix III: Additional Extinct Villages and other Forgotten Places, 2 pp. Domesday Book, 204 pp. Disputes, 31 pp. The Lindsey Survey, 24 pp. Index of Persons and Places, 44 pp. Index of Counties and Countries, 3 pp. Index of Subjects, 7 pp. Two folded maps of Lincolnshire loose in rear pocket.

Description

This is the oldest volume still in print and one of the easiest of the many editions of Domesday to use. Appendix II contains a comprehensive list of medieval place names including those that do not appear in Domesday. The English text includes the modern spelling of the place-names and other insertions to make the entries more easily understood. There are explanatory footnotes on most pages. For the sections relating to the City of Lincoln, the Boroughs of Stamford and Torksey, and the Disputes, the original Latin text is given, with a translation on the facing page.

Reprints
(1) 1976 facsimile case bound reprint, reproduced from the original edition by G. W. Belton, Gainsborough.

(2) 2005 paperback edition, published by Boydell Press for the Lincoln Record Society and printed by Antony Rowe Ltd, Eastbourne.

20

ROTULI | RICARDI GRAVESEND | EPISCOPI LINCOLNIENSIS | A.D. MCCLVIII–MCCLXXIX.

Edited by F. N. Davis, B.A., B.Litt., F.S.A., Rector of Rowner, with additions by C. W. Foster, M.A., F.S.A., Canon of Lincoln and Vicar of Timberland, and A. Hamilton Thompson, M.A., D.Litt., F.S.A., Professor of Medieval History in the University of Leeds, and an Introduction by A. Hamilton Thompson. Pp. xliv + 405. Printed by W. K. Morton & Sons, Horncastle. Issued in 1925. For the year ending 30 September 1922.

Content
Preface (1 December 1925), 1 p. Contents, 1 p. Abbreviations and Errata, 1 p. Introduction, 40 pp. Institutions: Archdeaconry of Lincoln, 87 pp. Archdeaconry of Stow, 10 pp. Archdeaconry of Northampton, 40 pp. Archdeaconry of Leicester, 29 pp. Archdeaconry of Huntingdon, 23 pp. Archdeaconry of Bedford, 23 pp. Archdeaconry of Oxford, 23 pp. Archdeaconry of Buckingham, 28 pp. Addenda and Corrigenda, 83 pp. Appendix I: Additional Roll for the Archdeaconry of Stow, 7 pp. Appendix II: Itinerary, 6 pp. Index: 47 pp.

Description
This volume continues the publication of the records of the thirteenth-century bishops of Lincoln. The Introduction sketches the career of Bishop Gravesend and his activities as diocesan bishop, including his relations with religious houses and with Lincoln Cathedral, are examined. The rolls themselves are calendared in English, while the Latin text of more important documents is transcribed in full. The reason for the extensive section of Addenda and Corrigenda is noted in Chapter 3 above.

21

VISITATIONS | OF | RELIGIOUS HOUSES | IN THE | DIOCESE OF LINCOLN | VOLUME III | RECORDS OF VISITATIONS | HELD BY | WILLIAM ALNWICK | BISHOP OF LINCOLN | A.D. 1436 TO A.D. 1449 | PART II.

Edited by A. Hamilton Thompson, M.A., D.Litt., F.B.A., F.S.A., Professor of History in the University of Leeds. Pp. viii + [462]. Printed by J. W. Ruddock & Sons, 287 High Street, Lincoln. Issued in 1929. For the year ending 30 September 1923.

Content
Preface (Leeds, 8 October 1928), 1 p. Contents, 2 pp. Bishop Alnwick's Visitations: Markby Priory to Wymondley Priory, 179 pp. in Latin, 179 pp. in English. Appendix I: Supplementary Documents, 6 pp. Appendix II: Records of Alnwick's Episcopate at Norwich, 14 pp. Appendix III: The Official Staff at Alnwick's Visitations, 3 pp. Appendix IV: Addenda and Corrigenda, 6 pp. Index of Persons and Places, 49 pp. Index of Counties, 9 pp. Index of Subjects, 15 pp.

Description
See LRS Volume 14 (*Visitations of Religious Houses*, Vol. II).

22

THE EARLIEST | LINCOLNSHIRE ASSIZE ROLLS | A.D. 1202–1209.

Edited by Doris M. Stenton, Lecturer in History in the University of Reading. Pp. lxxxii + 357. [Printed by The Hereford Times Ltd, Hereford.] Issued in 1926. For the year ending 30 September 1924.

Content
Preface (The University, Reading, August 1926), 2 pp. Contents, 2 pp. Rules and Abbreviations, 1 p. Errata, 1 p. Introduction, 63 pp. Appendix: The Family of Crevequer of Lincolnshire, 3 pp. Assize Roll 478: Pleas and Assizes at Lincoln, Trinity 1202, 92 pp. Assize Roll 479: Pleas of the Crown at Lincoln, Trinity 1202, 102 pp. Assize Roll 613: Pleas and Assizes at Northampton, September 1202: 18 pp. Assize Roll 1: Pleas at Bedford, October 1202, 3 pp. Curia Regis Roll 28: Pleas at Westminster, Michaelmas 1202, 1 p. Curia Regis Roll 27: Pleas at Westminster, Michaelmas 1202, 4 pp. Curia Regis Roll 29: Pleas at Westminster, Hillary 1202–3, 6 pp. Curia Regis Roll 26: Pleas at Westminster, Easter 1203, 8 pp. Assize Roll 480: Assizes at Lincoln, August 1206, 43 pp. Assize Roll 817: Pleas at Northampton, Summer 1203, 1 p. Assize Roll 799: Pleas at Lichfield, Autumn 1203, 1 p. Assize Roll 558: Pleas at Norwich, 1208–9, 4 pp. Index of Persons and Places, 55 pp. Index of Subjects, 17 pp.

Description
In 1916 when it was decided to publish this volume the intention had been to print it in Latin with an English translation. The editor realised that the translation would not be a great deal more intelligible that the original to those not versed in medieval law and Latin. It was decided to print the rolls in Latin transcribed according to a set of rules and add English explanatory notes to the cases where any especial difficulty arose, and to print an introduction explaining as far

as possible the type of case which is dealt with, and the various stages of a suit in its passage through the Court. The editor notes that the rising cost of printing was a contributory factor in reducing the size of the volume.
[Adapted from the Preface to the Volume.]

23

THE | STATE OF THE CHURCH | IN THE | REIGNS OF ELIZABETH AND JAMES I | AS ILLUSTRATED BY DOCUMENTS | RELATING TO | THE DIOCESE OF LINCOLN | VOLUME I.

Edited by C. W. Foster, M.A., F.S.A., Canon of Lincoln and Vicar of Timberland. Pp. cxlviii + 562. Printed by W. K. Morton & Sons, Horncastle. Issued in 1926. For the years ending 30 September 1925 and 30 September 1926.

Content
Contents, 4 pp. Preface (Timberland, 20 August 1926), 1 p. Abbreviations, 4 pp. Addenda and Corrigenda, 3 pp. Introduction, 84 pp. List No I: The Names of 'The Better Sort' of Ministers, who were required to contribute for the provision of Light Horse for Ireland, A.D. 1601–2, 5 pp. List No II: Nonconforming Ministers, 31 pp. Index of Persons and Places in the Introduction, 16 pp. Clerical Subsidy Rolls, 32 pp. Liber Cleri, A.D. 1576, 14 pp. Subscriptions of the Clergy in Buckinghamshire to the Three Articles, A.D. 1584, 5 pp. Liber Cleri, A.D. 1584: The State of the whole of the Clergy of the Archdeaconry of Huntingdon, 9 pp. Liber Cleri, A.D. 1585, 82 pp. Subsidy of Armour, A.D. 1590, 24 pp. Liber Cleri, A.D. 1595: Buckingham, 1 p. Liber Cleri, A.D. 1597–1600: Bedford and Buckingham, 1 p. Elections of Proctors for Convocation, A.D. 1597, 1601, 1603–4, 48 pp. The State of the Churches, A.D. 1602, 18 pp. Double Benefices, A.D. 1602–3, 7 pp. The Brown Book, 8 pp. Liber Cleri, A.D. 1603, 76 pp. Liber Cleri, A.D. 1598: Stow, 7 pp. Liber Archidiaconatus Stowe, A.D. 1603, 17 pp. Valuatio Beneficiorum, A.D. 1603–4, 8 pp. Nonconforming Ministers, A.D. 1604–1606, 9 pp. Clerical Subsidy Roll, A.D. 1583, 2 pp. Liber Cleri, A.D. 1594, 21 pp. Liber Cleri, A.D. 1604: Lincoln, 18 pp. Liber Cleri, A.D. 1607, 17 pp. Liber Cleri of the Cathedral Church, A.D. 1585, 1588, 1591, 1599–1600, 8 pp. Statistics, 23 pp. Appendix I: Liber Cleri, A.D. 1585, 4 pp. Appendix II: A Brief of Grievances, A.D. 1606, 2 pp. Index of Persons and Places in the Text, 85 pp. Index of Subjects to the Introduction and Text, 6 pp.

Description
The documents printed in this volume help to compensate for the loss of the registers of the bishops of Lincoln for the period 1585–98. They also illustrate the state of the Church in the days of Queen Elizabeth and James I. The entries in these documents relate to a vast and unwieldy diocese, comprising the counties of Lincoln, Leicester, Bedford, Buckingham, Huntingdon, & part of Hertford. At this time the bishop's principal place of residence was the manor of Buckden in Huntingdonshire. The material covers the period from 1571 to 1607, spanning the

episcopates of Bishops Cooper (1571–1584), Wickham (1584–1595) and Chaderton (1595–1608). The Introduction sets out the background to the documents, printing extracts from other material, including visitation books, with particular reference to cases of nonconformity.
[Adapted from the Introduction.]

24

LINCOLN WILLS | REGISTERED IN THE | DISTRICT PROBATE REGISTRY AT LINCOLN | VOLUME III | A.D. 1530 TO 1532.

Edited by C. W. Foster, Canon of Lincoln and Vicar of Timberland. Pp. [viii] + 301. Printed by J. W. Ruddock & Sons, Lincoln. Issued in 1930. For the year ending 30 September 1927.

Content
Preface (Timberland, 3 June 1930), 1 p. Contents, 1 p. Abbreviations and Explanations, 1 p. Lincoln Wills, 235 pp. Index of Persons and Places, 57 pp. Index of Places outside Lincolnshire, 2 pp. Index of Subjects, 5 pp.

Description
This volume continues the series of wills published in Volumes 5 & 10. A few wills which escaped notice when Volume II was printed have also been included.

25

MINUTES OF PROCEEDINGS | IN | QUARTER SESSIONS | HELD FOR | THE PARTS OF KESTEVEN | IN THE | COUNTY OF LINCOLN | 1674–1695 | VOLUME I.

Edited by S. A. Peyton. Pp. cxliv + 159. Printed by J. W. Ruddock & Sons, Lincoln. Issued in 1931. For the year ending 30 September 1928.

Content
Preface (University Library, Reading, 27 October 1931), 2 pp. Contents, 2 pp. Abbreviations and Explanations, 6 pp. Introduction, 118 pp. Appendix A: The Population of Parishes in Kesteven, 8 pp. Appendix B: Justices of the Peace in Kesteven, 6 pp. Proceedings in Quarter Sessions, Book I: Michaelmas 1674 to Midsummer 1683, 159 pp.

Description
In addition to the text of the proceedings the strength of this volume is in its long introduction. This is a text on county and parish law in the seventeenth century. The Introduction, comprising 64 sections, outlines the duties of the Sheriff, Coroner and Justices of the Peace as well as churchwardens, overseers and other

parish officers. The operation of the quarter sessions is described. There are entries concerning the maintenance of roads and bridges and poor relief. The Tudor poor laws are described in some detail and there are sections on recusancy and nonconformity. The text, mainly in Latin and partly in English, is printed in full with the exception of the dating formula, and in repeated cases, where an English summary is given.

26

MINUTES OF PROCEEDINGS | IN | QUARTER SESSIONS | HELD FOR | THE PARTS OF KESTEVEN | IN THE | COUNTY OF LINCOLN | 1674–1695 | VOLUME II.

Edited by S. A. Peyton. Pp. 386. Printed by J. W. Ruddock & Sons, Lincoln. Issued in 1931. For the year ending 30 September 1929.

Content
Proceedings in Quarter Sessions, Book II: Michaelmas 1683 to Midsummer 1686, 124 pp. Book III: Michaelmas 1686 to Michaelmas 1695, 212 pp. Index Personarum, 35 pp. Index Locorum, 9 pp. Index Locorum in Comitatibus Diversis, 1 p. Index Rerum, 4 pp.

Description
See LRS Volume 25.

27

THE | REGISTRUM ANTIQUISSIMUM | OF THE | CATHEDRAL CHURCH OF LINCOLN | VOLUME I.

Edited by C. W. Foster, Canon of Lincoln and Prebendary of Leicester St Margaret. Pp. lxxi + 351. Printed by The Hereford Times Limited, Hereford. Issued in 1931. For the year ending 30 September 1930.

Content
Frontispiece: Registrum Antiquissimum, part of Charter No 3, 1 foldout plate. Inscription from the Martilogium of John de Schalby: CATHEDRALIS ECCLESIE LINCOLNIENSIS FIDELIBVS VNIVERSIS IOHANNES DE SCHALBY CANONICVS EIVSDEM ECCLESIE VITAM BONAM EXITVMQUE FELICEM, 1 p. Preface (Timberland, 3 June 1931), 3 pp. Contents, 3 pp. List of illustrations, 1 p. There are 34 facsimiles of the most important original charters and 8 other illustrations. Abbreviations and Notes, 4 pp. Addendum, 1 p. Introduction, 36 pp. Table of Contents of the Registrum Antiquissimum, 5 pp. Analysis of the Quires of the Registrum Antiquissimum, 2 pp. Charters of Inspeximus, 7 pp. Lists of Charters, 9 pp. Documents, I: Royal, 186 pp. II: Papal, 64 pp. III:

Episcopal, 17 pp. Addendum, 1 p. Appendix I: Episcopal Residences at Lincoln, 10 pp. Appendix II: Thorngate and the Family of Condet, 19 pp. Index of Persons and Places, 42 pp. Index of Counties and Countries, 5 pp. Index of Subjects, 7 pp.

Description
The Registrum Antiquissimum is the earliest complete cartulary of Lincoln Cathedral. It was written mainly in the third decade of the thirteenth century. It was prepared from the original texts, many of which have not survived. Canon Foster noted that its writer 'copied with literal accuracy. As a consequence his texts may be relied upon.' The period originally proposed to be covered extended from the year 1061, the date of the only pre-Conquest document to the death of Bishop Hugh of Wells in 1235. However it was found convenient, and indeed necessary, to print many documents which are later in date. The Latin text of the charters is printed in full, headed in most cases by a short English summary.

The charters illustrate the history of an English secular cathedral church in respect of its organisation and personnel, its endowments and its franchises. The Introduction notes that the texts of 7,826 charters have survived of which 4,200 are the original documents. There are 1,073 charters in the Registrum Antiquissimum. Volume I contains the texts of 308 documents. The documents in the Registrum Antiquissimum include charters of the possessions not only of the common of the canons, and of the prebends, but also of the see of Lincoln. These possessions lay dispersed throughout the diocese of Lincoln which, as constituted by William the Conqueror, stretched, until the middle of the sixteenth century, from the Humber to the Thames. Outside the diocese, the charters relate to land in London and in the counties of Berkshire, Derbyshire, Hampshire, Kent, Nottinghamshire, Surrey, and Yorkshire. But it is for the history of the Northern Danelaw that the Lincoln charters are of first-rate importance.
[Adapted from the Introduction to the Volume.]

Reprint
2008 paperback edition, published by Boydell Press for the Lincoln Record Society and printed by 4edge Ltd, Hockley, Essex.

28

THE | REGISTRUM ANTIQUISSIMUM | OF THE | CATHEDRAL CHURCH OF LINCOLN | VOLUME II.

Edited by C. W. Foster, M.A., Hon. D.Litt., F.S.A., Canon of Lincoln and Prebendary of Leicester St Margaret. Pp. xlviii + 403. Printed by The Hereford Times Limited, Hereford. Issued in 1933. For the year ending 30 September 1931.

Content
Frontispiece: Seal of Bishop Hugh of Wells (1209–1235); Seal of the Chapter of

Lincoln (12th and 13th centuries), 1 plate. Dedication to Frank Merry Stenton, 1 p. Preface (Timberland, 28 November 1933), 3 pp. Contents, 15 pp. List of Illustrations, 2 pp. There are facsimiles of 31 documents. Abbreviations and Notes, 4 pp. Manuscripts additional to those described in the Introduction to Volume I, 1 p. List of Charters, 11 pp. Corrections and Additions for Volume I, 3 pp. Corrections and Additions for Volume II, 1 p. Documents: Magnates, 50 pp. Bishop Hugh II, 37 pp. Bishop Robert Grosseteste, 9 pp. Bishop Henry Lexington, 25 pp. Bishop Richard Gravesend, 3 pp. Indulgences, 17 pp. Registrum Choristarum II, 17 pp. Registrum Choristarum I, 39 pp. Lincolnshire: Asgarby, 20 pp. Bottesford, 30 pp. North Carlton, 10 pp. Middle Carlton, 3 pp. South Carlton, 5 pp. Hougham, 2 pp. Fillingham, Brattleby, Great Carlton, Riseholme, 4 pp. Frodingham, 2 pp. Gainsborough, 12 pp. Chapelry of Horncastle, 2 pp. Kingerby, Elsham, Owersby, 2 pp. Melton Ross, Scamblesby, Ulceby, 9 pp. Marton, North Ormsby, Wyham, Utterby, 25 pp. Nettleham, 12 pp. Bishop Norton, 11 pp. Norton Disney, 3 pp. Sturgate, 2 pp. Addenda, 3 pp. Appendix I: Facsimiles of the charters of Henry II of which facsimiles were not supplied in Volume I, 1 p. plus 8 pp pf plates. Appendix II: Seals, 5 pp. Index of Persons and Places, 49 pp. Index of Counties and Countries, 5 pp. Index of Subjects, 5 pp.

Description
See LRS Volume 27 (*Registrum Antiquissimum* Volume I). This volume, unlike the first volume which contained many charters that had been previously printed, consists of texts very few of which had been published before. The documents comprise charters of bishops and lay magnates, indulgences, the Choristers' charters and cartularies relating to Episcopal lands and administration, and to some of the prebendal estates in Lincolnshire.
[Adapted from the Preface.]

Reprint
2008 paperback edition, published by Boydell Press for the Lincoln Record Society and printed by 4edge Ltd, Hockley, Essex.

29

THE | REGISTRUM ANTIQUISSIMUM | OF THE | CATHEDRAL CHURCH OF LINCOLN | VOLUME III.

Edited by C. W. Foster, M.A., Hon. D.Litt., F.S.A., Canon of Lincoln and Prebendary of Leicester St Margaret. Pp. xl + 487. Printed by The Hereford Times Limited, Hereford. Issued in 1935. For the year ending 30 September 1932.

Content
Inscription: DORIDI MARIÆ STENTON | CUM MARITO PRÆCLARO | IN ÆVI MEDII STUDIIS | FELICISSIME CONIUNCTÆ | INTER AMICOS AMICISSIMÆ | HOC OPUS DEDICAT | C.W.F. Preface (Timberland, 21 June

1935), 5 pp. Contents, 8 pp. List of Illustrations, 1 p. There are facsimiles of 17 documents. Abbreviations and Notes, 4 pp. List of Charters, 14 pp. Corrections and Additions, 2 pp. Documents: Bedfordshire, 17 pp. Buckinghamshire, 21 pp. Derbyshire, 98 pp. Gloucestershire, 2 pp. Hampshire, 7 pp. Hertfordshire, 5 pp. Huntingdonshire, 64 pp. Kent, 4 pp. Leicestershire, 27 pp. Northamptonshire, 6 pp. Nottinghamshire, 23 pp. Oxfordshire, 31 pp. Somersetshire, 2 pp. Staffordshire, 1 p. Yorkshire, 4 pp. Miscellaneous Documents, 7 pp. Appropriations of Churches, 70 pp. Tithes, 8 pp. Vicarages of Churches of the Common, 14 pp. Pensions, 7 pp. Patronage, 3 pp. Index of Persons and Places, 62 pp. Index of Counties and Countries, 6 pp. Index of Subjects, 11 pp.

Description
See LRS Volume 27 (*Registrum Antiquissimum* Volume I). Of the four hundred and thirty-three documents in this volume only ten have been previously printed *verbatim*.

30

RECORDS OF SOME SESSIONS | OF THE PEACE IN LINCOLNSHIRE | 1360–1375.

Edited by Rosamond Sillem B.A. (Oxon.), M.A. (Mount Holyoke). Pp. xcii + 325. Printed by The Hereford Times Limited, Hereford. Issued in 1936. For the year ending 30 September 1933.

Content
Preface (Sutton, Surrey, November 1935), 1 p. Contents, 2 pp. Rules for Transcription, 1 p. Introduction, 84 pp. Roll L (Assize Roll 529, mm. 1 and 2), 11 pp. Roll LL (Assize Roll 530), 142 pp. Roll K (Ancient Indictments, K.B.9/57), 39 pp. Roll KK (Assize Roll 531), 26 pp. Roll H (Assize Roll 529, mm. 10–14), 31 pp. Index of Persons and Places, 64 pp. Index of Subjects, 11 pp.

Description
Rolls of proceedings before justices of the peace in the fourteenth century were found by Professor B. H. Putnam at the beginning of the twentieth century in the Public Record Office, preserved in a class of documents known then as *Assize Rolls*. The preservation of this material among the archives of central government is explained by a study of the migration of the court of King's Bench, which, during the fourteenth and early fifteenth centuries, went on tour at frequent but irregular intervals. On their return to Westminster they would naturally take with them these records, which thus remained among other the other rolls of the central courts. Of the five Lincolnshire peace rolls published in this volume, three – the Holland roll, the later Lindsey roll and the later Kesteven roll – were compiled in preparation for the visit of the King's Bench to Lincoln in 1375. The earlier Kesteven *roll* is not, strictly speaking, a roll at all, but a collection of strips of parchment of varying size which afford an excellent example of the

type of raw material from which the other rolls were compiled. The early Lindsey roll is a particularly neat and methodical record of indictments for trespass made in 1360–61 with the fines by which they were terminated. The group taken as a whole constitutes an invaluable source of information as to the activities of the justices of the peace in Lincolnshire during the latter part of the reign of Edward III. The text of the rolls is transcribed in full; some English summaries are given. [Adapted from the Preface and Introduction.]

31

LINCOLNSHIRE CHURCH NOTES | MADE BY | WILLIAM JOHN MONSON | F.S.A. | AFTERWARDS SIXTH LORD MONSON OF BURTON | 1828–1840 | EDITED BY HIS GRANDSON | JOHN NINTH LORD MONSON | F.S.A.

Edited by John, Ninth Lord Monson, F.S.A. Pp. xx + 474. Printed by The Hereford Times Limited, Hereford. Issued in 1936. For the year ending 30 September 1934.

Content
Frontispiece: plate, William John Monson, afterwards 6th Baron Monson, 1826. Preface (Burton by Lincoln, Michaelmas 1935), 2 pp. Contents, 1 p. Slip pasted in: 'The Council of the Lincoln Record Society wish to make their grateful acknowledgements to Lord Monson, the Society's President, for generously defraying the cost of printing this edition of his Grandfather's Church Notes'. Abbreviations, 1 p. Introduction, 12 pp. Church Notes, 429 pp. Index of Persons and Places, 37 pp. Index of Coats of Arms, 6 pp. Rear pocket: Map of Churches mentioned in the text.

Description
These Lincolnshire Church Notes, compiled by William John Monson, were started in 1828 during his honeymoon following his marriage to Eliza, daughter of Edmund Larken. The first notes were made with a view to obtaining material for his Family History., but by the time he had finished these early visitations he realised what vast sources of information Lincolnshire churches could supply for the compilation of a County History. The Church Notes contain details of monumental inscriptions, to which particulars of coats of arms and extracts from parish registers are added. The notes deal with 227 parishes, the distribution of which is shown on the map accompanying the volume.
[Adapted from the Introduction.]

Reprint
2005 paperback edition, published by Boydell Press for the Lincoln Record Society and printed by Antony Rowe Ltd, Eastbourne.

32

THE | REGISTRUM ANTIQUISSIMUM | OF THE | CATHEDRAL CHURCH OF LINCOLN | VOLUME IV | ... | WITH A MEMOIR OF CANON FOSTER.

Edited by the late C. W. Foster, M.A., Hon. D.Litt., F.S.A., Canon of Lincoln and Prebendary of Leicester St Margaret, and Kathleen Major, M.A., B.Litt., Archivist to the Bishop of Lincoln, Research Fellow of St Hilda's College, Oxford. Pp. xxxix + 344. Printed by The Hereford Times Limited, Hereford. Issued in 1937. For the year ending 30 September 1935.

Content
Frontispiece: plate, C. W. Foster. Inscription: THIS VOLUME IS DEDICATED | TO THE MEMORY OF | CHARLES WILMER FOSTER | 1866–1935 | THE FOUNDER OF THIS SOCIETY. Preface (Lincoln, October 1937), 4 pp. Memoir of the late Canon C. W. Foster, by F. M. Stenton, 6 pp. Contents, 6 pp. List of Illustrations, 1 p. There are facsimiles of 21 documents. Abbreviations and Notes, 4 pp. List of Charters, 12 pp. Corrections and Additions, 1 p. Documents: The West Riding, 122 pp. The North Riding, 158 pp. Appendix I: The Succentors, Sacrists, and Provosts of the Common, in the Cathedral Church of Lincoln, during the twelfth and thirteenth centuries, 4 pp. Appendix II: Letter from Bishop Wake to his Registrar, 1 p. Index of Persons and Places, 46 pp. Index of Counties and Countries, 4 pp. Index of Subjects, 8 pp. List of Subscribers to the Canon Foster Memorial Fund, 2 pp.

Description
See LRS Volume 27 (*Registrum Antiquissimum* Volume I). This volume contains three hundred and fifty-seven charters relating to the West and North Ridings of Lindsey. The documents in this volume are far less varied in subject than those of Volume III. With few exceptions they record the small gifts, often only of a few acres only, by the lesser gentry and the free peasantry of Lincolnshire. There are many grants of pasture rights and a few mills, generally water-mills, but once a wind-mill. The two field system was evidently the normal form of cultivation – no charter gives any hint of a three field village.
[Adapted from the Preface.]

33

VISITATIONS | IN THE | DIOCESE OF LINCOLN | 1517–1531 | VOLUME I | VISITATIONS OF RURAL DEANERIES BY WILLIAM ATWATER, | BISHOP OF LINCOLN, AND HIS COMMISSARIES, | 1517–1520.

Edited by A. Hamilton Thompson, C.B.E., M.A., D.Litt., F.S.A. Pp. civ + 203. Printed by The Hereford Times Limited, Hereford. Issued in 1940. For the year ending 30 September 1936.

Content
Preface (August 1940), 2 pp. Table of Contents, 2 pp. Introduction, 96 pp. Diocesan Visitations, 140 pp. Appendix I: Visitation Time-Table, April to July 1518, 7 pp. Appendix II: Miscellaneous Documents, 7 pp. Index of Persons and Places, 37 pp. Index of Counties and Countries, 11 pp.

Description
The sources of the records in this edition are three volumes in which Canon Foster collected and arranged the reports of visitations held by the last two pre-Reformation bishops of Lincoln and their officers. These, including visitations of rural deaneries as well as of monasteries and colleges, cover a wider ground than the three volumes of *Visitations of Religious Houses* (LRS Volumes 7, 14 & 21), which belong to the first half of the previous century. The records for the whole diocese are incomplete. Out of seventy-one religious houses of any importance visited by either Bishop Atwater or Bishop Longland, records remain for thirty-three which were visited by both. The returns from parishes are less full. Those of Longland's episcopate refer to only five archdeaconries, omitting those of Lincoln, Stow and Leicester, while from those of Atwater's episcopate, returns from the Archdeaconry of Northampton are missing. Nevertheless, it is doubtful whether any English diocese can supply an equally valuable source of information for the state of parochial and religious life at this highly critical period in the history of the Church. The first volume contains the visitations of rural deaneries from the Atwater manuscript. The Latin text is printed in full.
[Adapted from the Preface.]

34

THE | REGISTRUM ANTIQUISSIMUM | OF THE | CATHEDRAL CHURCH OF LINCOLN | VOLUME V.

Edited by Kathleen Major, M.A., B.Litt., on the plan laid down by the late Charles Wilmer Foster. Pp. xxviii + 249. Printed by The Hereford Times Limited, Hereford. Issued in 1940. For the year ending 30 September 1937.

Content
Preface (July 1940), 4 pp. Contents, 6 pp. Abbreviations and Notes, 3 pp. List of Charters, 9 pp. Corrections and Additions, 2 pp. Documents: The South Riding (Wraggoe and Louthesk Wapentakes), 203 pp. Index of Persons and Places, 33 pp. Index of Counties and Countries, 3 pp. Index of Subjects, 7 pp.

Description
See LRS Volume 27 (*Registrum Antiquissimum* Volume I). This volume contains two hundred and ninety charters relating to the wapentakes of Wraggoe and Louthesk in the South Riding of Lincolnshire. Owing to the war there are no plates in this volume.
[Adapted from the Preface.]

35

VISITATIONS | IN THE | DIOCESE OF LINCOLN | 1517–1531 | VOLUME II | VISITATIONS OF RURAL DEANERIES BY JOHN LONGLAND, BISHOP | OF LINCOLN, AND OF RELIGIOUS HOUSES BY BISHOPS | ATWATER AND LONGLAND, AND BY HIS AND THEIR | COMMIS-SARIES, | 1517–1531.

Edited by A. Hamilton Thompson, C.B.E., M.A., D.Litt., LL.D., F.B.A., F.S.A., Honorary Fellow of St John's College, Cambridge. Pp. x + 263. Printed by The Hereford Times Limited, Hereford. Issued in 1944. For the year ending 30 September 1938.

Content
Preface (December 1942), 1 p. Table of Contents, 4 pp. Diocesan Visitations, 195 pp. Appendix I: Chronology of Longland's Visitations, 5 pp. Appendix II: Injunctions and Other Documents relating to Monasteries, 18 pp. Appendix III: The Chancellors and Commissaries of Bishops Atwater and Longland, 4 pp. Appendix IV: Contents of the MS Volumes of Atwater's and Longland's Visitations, 5 pp. Index of Persons and Places, 35 pp.

Description
See LRS Volume 33 (*Diocesan Visitations*, Volume I).

36

A LINCOLNSHIRE ASSIZE ROLL | FOR 1298 | (P.R.O. ASSIZE ROLL No 505) | EDITED | WITH AN INTRODUCTION ON | ROYAL LOCAL GOVERNMENT IN LINCOLNSHIRE | DURING THE WAR OF 1294–8.

Edited by the late Walter Sinclair Thomson, M.A., Ph.D., History Department, University of Edinburgh. Pp. cxxvii + 305. Printed by The Hereford Times Limited, Hereford. Issued in 1944. For the year ending 30 September 1939.

Content
In Memoriam: Memoir of Walter Sinclair Thomson by Harry Rothwell, 3 pp. Preface (July 1940), 3 pp. Table of Contents, 1 p. Abbreviations and Notes, 2 pp. Introduction, 119 pp. Text of Assize Roll 505, 135 pp. Appendix I: Royal Ordinance of 4 April 1298 setting up a Commission of Enquiry into Acts of Royal Ministers during the War with France 1294–8, 1 p. Appendix II: Royal Officials in Lincolnshire 1294–1298, 42 pp. Appendix III: Analysis of Burdens Imposed on Lincolnshire 1294–8, 5 pp. Appendix IV: P.R.O. Sheriffs' Administrative Accounts No 568/1, 7 pp. Bibliography, 4 pp. Biographical Index of

Persons, 79 pp. Index of Subjects, 11 pp. Index of Places, 16 pp. Index of Counties and Countries, 5 pp.

Description
This study is of royal government in Lincolnshire during the years 1294–8, when Edward I was at war with Philip IV of France. It is based primarily upon the existing records (at the Public Record Office) of a general enquiry, ordered by Edward in March 1298, into the conduct of royal ministers in the counties since the war began. This volume presents a picture of the war-time administration of Lincolnshire which was not so very different from peace-time administration, save in the number and kind of restrictions and burdens imposed. There are vignettes of the lives of obscure individuals and the volume shows that what affected the lives of the people of Lincolnshire had also a significance far other than local.
[Adapted from the Preface.]

37

VISITATIONS | IN THE | DIOCESE OF LINCOLN | 1517–1531 | VOLUME III | VISITATIONS OF RELIGIOUS HOUSES (CONCLUDED) BY BISHOPS ATWATER | AND LONGLAND AND BY THEIR COMMISSARIES | 1517–1531.

Edited by A. Hamilton Thompson, C.B.E., M.A., D.Litt., LL.D., F.B.A., F.S.A., Honorary Fellow of St John's College, Cambridge. Pp. ix + 289. Printed by The Hereford Times Limited, Hereford. Issued in 1947. For the year ending 30 September 1940.

Content
Preface (January 1947), 1 p. Table of Contents, 3 pp. Visitations of Monasteries by Bishops Atwater and Longland, 122 pp. Visitation of the Newarke College at Leicester 1525, 116 pp. Appendix: Injunctions issued by Bishop Longland after his Visitation of the Newarke College in 1525, 11 pp. Index of Persons and Places, 19 pp. Index of Counties and Countries, 4 pp. Index of Subjects for Volumes I-III, 17 pp.

Description
See LRS Volume 33 (*Diocesan Visitations*, Volume I).

38

THE FIRST MINUTE BOOK OF THE | GAINSBOROUGH MONTHLY MEETING | OF THE SOCIETY OF FRIENDS | 1669–1719 | VOLUME I | 1669–1689.

Edited by Harold W. Brace, Clerk of Lincolnshire Monthly Meeting. Pp. xxiii + 149. Printed by The Hereford Times Limited, Hereford. Issued in 1948. For the year ending 30 September 1941.

Content
Frontispiece: Map of Places Mentioned in the Text. Table of Contents, 1 p. Extracts from Minutes of Gainsborough Meetings of November 1945, approving the publication of the Minute Book, 1 p. Introduction, 15 pp. The Minute Book, 137 pp. Index of Persons and Places, 7 pp. Index of Subjects, 3 pp.

Description
The Minute Book opens with the following statement: *A booke of records for the Monthly Meeting on the North West parts of the County of Lyncolne wherein for the information of such as are concerned is Recorded severall things as well of Publique as of particular concernment in relation to the pretious truth & those that make profession thereof.* In these three volumes are recorded in detail the activities of the Friends including their income, charitable giving, marriages and admonition of those not meeting their high standards.

39

THE | ROLLS AND REGISTER | OF | BISHOP OLIVER SUTTON | 1280–1299 | VOLUME I | INSTITUTIONS TO BENEFICES AND CONFIRMATIONS OF HEADS | OF RELIGIOUS HOUSES IN THE ARCHDEACONRY OF LINCOLN.

Edited by Rosalind M. T. Hill, M.A., B.Litt., F.S.A., Lecturer in Mediæval History, Westfield College, University of London. Pp. xxvii + 295. Printed by The Hereford Times Limited, Hereford. Issued in 1948. For the year ending 30 September 1942.

Content
Preface (Westfield, St Dunstan's Day 1948, 2 pp. Contents, 1 p. Abbreviations and Notes, 3 pp. Introduction, 15 pp. The Text, 247 pp. Index of Persons and Places, 34 pp. Index of Subjects, 4 pp. Index of Counties and Countries, 9 pp.

Description
This is the first of eight volumes containing the register of Oliver Sutton, Bishop of Lincoln from 1280 to 1299. Subsequent volumes in addition to the institutions include memoranda dealing with the administration of the see, together with an account of his life. The introduction to the first volume includes a brief description of the manuscripts from which the contents of the volumes is drawn. Sutton's register describes incidents in the course of which clerks were maltreated and sometimes killed, rights of sanctuary violated and churches desecrated by bloodshed. There is no reason to think that in offences such as these the diocese of

Lincoln had an especially bad record. Sutton was not a saint, and as a scholar he appears to have been competent rather than distinguished. He was, however, a thoroughly good man, a trained canonist who was determined to uphold the law, and an administrator at once efficient and humane. For nearly twenty years he devoted himself almost completely to his diocese, ruling it with unending patience and a determined sense of justice.
[Adapted from the Preface.]

40

THE FIRST MINUTE BOOK OF THE | GAINSBOROUGH MONTHLY MEETING | OF THE SOCIETY OF FRIENDS | 1669–1719 | VOLUME II | 1689–1709.

Edited by Harold W. Brace, F.R.Hist.S., Clerk of Lincolnshire Monthly Meeting. Pp. viii + 222. Printed by The Hereford Times Limited, Hereford. Issued in 1949. For the year ending 30 September 1943.

Content
Table of Contents, 1 p. Preface (28 July 1949), 2 pp. The Minute Book, 207 pp. Appendix, 1 p. Index of Persons and Places, 8 pp. Index of Subjects, 4 pp.

Description
The text of this volume covers a period of consolidation. The Toleration Act of 1689 enabled Meeting Houses to be built and licensed, so business concerning real property begins to appear in Monthly Meeting Minutes. Preoccupation with discipline, leading to the appointment of Overseers; structural elaboration as in the establishment of Preparative Meetings; meticulous recording of names of Representatives, to Monthly and Quarterly Meetings, and of those appointed to inquire into the 'clearness' of the parties to a marriage, are all indicative of congelation from a movement into an organisation.
[Adapted from the Preface.]

41

THE | REGISTRUM ANTIQUISSIMUM | OF THE | CATHEDRAL CHURCH OF LINCOLN | VOLUME VI.

Edited by Kathleen Major, M.A., B.Litt., F.S.A., on the plan laid down by the late Charles Wilmer Foster. Pp. xxv + 230. Printed by The Hereford Times Limited, Hereford. Issued in 1950. For the year ending 31 August 1944.

Content
Preface (January 1950), 3 pp. Contents, 5 pp. Abbreviations and Notes, 3 pp. List of Charters, 6 pp. Addenda et Corrigenda, 1 p. Documents: The South Riding

(Calcewath, Candleshoe, Bolingbroke, Hill, Horncastle and Gartree Wapen-takes), 167 pp. Appendix I: The Date of the Second Seal of the Chapter, 2 pp. Suggested Descent of the Family of Scoteni in the 12th and 13th Centuries, 1 foldout page. Appendix II: The Family of Scoteni, 16 pp. Index of Persons and Places, 32 pp. Index of Counties and Countries, 4 pp. Index of Subjects, 8 pp.

Description
See LRS Volume 27 (*Registrum Antiquissimum* Volume I). This volume contains two hundred and one charters. The plates for Volumes V and VI of *Registrum Antiquissimum* are in Volume 42.
[Adapted from the Preface.]

42

THE | REGISTRUM ANTIQUISSIMUM | OF THE | CATHEDRAL CHURCH OF LINCOLN | FACSIMILES OF CHARTERS | IN | VOLUMES V AND VI.

Pp. [vi] + 20. Issued in 1950. For the year ending 31 August 1945.

Content
List of Facsimiles, 2 pp. Facsimiles, 20 pp of plates.

Description
A collection of 20 plates containing facsimiles of 30 charters from Volumes V and VI of *Registrum Antiquissimum*.

43

THE | ROLLS AND REGISTER | OF | BISHOP OLIVER SUTTON | 1280–1299 | VOLUME II | INSTITUTIONS TO BENEFICES AND CONFIRMA-TIONS OF HEADS OF | RELIGIOUS HOUSES IN THE ARCHDEACONRY OF NORTHAMPTON.

Edited by Rosalind M. T. Hill, M.A., B.Litt., F.S.A., Lecturer in Mediæval History, Westfield College, University of London. Pp. xix + 205. Printed by The Hereford Times Limited, Hereford. Issued in 1950. For the year ending 31 August 1946.

Content
Contents, 1 p. Abbreviations and Notes, 3 pp. Introduction, 7 pp. The Text, 166 pp. Index of Persons and Places, 27 pp. Index of Subjects, 4 pp. Index of Counties and Countries, 7 pp.

Description
See LRS Volume 39. This is the second in the eight-volume edition of Bishop Sutton's records. The institutions in the archdeaconry of Northampton (which consisted of the counties of Northampton and Rutland) are complete, beginning with a few *sede vacante* institutions in the early months of 1280 and ending with the Bishop's death in November 1299.
[Adapted from the Introduction.]

44

THE FIRST MINUTE BOOK OF THE | GAINSBOROUGH MONTHLY MEETING | OF THE SOCIETY OF FRIENDS | 1669–1719 | VOLUME III | 1709–1719.

Edited by Harold W. Brace, F.R.Hist.S., Clerk of Lincolnshire Monthly Meeting. Pp. xi + 217. Printed by The Hereford Times Limited, Hereford. Issued in 1951. For the year ending 31 August 1947.

Content
Table of Contents, 1 p. Preface (Gainsborough, 2 May 1951), 4 pp. Note on the Devolution of Monthly Meetings in Lincolnshire, 1 p. The Minute Book, 123 pp. Appendix I: Dissenting Influences prior to the Introduction of Quakerism, 2 pp. Appendix II: Material abstracted from various Sources to show the Progress of Quakerism, within the Compass of Gainsborough Monthly Meeting, from its Introduction until the Commencement of the Minute Book, 44 pp. Appendix III: Records in the custody of the Clerk of Lincolnshire Monthly Meeting, 4 pp. Appendix IV: Books mentioned in the Text, 3 pp. Index of Persons, 31 pp. Index of Places, 3 pp. Index of Subjects, 3 pp.

Description
This is the final volume in the trilogy covering the last ten years of the text. The index of persons has been expanded to give some biographical details of Lincolnshire Quakers mentioned in the three volumes. Appendices I and II contain matter from other contemporary sources to illustrate or amplify features not covered by the Minutes themselves. Various printed books are referred to incidentally in Volumes II and III and these have been fully identified in Appendix IV.
[Adapted from the Preface.]

45

THE LETTERS AND PAPERS | OF THE | BANKS FAMILY OF REVESBY ABBEY | 1704–1760.

Edited by J. W. F. Hill, LL.M., Litt.D., F.S.A. Pp. xxxi + 330. Printed by The Hereford Times Limited, Hereford. Issued in 1952. For the years ending 31 August 1948 and 31 August 1949.

Content
Frontispiece: Joseph Banks I (1665–1727), from a bust by John Nost in Revesby Church (black-and-white photograph by Thomas Jones). Table of Contents, 1 p. Preface (Lincoln, May 1952), 2 pp. Introduction, 27 pp. Banks Family Papers, 242 pp. Appendix: Copy of the Will of Joseph Banks Esquire, 27 July 1726, with other documents, 57 pp. Index of Persons, Places and Subjects, 30 pp.

46

THE | REGISTRUM ANTIQUISSIMUM | OF THE | CATHEDRAL CHURCH OF LINCOLN | VOLUME VII.

Edited by Kathleen Major, M.A., B.Litt., F.S.A., on the plan laid down by the late Charles Wilmer Foster. Pp. xxvii + 284. Printed by The Hereford Times Limited, Hereford. Issued in 1953. For the year ending 31 August 1950.

Content
Preface (Lincoln, 1 January 1953), 4 pp. Contents, 4 pp. List of Illustrations, 1 p. Abbreviations and Notes, 3 pp. List of Charters, 7 pp. Addenda and Corrigenda, 1 p. Documents: The Parts of Holland and The Parts of Kesteven, 200 pp. Appendix I: The Chronology of the Archdeacons of Lincoln in the Twelfth Century, 8 pp. Appendix II: The Alselin and Caux Estates, An attempt to disentangle some confusions, 17 pp. Index of Persons and Places, 41 pp. Index of Counties and Countries, 4 pp. Index of Subjects, 12 pp.

Description
See LRS Volume 27 (*Registrum Antiquissimum* Volume I). This volume contains two hundred and thirty-six charters.
[Adapted from the Preface.]

47

PAPAL DECRETALS | RELATING TO THE | DIOCESE OF LINCOLN | IN THE TWELFTH CENTURY.

Edited with an introduction on the sources by Walther Holtzmann, Professor in Bonn, with translations of the texts and an introduction on the Canon Law and its administration in the twelfth century by Eric Waldram Kemp, Canon of Lincoln and Prebendary of Caistor, Fellow and Chaplain of Exeter College, Oxford. Pp. xxviii + 65. Printed by The Hereford Times Limited, Hereford. Issued in 1954. For the year ending 31 August 1951.

Content
Preface, 1 p. General Editor's Note, 1 p. Introduction, 20 pp. Papal Decretals, 60 pp. Index, 3 pp.

Description
Papal correspondence of this period has been preserved in three ways: in the archives of those to whom the letters were addressed; through the papal registers, beginning with those of Innocent III (1198–1216); and through collections of legally important documents, originally compiled by private initiative and later on officially acknowledged by the curia and used as law books in the church courts and as text books in the Universities. This volume is concerned with the third class of texts. Papal letters transmitted in this way may be called decretals (*epistolæ decretales*). In most cases a decretal is nothing but an ordinary papal letter which happened to attract the attention of a compiler because some principle of law was expressed in it.
[Adapted from the Introduction.]

48

THE | ROLLS AND REGISTER | OF | BISHOP OLIVER SUTTON | 1280–1299 | VOLUME III | MEMORANDA, MAY 19 1290 - MAY 18 1292.

Edited by Rosalind M. T. Hill, M.A., B.Litt., F.S.A., Lecturer in Mediæval History, Westfield College, University of London. Pp. lxxxvi + 250. Printed by The Hereford Times Limited, Hereford. Issued in 1954. For the year ending 31 August 1952.

Content
Contents, 1 p. Abbreviations and Notes, 1 p. Corrections for Volume I and Volume II, 2 pp. Introduction, 74 pp. The Text, 206 pp. Itinerary of Bishop Sutton, 8 pp. Index of Persons and Places, 25 pp. Index of Subjects, 4 pp. Index of Counties and Countries, 6 pp.

Description
See LRS Volume 39. The formal entries in Bishop Sutton's memoranda consist of notes of dispensations, letters dimissory, grants of indulgences or ratifications of such grants, appointments of commissaries, licences, the reports of the benediction of abbots, and a few similar matters of diocesan administration.
[Adapted from the Notes.]

49

RECORDS OF SOME | SESSIONS OF THE PEACE | IN LINCOLNSHIRE | 1381–1396 | VOLUME I | THE PARTS OF KESTEVEN | AND THE PARTS OF HOLLAND.

Edited by Elisabeth G. Kimball, M.A. (Mount Holyoke), B.Litt. (Oxon), Ph.D. (Yale). Pp. lxvi + 110. Printed by The Hereford Times Limited, Hereford. Issued in 1955. For the year ending 31 August 1953.

Content
Preface (Princeton, New Jersey, 1 July 1953), 1 p. Table of Contents, 1 p. List of Abbreviations, 1 p. Rules for Transcription and Note of Explanation, 1 p. Introduction, 54 pp. Appendix: Sessions of the Peace in Kesteven, 1392–1396; Sessions of the Peace in Holland, 1387, 1390–1396; Sessions of the Peace in Lindsey, 1381–1388, 1395–1396, 4 pp. Text: The Kesteven Roll, 37 pp. The Holland Roll, 45 pp. Index of Persons and Places, 21 pp. Index of Subjects, 7 pp.

Description
The three Lincolnshire peace rolls for the reign of Richard II printed in this volume and in Volume 56 were discovered (as were the Edward III rolls published in Volume 30) by Professor B. H. Putnam. The preservation of these rolls is undoubtedly due to the visit of the King's Bench to Lincoln in Easter term, 1396. When the bench came into a county all lesser judicial agencies were suspended and their unfinished business brought before the superior court. Undoubtedly the peace rolls were carried back to London with the records of the bench and so preserved. These rolls contain much material that will be of value to legal and economic historians as well as to local historians and to those interested in genealogy.
[Adapted from the Preface and the Introduction.]

50

THE | PORT BOOKS OF BOSTON | 1601–1640.

Edited by R. W. K. Hinton, Fellow of Peterhouse, Cambridge. Pp. liii + 336. Printed by The Hereford Times Limited, Hereford. Issued in 1956. For the years ending 31 August 1954 and 31 August 1955.

Content
Preface, 2 pp. Contents, 1 p. Abbreviations, etc., used in the text, 2 pp. List of the Port Books, 1 p. Introduction, 31 pp. Appendix A: A Comparison of Boston Port Books and the Danish Sound Toll Registers, 8 pp. Appendix B: Some Figures of Tonnage and Poundage in Selected Years, 2 pp. The Port Books, 321 pp. Index of Persons, 6 pp. Index of Places, 3 pp. Index of Subjects, 5 pp.

Description
These Port Books make available in a clear and useful fashion the materials for a study of the foreign trade of Boston in the first half of the seventeenth century. At one time the port of Boston was second in importance only to London, but by the seventeenth century its trade was much smaller than that of Hull. The great inland area once served by Boston had come to depend on the rivers of Humber

and Thames, and Boston now exported mainly the produce of a limited hinter-
land, and imported goods apparently for local consumption. These port books,
displaying what is indeed a negligible proportion of the total trade of the United
Kingdom, are therefore a contribution to the economic study of Lincolnshire.
This does not necessarily mean that they are only of local value. If the merchants
of Boston in their relatively small trade were subject to the same influences as the
merchants of greater ports, to study the trade of Boston is in some sort to study
a national trade in miniature.
[Adapted from the Preface.]

51

THE | REGISTRUM ANTIQUISSIMUM | OF THE | CATHEDRAL
CHURCH OF LINCOLN | VOLUME VIII.

Edited by Kathleen Major, M.A., B.Litt., F.S.A., on the plan laid down by the
late Charles Wilmer Foster. Pp. xxiii + 258. Printed by The Hereford Times
Limited, Hereford. Issued in 1958. For the year ending 31 August 1956.

Content
On reverse of title-page: 'This Volume has been produced with the assistance of
a grant from the Pilgrim Trust'. Preface (21 January 1958), 3 pp. Contents, 2
pp. Abbreviations and Notes, 4 pp. List of Charters, 6 pp. Corrections and Additions, 3 pp. Documents: The City of Lincoln, 198 pp. Appendix: The Mayors and
Bailiffs of Lincoln in the Thirteenth Century, 11 pp. Index of Persons and Places,
36 pp. Index of Counties and Countries, 4 pp. Index of Subjects, 8 pp.

Description
See LRS Volume 27 (*Registrum Antiquissimum* Volume I). This is the first of
three volumes containing charters of the chapter property in the city of Lincoln.
Documents connected with chantries other than those administered by the
Common Fund have been omitted. This volume contains documents relating to
the Common Fund, the chantry and obit property included in the Common Fund
accounts, the charters of prebends, of the Fabric Fund and of the Bishop's fee
within the city.
[Adapted from the Preface.]

52

THE | ROLLS AND REGISTER | OF | BISHOP OLIVER SUTTON | 1280–
1299 | VOLUME IV | MEMORANDA, MAY 19 1292 - MAY 18 1294.

Edited by Rosalind M. T. Hill, M.A., B.Litt., F.S.A., Reader in Mediæval
History, Westfield College, University of London. Pp. viii + 221. Printed by

The Hereford Times Limited, Hereford. Issued in 1958. For the year ending 31 August 1957.

Content
Contents, 1 p. Abbreviations and Notes, 1 p. Correction for Volume III, 1 p. The Text, 192 pp. Index of Persons and Places, 20 pp. Index of Subjects, 4 pp. Index of Counties and Countries, 5 pp.

Description
See LRS Volumes 39 and 48.

53

THE STATE OF THE EX-RELIGIOUS | AND FORMER CHANTRY PRIESTS | IN THE | DIOCESE OF LINCOLN | 1547–1574 | FROM RETURNS IN THE EXCHEQUER.

Edited by G. A. J. Hodgett, M.A., F.R.Hist.S., Lecturer in History in the University of London, King's College. Pp. xxii + 181. Printed by The Hereford Times Limited, Hereford. Issued in 1959. For the year ending 31 August 1958.

Content
On reverse of title-page: 'This Volume has been produced with the assistance of a grant from the British Academy'. Preface (King's College, London, 8 May 1957), 1 p. Contents, 2 pp. Abbreviations and Notes, 2 pp. Introduction, 12 pp. The Text, 150 pp. Index of Persons and Places, 26 pp. Index of Counties, 5 pp.

Description
The documents calendared in this volume provide, in the main, information concerning the material state of the ex-religious, but from some returns there is a glimpse of something more of the way of life of a few individual pensioners. Two types of documents were used in editing this volume: lists of pensions compiled in the Court of Augmentations and lists, drawn up in the various counties of the diocese, sent to the Court.
[Adapted from the Introduction.]

54

THE RECORDS OF | THE COMMISSIONERS | OF SEWERS | IN THE | PARTS OF HOLLAND | 1547–1603 | VOLUME I.

Edited by A. Mary Kirkus, Ph.D., Librarian of the University of Reading. Pp. xci + 168. Printed by J. W. Ruddock & Sons Ltd, Lincoln. Issued in 1959. For the year ending 31 August 1959.

Content
Preface (Reading), 1 p. Contents, 1 p. Abbreviations and Notes, 1 p. Map: The
Fenlands of Lincolnshire, 1 p. Introduction, 85 pp. Text, 134 pp. Index of Persons
and Places, 27 pp. Index of Counties and Countries, 3 pp. Index of Subjects, 4 pp.

Description
The records of the Courts of Sewers concern the district bounded by Friskney,
Stickney, Dogdike, Kyme, Heckington, Helpringham, Swaton, Horbling, Bourne,
Stamford, the Deepings, Crowland, Tydd St Mary, Long Sutton, Lutton and
Gedney. They consist of verdicts, 'laws' and ordinances, joyce books and acre
books, and accounts. The joyce books (which took their name from the word
'agistment') give the names of the landholders with the length of the dike or bank
for which they were responsible. Acre books list the names of the landholders
with the acreage on which they were rated. The three volumes in the series throw
light on the Courts of Sewers, and more generally on local administration in the
later sixteenth century. The Introduction contains a description of the physical
conditions that eventually led to the setting up of the Courts, and of the early
methods used to try to prevent flooding getting worse.
[Adapted from the Introduction.]

55

THE | BUILDING ACCOUNTS | OF | TATTERSHALL CASTLE | 1434–
1472.

Edited by W. Douglas Simpson, O.B.E., D.Litt., Librarian of the University
of Aberdeen. Pp. xxxii + 87, 7 pp. of plates. Printed by The Hereford Times
Limited, Hereford. Issued in 1960. For the year ending 31 August 1960.

Content
Frontispiece: sketch plan of Tattershall Castle (by J. M. McDonald, 1957), 1
foldout page. Preface (King's College, Old Aberdeen, Easter 1960), 1 p. Contents,
1 p. List of Illustrations, 1 p. Introduction, 21 pp. Notes on the Manuscripts, 1 p.
Text (Latin, followed by English translation), 78 pp. Index of Persons and Places,
6 pp. Index of Subjects, 3 pp.

Description
The building accounts of Tattershall Castle are preserved among the manuscripts
belonging to Lord De L'Isle and Dudley at Penshurst Place in Kent. They were
first recognised by the Historical Manuscripts Commission and summarized in
their 1925 report. A precise transcription was prepared in 1943.
The Preface begins:
'The publication of this work has been inordinately delayed. This is partly due to
my own ill-health and partly to various mishaps, of which the most spectacular
is perhaps unique in the record of such undertakings. My house was invaded
by a monkey, escaped from a travelling circus a mile or more away: and, in the

fracas consequent on efforts to recapture it, some of the transcripts were so badly damaged that they had to be re-written!'
[Adapted from the Preface and Introduction.]

Reprint
2010 paperback edition, published by Boydell Press for the Lincoln Record Society and printed by 4edge Ltd, Hockley, Essex.

56

RECORDS OF SOME | SESSIONS OF THE PEACE | IN LINCOLNSHIRE | 1381–1396 | VOLUME II | THE PARTS OF LINDSEY.

Edited by Elisabeth G. Kimball, M.A. (Mount Holyoke), B.Litt. (Oxon), Ph.D. (Yale). Pp. xi + 331. Printed by The Hereford Times Limited, Hereford. Issued in 1962. For the year ending 31 August 1961.

Content
On reverse of title-page: 'This Volume has been produced with the assistance of a grant from the British Academy'. Table of Contents, 1 p. List of Abbreviations, 1 p. Rules for Transcription and Note of Explanation, 1 p. Appendix: Sessions of the Peace in Lindsey, 1381–1388, 1395–1396, 3 pp. Text: The Lindsey Roll, 261 pp. Index of Persons and Places, 64 pp. Index of Subjects, 5 pp.

Description
See LRS Volume 49.

57

THE REGISTER OF | BISHOP PHILIP REPINGDON | 1405–1419 | VOLUME I | MEMORANDA 1405–1411.

Edited by Margaret Archer, M.A. (Liverpool), B.Litt. (Oxon), Lecturer in Medieval History, University of Birmingham. Pp. li + 209. Printed by The Hereford Times Limited, Hereford. Issued in 1963. For the year ending 31 August 1962.

Content
Editor's Preface, 1 p. General Editor's Preface, 1 p. Contents, 1 p. Notes Concerning the Method of Transcription, 3 pp. Principal Abbreviations Used in the Footnotes, 2 pp. Introduction, 37 pp. Memoranda 1405–1411, 209 pp.

Description
The Register of Philip Repingdon, bishop of Lincoln from 1405 to 1419, consists of two volumes, the Institutions and the Memoranda, both in the Lincolnshire

Archives. The Memoranda volume contains the miscellaneous business of the diocese. It gives a clear picture of diocesan administration and the state of religious life in the See of Lincoln between 1405 and 1420. The Memoranda lacks, perhaps, the richness of material found in earlier episcopal registers, and in some respects it may be a little disappointing. The selection of entries was determined by the registrar; thus, much space is given to the transcription of formal and sometimes repetitive documents, and inevitably much that would be of greater interest to us is omitted. Despite its shortcomings and omissions, however, the Memoranda is a fascinating and valuable record of ecclesiastical administration and religious life, not only in the diocese of Lincoln but in the English Church as a whole in the early fifteenth century. Documents in common form are calendared in English. Others are printed in full, with brief English summaries. [Adapted from the Introduction.]

58

THE REGISTER OF | BISHOP PHILIP REPINGDON | 1405–1419 | VOLUME II | MEMORANDA 1411–1414.

Edited by Margaret Archer, M.A. (Liverpool), B.Litt. (Oxon), Lecturer in Medieval History, University of Birmingham. Pp. xii + 231 (paginated continuously with Volume I as 211–441). Printed by The Hereford Times Limited, Hereford. Issued in 1963. For the year ending 31 August 1963.

Content
Notes Concerning the Method of Transcription, 3 pp. Principal Abbreviations Used in the Footnotes, 2 pp. Introduction, 37 pp. Memoranda 1411–1414, 171 pp. Index of Persons and Places, 45 pp. Index of Subjects, 5 pp. Index of Counties and Countries, 7 pp.

Description
See LRS Volume 57.

59

LETTERS AND PAPERS | OF THE CHOLMELEYS FROM | WAINFLEET | 1813–1853.

Collected and edited by Guy Hargreaves Cholmeley. Pp. xvi + 130, plus 5 pp of plates and 5 foldout pages of pedigrees. Printed by The Hereford Times Limited, Hereford. Issued in 1964. For the year ending 31 August 1964.

Content
Table of Contents, 1 p. List of Illustrations and List of Pedigrees, 1 p. General Editor's Preface (St Hilda's College, Oxford, 9 May 1964), 1 p. Preface, 1 p.

Acknowledgements, 2 pp. Contents of Part I, 2 pp. The Letters and Papers, 118 pp. Appendix, 1 p. General Index, 10 pp. Pedigrees, 5 foldout pages.

Description
This chronicle was not intended to be a family history. Its object was to make easy to read some family letters and to help a reader to identify persons, places and events mentioned in them. The letters which cover the years 1813 to 1874 come from three sources - the family of Stephen (the eldest of Revd Robert Cholmeley's nine sons), that of Mountague his third son, and that of Maria the eldest of his six daughters, including some preserved by his eighth son Humphrey. At the end are six pedigrees. Without the first four - and even with them - the reader might get lost in an impenetrable maze. The last two indicate the relatives of Revd Robert's wife.
[Adapted from the Preface.]

60

THE | ROLLS AND REGISTER | OF | BISHOP OLIVER SUTTON | 1280–1299 | VOLUME V | MEMORANDA, MAY 19 1294 - MAY 18 1296 [*recte* 1297].

Edited by Rosalind M. T. Hill, M.A., B.Litt., F.S.A., Reader in Mediæval History, Westfield College, University of London. Pp. vii + 255. Printed by The Hereford Times Limited, Hereford. Issued in 1965. For the year ending 31 August 1965.

Content
Contents, 1 p. Abbreviations and Notes, 1 p. The Text, 218 pp. Index of Persons and Places, 25 pp. Index of Subjects, 4 pp. Index of Counties and Countries, 7 pp.

Description
See LRS Volumes 39 and 48.

Reprint
2005 paperback edition, published by Boydell Press for the Lincoln Record Society and printed by 4edge Ltd, Hockley, Essex.

61

AN EPISCOPAL | COURT BOOK | FOR THE DIOCESE OF LINCOLN | 1514–1520.

Edited by Margaret Bowker, B.Litt., M.A., Fellow of Girton College, Cambridge. Pp. xxxii + 161. Printed by J. W. Ruddock & Sons Ltd, Lincoln. Issued in 1967. For the year ending 31 August 1966.

Content

On reverse of title-page: 'This Volume has been produced with the assistance of grants from the British Academy and from Girton College, Cambridge'. Preface (Cambridge, 1967), 1 p. Contents, 1 p. Notes on the Edition, 1 p. List of Abbreviations, 1 p. Introduction, 17 pp. Appendix: Bishop Atwater's Itinerary, 9 pp. The Book of the Court of Audience of Bishop William Atwater 1514–1520, 141 pp. Index of Persons and Places, 15 pp. Index of Subjects, 3 pp.

Description

The visitation records of the diocese of Lincoln for the early part of the sixteenth century, published in LRS Volumes 33, 35 and 37, provide some useful information about the state of the church in the last two decades before the break with Rome, particularly about the state of affairs in the parishes. Although they are an important source of evidence they have considerable limitations, which are discussed in the introduction to this volume. Diocesan Court Books take up the story where the visitations leave off. The real meaning of the visitation returns does not emerge until their sequel, contained in the court books, is studied. The proceedings recorded in this volume seem to be those of the bishop's court of audience. This was the court held before the bishop himself or before his chancellor, vicar general or any household clerk specifically deputed by him.
[Adapted from the Introduction.]

62

THE | REGISTRUM ANTIQUISSIMUM | OF THE | CATHEDRAL CHURCH OF LINCOLN | VOLUME IX | WITH A MEMOIR OF SIR FRANK MERRY STENTON.

Edited by Kathleen Major, M.A., D.Litt., on the plan laid down by the late Charles Wilmer Foster. Pp. xxxii + 329. Printed by Northumberland Press Ltd, Gateshead, Co. Durham. Issued in 1968. For the year ending 31 August 1967.

Content

Frontispiece, 'Sir Frank Merry Stenton, Aetat. 70' (black and white photograph). On reverse of title-page: 'This Volume has been produced with the assistance of a grant from the Pilgrim Trust, a grant from the Dean and Chapter of Lincoln and a legacy from the late Miss Florence Thurlby'. Preface (Lincoln, 4 January 1968), 5 pp. Memoir of Sir Frank Merry Stenton, by Kathleen Major, 2 pp. Contents, 3 pp. Abbreviations and Notes, 4 pp. List of Charters, 8 pp. Corrections and Additions, 4 pp. Documents: The City of Lincoln, 254 pp. Appendix: The Archdeacons of Stow, 8 pp. Index of Persons and Places, 49 pp. Index of Counties and Countries, 5 pp. Index of Subjects, 11 pp.

Description

See LRS Volume 27 (*Registrum Antiquissimum* Volume I). This is the second volume of charters of Chapter property in the city of Lincoln.

63

THE RECORDS OF | THE COMMISSIONERS | OF SEWERS | IN THE | PARTS OF HOLLAND | 1547–1603 | VOLUME II.

Edited by A. E. B. Owen, M.A., Under-Librarian, Cambridge University Library. Pp. ix + 187. Printed by J. W. Ruddock & Sons Ltd, Lincoln. Issued in 1968. For the year ending 31 August 1968.

Content

On reverse of title-page: 'This Volume has been produced with the assistance of a grant from the British Academy'. General Editor's Preface, 1 p. Contents, 1 p. Introduction to Volume II, 3 pp. List of Documents Printed in Volume I, 1 p. Synopsis of Documents in Volume II, 1 p. Text, 159 pp. Index of Persons and Places, 23 pp. Index of Counties, 1 p. Index of Subjects, 3 pp.

Description

See LRS Volume 54. This is the second volume of the trilogy.

64

THE | ROLLS AND REGISTER | OF | BISHOP OLIVER SUTTON | 1280– 1299 | VOLUME VI | MEMORANDA, MAY 19 1297 - SEPTEMBER 12 1299.

Edited by Rosalind M. T. Hill, M.A., B.Litt., F.S.A., Reader in Mediæval History, Westfield College, University of London. Pp. ix + 236. Printed by J. W. Ruddock & Sons Limited, Lincoln. Issued in 1969. For the years ending 31 August 1969 and 31 August 1970.

Content

On reverse of title-page: 'This Volume has been produced with the assistance of grants from the British Academy and Westfield College, University of London'. Acknowledgement, 1 p. Contents, 1 p. Abbreviations and Notes, 1 p. The Text, 205 pp. Index of Persons and Places, 19 pp. Index of Subjects, 3 pp. Index of Counties and Countries, 6 pp.

Description

See LRS Volumes 39 and 48.

Reprint
2005 paperback edition, published by Boydell Press for the Lincoln Record
Society and printed by Antony Rowe Ltd, Eastbourne.

65

RECORDS OF SOME | SESSIONS OF THE PEACE | IN THE CITY OF
LINCOLN | 1351–1354 | AND THE BOROUGH OF STAMFORD | 1351.

Edited by Elisabeth G. Kimball, M.A. (Mount Holyoke), B.Litt. (Oxon),
Ph.D. (Yale). Pp. xxx + 67. Printed by J. W. Ruddock & Sons Ltd, Lincoln.
Issued in 1971. For the year ending 31 August 1971.

Content
Frontispiece: Plate, The Seals of the Jurors on the Lincoln Roll. On reverse of
title-page: 'This Volume has been produced with the assistance of grants from the
British Academy and the Corporation of the City of Lincoln'. Preface (Princeton,
New Jersey, June 1971), 1 p. Contents, 1 p. List of Abbreviations, 1 p. Rules for
Transcription, 1 p. Introduction, 22 pp. Text: The City of Lincoln Roll, 49 pp. The
Stamford Roll, 6 pp. Index of Persons and Places, 7 pp. Index of Subjects, 4 pp.

Description
This volume contains a peace roll for the city of Lincoln and a single membrane
from a Gaol Delivery Roll which contains a peace commission for the borough
of Stamford and the record of two sessions held under this commission. These
enrolments are among the few extant medieval peace records for urban jurisdic-
tions.
[Adapted from the Preface.]

66

LETTERS FROM JOHN WALLACE | TO | MADAM WHICHCOT | AND
| SOME CORRESPONDENCE OF | JOHN FARDELL | DEPUTY REGIS-
TRAR, 1802–1805.

Edited by C. M. Lloyd, M.A., and Mary E. Finch, M.A., Ph.D. Pp. 74.
Printed by J. W. Ruddock & Sons Limited, Lincoln. Issued in 1973. For the
year ending 31 August 1972.

Content
Frontispiece: Plate, Harpswell Hall in the late Eighteenth Century (drawing by
J. C. Nattes in Lincoln Public Library). On reverse of title-page: 'This Volume
has been produced with the assistance of a grant from the British Academy'.
Contents, 1 p. Some Correspondence of the Family of Whichcot of Harpswell:

Introduction, 7 pp. Letters, 30 pp. Some Correspondence of John Fardell, Deputy Registrar, 1802–1805: Editor's Notes, 1 p. Introduction, 11 pp. Letters, 15 pp. Index of Persons, Places and Subjects, 6 pp.

Description

The surviving records of the Whichcots of Harpswell, apart from title deeds and estate papers, include a large number of household vouchers and many family letters. Most of the latter cover a fairly short period between about 1710 and 1730. The small group of letters printed in this volume have been chosen because of the interesting picture they give of household life and also because of the information which they contain about politics and other county affairs.

John Fardell, recipient of the letters in the second part of this volume, was Deputy Registrar at Lincoln from 1783 until his sudden death in 1805, twelve days after the last of these letters. The small group of letters published here provides a glimpse of the functioning of one particular ecclesiastical office at the beginning of the nineteenth century and illustrates some long-established characteristics of office-holding in the Church.
[Adapted from the Introductions.]

67

THE | REGISTRUM ANTIQUISSIMUM | OF THE | CATHEDRAL CHURCH OF LINCOLN | VOLUME X.

Edited by Kathleen Major, M.A., D.Litt., on the plan laid down by the late Charles Wilmer Foster. Pp. lxx + 378. Printed by Northumberland Press Ltd, Gateshead, Co. Durham. Issued in 1973. For the year ending 31 August 1973.

Content

On reverse of title-page: 'This Volume has been produced with the assistance of grants from the Pilgrim Trust, the British Academy and the Dean and Chapter of Lincoln'. Preface (Lincoln, 22 February 1973), 8 pp. Contents, 2 pp. Abbreviations and Notes, 4 pp. List of Charters, 9 pp. Corrections and Additions for Volumes I to X, 43 pp. Documents: The City of Lincoln, 317 pp. Index of Persons and Places, 41 pp. Index of Counties and Countries, 4 pp. Index of Subjects, 14 pp.

Description

See LRS Volume 27 (*Registrum Antiquissimum* Volume I). This is the third volume of charters relating to properties in the city of Lincoln. The preface describes the history of the series together with details of the contents of Volume X.

68

THE | REGISTRUM ANTIQUISSIMUM | OF THE | CATHEDRAL CHURCH OF LINCOLN | FACSIMILES OF CHARTERS | IN | VOLUMES VIII, IX AND X.

Pp. [vi] + 28. Issued in 1973. Extra Volume for the year ending 31 August 1973.

Content
On reverse of title-page: 'IN MEMORIAM | CAROLI WILMER FOSTER | CANONICI ECCLESIAE LINCOLNIENSIS | HUIUS SOCIETATIS CONDI-TORIS | NECNON | HUIUSCE OPERIS EDITORIS PRIMI | HUNC CODICEM PIO ANIMO | DONO DEDIT DISCIPULA | K. M.' List of Facsimiles, 2 pp. Facsimiles, 28 pp of plates.

Description
A collection of 28 plates containing facsimiles of 36 charters from Volumes VIII, IX and X of *Registrum Antiquissimum*.

69

THE | ROLLS AND REGISTER | OF | BISHOP OLIVER SUTTON | VOLUME VII | ORDINATIONS, MAY 19 1290 - SEPTEMBER 19 1299.

Edited by Rosalind M. T. Hill, M.A., B.Litt., F.S.A., Professor of Medieval History, Westfield College, University of London. Pp. ix + 236. Printed by J. W. Ruddock & Sons Limited, Lincoln. Issued in 1975. For the year ending 31 August 1974.

Content
On reverse of title-page: 'This Volume has been produced with the assistance of a grant from the British Academy'. Contents, 1 p. Abbreviations and Notes, 1 p. Introduction, 15 pp. Ordination Lists, 123 pp. Appendix: Ordinations of members of, and titles granted by, religious houses and orders of friars, Templars and Hospitallers, mentioned in the ordination lists, 4 pp. Index of Persons and Places, 52 pp. Index of Counties and Countries, 12 pp.

Description
Bishop Sutton's ordination-lists, in common with the rest of his register, were kept on rolls for the first ten years of his episcopate. None of these rolls has survived, and the records therefore begin with the Whitsun ordinations of the eleventh year of Sutton's episcopate (which ran from 19 May 1290 to 18 May 1291) and continue until his death on 13 November 1299.
[Adapted from the Introduction.]

70

LETTERS AND PAPERS | CONCERNING THE ESTABLISHMENT OF THE | TRENT, ANCHOLME AND GRIMSBY | RAILWAY, 1860–1862.

Edited by Frank Henthorn, Ph.D. Pp. lv + 130, plus 9 pp of plates. Printed by J. W. Ruddock & Sons Limited, Lincoln. Issued in 1975. For the year ending 31 August 1975.

Content
Frontispiece: Plate, Rowland Winn, 1st Lord St Oswald. On reverse of title-page: 'This Volume has been produced with the assistance of grants from the British Academy, Lincolnshire and Humberside Arts and the former Council of the Borough of Scunthorpe. The blocks for the illustrations have been provided by Dr Henthorn.' Preface and Acknowledgements, 1 p. Contents and List of Illustrations, 1 p. Abbreviations, 1 p. Introduction, 47 pp. Map and Illustrations, 9 pp of plates. The Text, 120 pp. Index of Persons and Places, 10 pp.

Description
The documents published in this volume tell the story of the development of the railway from a legal, commercial, engineering and human perspective. Roland Winn promoted the line not as a railway pioneer or enthusiast but to exploit the ironstone underlying his land. The Trent, Ancholme and Grimsby railway was never really independent and had a short life. It was vested in the Manchester, Sheffield and Lincolnshire Railway in 1882. This volume has much to offer to local historians as it does to the railway enthusiast and transport historians.

Reprint
2005 paperback edition, published by Boydell Press for the Lincoln Record Society and printed by Antony Rowe Ltd, Eastbourne.

71

THE RECORDS OF | THE COMMISSIONERS | OF SEWERS | IN THE | PARTS OF HOLLAND | 1547–1603 | VOLUME III.

Edited by A. E. B. Owen, M.A., Senior Under-Librarian, Cambridge University Library. Pp. xiii + 140. Printed by Popper & Company Limited, Welwyn Garden City. Issued in 1977. For the year ending 31 August 1977.

Content
On reverse of title-page: 'The Society is grateful to the British Academy for a generous grant towards the cost of this publication'. Contents, 1 p. Introduction to Volume III, with Addenda and Corrigenda for Volumes I and II, 8 pp. Synopsis of Documents in Volume III, 1 p. Text, 117 pp. Index of Persons and Places, 19 pp. Index of Subjects, 3 pp.

Description
See LRS Volume 54. This is the third volume of the trilogy.

72

LINCOLNSHIRE RETURNS | OF THE CENSUS OF | RELIGIOUS WORSHIP | 1851.

Edited by R. W. Ambler, M.A. Pp. xcv + 317. Printed by Fakenham Press Limited, Fakenham, Norfolk. Issued in 1979. For the two years ending 31 August 1979.

Content
Opposite title-page: 'The Society is grateful to the British Academy for a generous grant towards the cost of this publication and to the Keeper of the Public Records for permission to publish this text.' Preface (April 1979) and Acknowledgement, 1 p. Contents, 1 p. Tables and List of Plates, 1 p. Introduction, 68 pp. Appendix: Lincolnshire Places arranged under Registration Districts and Sub-Districts giving Census Reference Numbers, 21 pp. The Text, 278 pp. Index of Persons and Places, 34 pp. Index of Subjects, 3 pp.

Description
Sunday 30 March 1851 was unique in British statistical history. This was the only day in British history when a census was taken of attendance at places of religious worship in the country. This volume contains transcriptions of the returns from Lincolnshire churches and chapels. The entries contain a wealth of religious and social detail. For instance attendance at St. Martin's in Lincoln was 'much diminished by the prevailing influenza and the evening service still further by a violent storm of thunder and lightning'.
[Adapted from the Introduction.]

73

THE MINUTE-BOOKS | OF | THE SPALDING GENTLEMEN'S SOCIETY | 1712–1755.

Selected and introduced by Dorothy M. Owen with the help of S. W. Woodward. Pp. xvii + 53. Printed by Fakenham Press Limited, Fakenham, Norfolk. Issued in 1981. For the year ending 31 August 1980.

Content
On reverse of title-page: 'The Society is grateful to the late Sir Francis Hill and to the Twenty-Seven Foundation for generous grants towards the cost of this publication and to the Spalding Gentlemen's Society for permission to publish the text.' Contents, 1 p. Introduction, 11 pp. Facsimile of Minutes for the year

1732, 46 pp of plates. Place Index, 1 p. Index of Persons, 2 pp. Subject Index, 2 pp. Printed books referred to in introduction and text, a selective list, 1 p.

Description
The Spalding Gentlemen's Society has been in existence from 1710 and all its minute books survive. Early members, under the leadership of Secretary Maurice Johnson, included Sir Isaac Newton and William Stukeley. A quick glance through this volume soon indicates why it is of facsimile pages and is not a transcription. There are sketches of medals, coins, artefacts, heraldry and even a seahorse. Among the many subjects discussed at these early meetings were alphabets, a Roman Wall at Boston, a method for treating small pox, an urn found at Spalding and Gerves's Water Engine.
[Adapted from the Introduction.]

74

THE REGISTER OF | BISHOP PHILIP REPINGDON | 1405–1419 | VOLUME III | MEMORANDA 1414–1419.

Edited by Margaret Archer, M.A. (Liverpool), B.Litt. (Oxon), Formerly Senior Lecturer in Medieval History, University of Birmingham. Pp. viii + 327. Filmset by Northumberland Press Ltd, Gateshead, and Printed by Fletcher and Son Ltd, Norwich. Issued in 1982. For the two years ending 31 August 1982.

Content
Opposite title-page: 'The Society is grateful for grants in aid of publication to the University of Birmingham and to Lincolnshire County Council'. Editor's Preface, 1 p. Contents, 1 p. Notes Concerning the Method of Transcription, 2 pp. Principal Abbreviations Used in the Notes, 1 p. Memoranda 1414–1419, 289 pp. Index of Persons and Places, 28 pp. Index of Subjects, 4 pp. Index of Counties and Countries, 5 pp.

Description
See LRS Volume 57.

75

STOW CHURCH RESTORED | 1846–1866.

Edited by Mark Spurrell. Pp. xxxii + 220, plus 5 pp of plates. Published by The Boydell Press for the Lincoln Record Society. Printed by Short Run Press Ltd, Exeter, Devon. Issued in 1984. For the year ending 31 August 1983. ISBN 0–901503–39–8.

Content
Contents, 1 p. List of Plates, 1 p. Foreword, with Abbreviations and Signs, 2 pp. Introduction, 22 pp. Appendix 1: Church Dignitaries during the Period, 1 p. Appendix 2: Publications of the Revd George Atkinson, 1 p. The Documents, 206 pp. Index of Persons and Places, 10 pp. Index of Subjects, 4 pp.

Description
Stow church in Lincolnshire is one of the major surviving Anglo-Saxon churches in the country, and this volume of documents concerned with its restoration in the mid nineteenth century is of great interest to architectural historians and archaeologists as well as social historians. The records printed not only contain much evidence as to what was done at the time of restoration: they also unfold a fascinating picture of the battle between the perpetual curate, Revd George Atkinson, and the local farmers who wished to prevent any changes whatsoever. Further interest is added by the presence of John Loughborough Pearson, later to be famous as the architect of Truro Cathedral, as the architect in charge of the restoration.
[Adapted from Dust-Jacket.]

76

THE | ROLLS AND REGISTER | OF | BISHOP OLIVER SUTTON | VOLUME VIII | INSTITUTIONS, COLLATIONS AND SEQUESTRA-TIONS, ALL ARCHDEACONRIES EXCEPT LINCOLN AND NORTH-AMPTON.

Edited by Rosalind M. T. Hill, M.A., B.Litt., F.S.A., Formerly Professor of Medieval History, Westfield College, University of London. Pp. xii + 256. Published by The Boydell Press for the Lincoln Record Society. Printed by Short Run Press Ltd, Exeter, Devon. Issued in 1986. For the year ending 31 August 1985. ISBN 0–901503–40–1.

Content
Contents, 1 p. Corrigenda to Volumes I to VII, 4 pp. The Text, 228 pp. Index of Persons, 16 pp. Index of Places, 6 pp. Index of Subjects, 1 p.

Description
This volume completes the edition of the large and important register of Oliver Sutton, Bishop of Lincoln from 1280 to 1299. It includes institutions and promo-tions of heads of religious houses for the archdeaconries of Stow, Bedford, Leicester, Huntingdon, Buckingham and Oxford, collations of dignities and preb-ends within the cathedral, and a small section of *Sede Vacante* administration.
[Adapted from Dust-Jacket.]

77

THE | BOSTON ASSEMBLY MINUTES | 1545–1575.

Edited by Peter and Jennifer Clark from a transcript by John Bailey. Pp. xix + 139. Published by The Boydell Press for the Lincoln Record Society. Printed by Short Run Press Ltd, Exeter. Issued in 1987. For the year ending 31 August 1986. ISBN 0–901503–50–9.

Content
On reverse of title-page: 'This volume has been printed with the help of gifts from the late Mrs Dawson and the Lincolnshire County Council'. Contents, 1 p. Preface, 1 p. Introduction, 10 pp. Editorial Note, 1 p. Text of Calendar, 119 pp. Index of Persons and Places, 13 pp. Index of Subjects, 5 pp.

Description
This book constitutes a calendar prepared from a transcript made by a group led by the late John Bailey, as part of the History of Boston Project. Professor Peter Clark has supplied a brief introduction. The volume covers the first thirty years of the first minute book of the Boston Assembly (the corporation), and is of interest for the economic history of an important port, a centre of puritanical activity and the place from which some of the early Massachusetts settlers were drawn. It also throws light on local administrative conditions in East Lincolnshire, and on the relationship of the central administration with outlying provincial centres. [Adapted from Dust-Jacket.]

78

THE 1341 ROYAL INQUEST | IN LINCOLNSHIRE.

Edited by Bernard William McLane. Pp. xxxiii + 202. Published by The Boydell Press for the Lincoln Record Society. Printed by Short Run Press Ltd, Exeter. Issued in 1988. For the year ending 31 August 1987. ISBN 0–901503–51–7.

Content
Contents, 1 p. Preface (Dartmouth College, August 1988), 1 p. List of Abbreviations, 1 p. Introduction, 21 pp. Editorial Note, 3 pp. Calendar, 133 pp. Index of Persons and Places, 49 pp. Index of Subjects, 18 pp.

Description
This volume is a calendar edition of the judicial proceedings held in Lincoln in January, February, April and October 1341 as part of a nationwide investigation into official misconduct and local disorder. This inquest, conducted by specially appointed royal justices, royal officials and trusted local men, was held in the

aftermath of the opening campaign of the Hundred Years War and was intended by Edward III to uncover the reasons why he had not been adequately supported in his first Continental campaign, to quell popular unrest over corrupt officials and the unprecedented royal demands for money and supplies that had been imposed on the local communities during the late 1330s, and to deal with the constant problem of local disorder. The resulting proceedings at Lincoln provide detailed evidence of the problems posed by unscrupulous royal and local officials and criminals and the limited extent to which royal judicial mechanisms could be used to deal with them. In a more general sense, the proceedings also reveal the impact of the growth of royal government on local communities, a process that had begun in the twelfth century. Finally, this calendar serves as a companion piece to W. S. Thomson's edition of the 1298 royal inquest into official misconduct in Lincolnshire (LRS Volume 36, above).
[Adapted from Dust-Jacket.]

79

A | BIBLIOGRAPHY | OF PRINTED ITEMS RELATING TO | THE CITY OF LINCOLN.

Compiled by D. Mary Short, M.A. Pp. xx + 540. Published by The Boydell Press for the Lincoln Record Society and the Francis Hill Commemoration Trust. Printed by St Edmundsbury Press, Bury St Edmunds, Suffolk. Issued in 1990. For the year ending 31 August 1988. ISBN 0–901503–52–5.

Content
Contents, 6 pp. Sir Francis Hill (black-and-white photograph), 1 p. Memoir of Sir Francis Hill, by Joan Varley (reprinted from *Archives* 15, April 1981), 2 pp. Foreword (February 1989), by Philip Race, 1 p. Preface, 5 pp. Bibliography, 483 pp. Index, 57 pp.

Description
This bibliography builds on the material contained in Corns's *Bibliotheca Lincolniensis,* published in 1904, since which time the main contributions to the bibliographic coverage of the city have been commercial auction and booksellers' lists, the Lincolnshire section of the regional lists produced by the Library Association, and the *East Midlands Bibliography*. It is limited to the city itself, and the Cathedral is largely excluded, except where material relates to both the city and the Church. The bibliography is based on the collections of Lincoln Central Library, though numerous other sources have been consulted, and includes items from the Local Studies Collection such as broadsheets, postcards, scrapbooks and manuscript items. The bibliography of the city of Lincoln was commissioned by the Francis Hill Memorial Trust as a tribute to the work of the late Sir Francis Hill, historian of Lincoln, local solicitor, chairman of the council and later chancellor of the University of Nottingham. He was for many years treasurer of the Lincoln

Record Society and the Society is delighted to be able to publish this as a tribute to him.

[Adapted from the Dust-Jacket.]

80

PROBATE INVENTORIES OF | LINCOLN CITIZENS | 1661–1714.

Edited by J. A. Johnston. Pp. lxxx + 157. Published by The Boydell Press for the Lincoln Record Society. Printed by Woolnough Bookbinding Ltd, Irthlingborough, Northants. Issued in 1991. For the year ending 31 August 1989. ISBN 0–901503–53–3.

Content
Preface, 1 p. Contents, 1 p. Tables and Illustrations, 1 p. Editorial Method, 1 p. Introduction, map and plates, 68 pp. Inventories, 142 pp. Appendix I: The population of Lincoln 1642–1721, 2 pp. Glossary, 8 pp. Index of Persons and Places, 3 pp. Index of Subjects, 2 pp.

Description
The sixty inventories printed in this volume have been selected from the 590 that survive for the thirteen parishes of the City and County of Lincoln between 1661 and 1714. The parishes chosen are those in which urban occupations and residences rather than agricultural predominate. Probate inventories were drawn up to protect the heirs to an estate and to facilitate the distribution of bequests. The introduction includes a survey of the City of Lincoln and chapters on a wide range of occupations, among them butchers, farmers, gardeners, millers, bakers and goldsmiths.

[Adapted from the Introduction.]

81

CLERICAL POLL-TAXES | OF THE | DIOCESE OF LINCOLN | 1377–1381.

Edited by A. K. McHardy. Pp. xxxvii + 252. Published by The Boydell Press for the Lincoln Record Society. Printed by St Edmundsbury Press Ltd, Bury St Edmunds, Suffolk. Issued in 1992. ISBN 0–901503–54–1.

Content
Frontispiece: Lincoln Diocese, showing the areas covered by the text. Contents, 1 p. On reverse of Contents page: 'This volume is published with the help of a grant from the late Miss Isobel Thornley's Bequest to the University of London'. List of Maps, 1 p. Abbreviations, 1 p. Dedication: 'PATRI MEO | W. D. McH. | DONUM INDIGNUM', 1 p. Introduction, 27 pp. Maps of Leicestershire and

Lincolnshire, showing ecclesiastical divisions, 2 pp. Taxation of the Clergy 1377–1381, 174 pp. Note on the Parish Maps, 1 p. Parish Map of Leicestershire and Key to Leicestershire Parishes, 4 pp. Parish Map of Lincolnshire and Key to Lincolnshire Parishes, 9 pp. Appendix A: Arrangements for Collecting the Subsidy of £50,000, 1371, 2 pp. Appendix B: Collectors of Clerical Taxes in the Diocese of Lincoln 1370–1381, 3 pp. Index, 59 pp.

Description
The clergy of England, like the laity, were subjected to a series of poll-taxes within a short space of time. This volume prints the surviving assessments made of the clergy of the diocese of Lincoln in the years 1377, 1379 and 1381. Most of the material relates to the county of Lincoln but there are also surveys of Leicestershire, Rutland, most of Bedfordshire, and parts of Huntingdonshire and Hertfordshire. These poll-tax assessments represent what was virtually a census of the clerical population whose members were listed parish by parish. The documents show us not only that the number of clergy was very great, but that most were without benefices, and that they tended to gather in areas of high prosperity. Monks and nuns are also listed so that we can see how many members each monastery had. Publication of this material offers the opportunity to make a reassessment of the clergy and, hence the church of late medieval England. An extensive introduction describes the gathering of these taxes and the value and limitations of the documents themselves.
[Adapted from the Dust-Jacket.]

82

THE DIARIES OF | EDWARD LEE HICKS | BISHOP OF LINCOLN | 1910–1919.

Selected and edited by Graham Neville. Pp. xv + 287. Published by The Boydell Press for the Lincoln Record Society. Printed by St Edmundsbury Press Ltd, Bury St Edmunds, Suffolk. Issued in 1993. ISBN 0–901503–55-X.

Content
Contents, 1 p. Acknowledgement, 1 p. Introduction, Conventions used in transcription, Some abbreviations, 9 pp. The Diaries, 251 pp. Index of Persons, 17 pp. Index of Places, 12 pp. Index of Subjects, 7 pp.

Description
Bishop Edward Lee Hicks kept a diary throughout his episcopate at Lincoln, from 1910 to 1919. The two foolscap volumes from which this book is edited offer an honest picture of the daily life of a bishop in the period immediately before and during the First World War, a portrait of church and society in a largely rural diocese in the last phase before the radical transformation which the War hastened. Bishop Hicks had special interest in women's suffrage, the Labour movement and temperance reform. In church affairs he was an advocate

of liberal theology and biblical criticism, the development of women's work, a social gospel, and co-operation with the nonconformists; he was also President of the Peace League. The diary presents a largely church-centred picture, but it is also valuable as a personal view of Lincolnshire social life, including the impact of war on the county, conditions of travel at the beginning of the era of the motor car, and the characteristics of the clergy. There is frequent comment on items of archaeological and antiquarian interest.
[Adapted from the Dust-Jacket.]

83

GRANTHAM | DURING | THE INTERREGNUM | THE HALL BOOK OF GRANTHAM | 1641–1649.

Transcribed by Bill Couth. Pp. x + 149. Published by The Boydell Press for the Lincoln Record Society. Printed by St Edmundsbury Press Ltd, Bury St Edmunds, Suffolk. Issued in 1995. ISBN 0–901503–56–8.

Content
Contents, 1 p. General Editor's Note, 1 p. Acknowledgements, 1 p. Sketch plan of the centre of Grantham *c*.1640, 1 p. The Hall Book of Grantham 1641–1649, 140 pp. Index of Persons, Places and Subjects, 9 pp.

Description
Grantham had considerable local importance as a garrison town for both sides during the first Civil War. Its situation on the Great North Road gave it additional military and strategic significance. The Hallbook contains the recorded minutes of Grantham Corporation; it reflects the fates of successive aldermen who joined the Royal forces, went as hostage to Lincoln, and suffered imprisonment in Nottingham castle, and it provides a fascinating glimpse into the lives of the townspeople during this time of crisis. Householders were forced to pay taxes to both sides in the war, as well as shouldering their normal burden of taxation. Besides contributing to poor relief, their time and talents were also in demand for many tasks, including paving the streets, reinforcing the banks of the Witham, maintaining the town wells, doing watch and ward, paying quarteridge, and removing refuse from the streets. This volume provides much evidence about the local impact of hostilities on the social and economic life of the town.

84

THE PRINTED | MAPS OF LINCOLNSHIRE | 1576–1900 | A CARTO-BIBLIOGRAPHY | WITH AN APPENDIX | ON ROAD-BOOKS | 1675–1900.

By R. A. Carroll, formerly County Librarian of Lincolnshire. Pp. xlvi + 449.

Published by The Boydell Press for the Lincoln Record Society. Printed by St Edmundsbury Press Ltd, Bury St Edmunds, Suffolk. Issued in 1996. ISBN 0–901503–57–6.

Content
Dedication: 'To my father-in-law Ernest Sharman who looked after the dogs', 1 p. Contents, 3 pp. Preface, 3 pp. Introduction, 19 pp. Arrangement and Scope, 6 pp. Abbreviations, 1 p. Railways Shown on Lincolnshire Maps, 4 pp. List of Illustrations, 1 p. The Printed Maps of Lincolnshire 1576–1900, 358 pp. Appendix: Road Books 1675–1900, 52 pp. Addenda, 2 pp. Bibliography, 4 pp. Index, 33 pp.

Description
This volume provides a detailed catalogue of all the maps of Lincolnshire that show the county as a whole, from the first, issued by Christopher Saxton in 1576, to 1900, by which time the provision of maps of the county was largely in the hands of the Ordnance Survey. A detailed general essay outlines the history of the map-making as evidenced by the maps of Lincolnshire, and also provides much material on other maps, reflecting the various geographical changes in the county, such as the drainage of the fens, the building of canals and the coming of the railways. This is followed by a complete record of all the county maps in chronological order, with detailed notes on the differences between the states of each plate, the titles of the books or atlases in which they were issued, and information on the location of copies of the maps, both in book/atlas form and as individual sheets. The work provides a key for map enthusiasts to the book and cartographic resources held in the national, university and local collections throughout the country. Each section is equipped with notes on the surveyors, engravers, publishers and booksellers involved in the issue of each map, and the circumstances of publication; some idea is therefore gained of the ramifications of early publishing and the book and print trade. An appendix describes the road strip maps from the time of Ogilby's first national survey (1675) to the maps prepared for cyclists at the end of the nineteenth century.
[Adapted from the Dust-Jacket.]

Reprint
2005 paperback edition, published by Boydell Press for the Lincoln Record Society and printed by Antony Rowe Ltd, Eastbourne.

85

THE MEDIEVAL | LINDSEY MARSH | SELECT DOCUMENTS.

Edited by A. E. B. Owen, formerly Keeper of Manuscripts at Cambridge University Library. Pp. xxi + 185. Published by The Boydell Press for the Lincoln Record Society. Printed by St Edmundsbury Press Ltd, Bury St Edmunds, Suffolk. Issued in 1996. ISBN 0–901503–58–4.

Content

Frontispiece: Grant by Rengot of Wainfleet to Thomas son of Herward of property next to the port of Wainfleet, *c.* 1200 (black-and-white photograph). Contents, 2 pp. Preface (Thimbleby, October 1995), 2 pp. References, 3 pp. Sketch of the Lindsey coast between the Humber and the Wash, showing principal places mentioned in the text, 1 p. Introduction, 9 pp. The Documents, 144 pp. Selective Glossary, 4 pp. Index of Persons and Places, 29 pp. Index of Subjects, 8 pp.

Description

The Marsh District of Lindsey in Lincolnshire is a coastal belt some six to nine miles wide between the sea and the Wolds. This volume is an edition of almost 100 documents derived mainly from collections in the Lincolnshire Archives Office, British Library and Public Record Office, relating principally to the southern half of the Marsh. Dating from the late twelfth century to the first years of the sixteenth, with a few exceptions they have never previously been published. They are of particular interest for the history of land drainage and the upkeep of the sea defences, for both of which the medieval Commissioners of Sewers (watercourses) had an overall responsibility on a coast especially liable to erosion and flooding. Other topics dealt with include charters concerning the keeping of sheep outside the sea banks; material on local religious houses; extracts from manor court rolls; and will abstracts. The editor provides explanatory notes ranging from a simple précis to a nearly full translation to the documents, which are mostly in Latin. There is also a selective glossary covering items in the vernacular, an introduction, and full indexes of subjects, persons and places.

[Adapted from the Dust-Jacket.]

86

ROYAL WRITS ADDRESSED TO | JOHN BUCKINGHAM | BISHOP OF LINCOLN | 1363–1398 | LINCOLN REGISTER 12B | A CALENDAR.

Edited by A. K. McHardy, Senior Lecturer in Medieval History, University of Nottingham. Pp. xxix + 197. Published by The Boydell Press as a Joint Publication of the Canterbury and York Society and the Lincoln Record Society. Printed by St Edmundsbury Press Ltd, Bury St Edmunds, Suffolk. Issued in 1997. ISBN 0–901503–63–0.

Content

Contents, 1 p. Acknowledgement, 1 p. Dedication: 'To Pat Crimmin, for twenty years of supportive friendship', 1 p. Abbreviations, 2 pp. Introduction, 19 pp. Royal Writs, 158 pp. Appendix A: Some Writs Addressed to John Buckingham now in the Public Record Office, 13 pp. Appendix B: Select Writs Addressed to Bishop Buckingham which were copied into his other Registers, 3 pp. Appendix C: Attesting Judges, 4 pp. Index of Persons and Places, 17 pp. Index of Subjects, 2 pp.

Description

The many commands which the crown addressed to bishops represent a rich source of information about the history of government, law, and lay society, as well as about the church itself. The material, previously neglected, offers rich rewards to scholars in a variety of disciplines, and the writs collected here touch on many aspects of life in the later fourteenth century, including tax gathering, political upheaval, property disputes, Lollardy and foreign warfare. The bishop is seen swearing in local officials, setting up commissions of enquiry, organising the attendance of the clergy in parliament and the saying of patriotic prayers, and consulting episcopal archives to answer queries from the lay courts. There is also a vivid series of vignettes of family life among the gentry class from Yorkshire to Hampshire. An extensive introduction places the writs in their historical and archival contexts, and suggests further lines of research.
[Adapted from the Dust-Jacket.]

87

THE REGISTERS OF | BISHOP HENRY BURGHERSH | 1320–1342 | VOLUME I | INSTITUTIONS TO BENEFICES IN | THE ARCHDEACON- RIES OF LINCOLN, STOW AND LEICESTER.

Edited by Nicholas Bennett, Vice-Chancellor and Librarian of Lincoln Cathe- dral. Pp. xxxii + 223. Published by The Boydell Press for the Lincoln Record Society. Printed by St Edmundsbury Press Ltd, Bury St Edmunds, Suffolk. Issued in 1999. ISBN 0–901503–64–9.

Content

Contents, 1 p. Abbreviations, 3 pp. Introduction, 22 pp. The Text, 149 pp. Index of Persons and Places, 66 pp. Index of Subjects, 7 pp.

Description

Henry Burghersh, Bishop of Lincoln from 1320 until 1340, has not been treated kindly by historians. The largely hostile view expressed by early fourteenth- century chroniclers has coloured most subsequent accounts of his career; they give us a portrait of a man unqualified by age or ability to be a bishop, yet promoted to that office by the pope as a result of family influence and royal intervention; a man who nonetheless betrayed the monarch who had so conspicu- ously favoured him by lending support to the rebellion of Thomas of Lancaster in 1322 and thereafter by plotting with Queen Isabella to overthrow her husband. This edition of Burghersh's episcopal register reveals a different character. The bishop emerges as a conscientious diocesan and an administrator of considerable ability, while the evidence of his itinerary throws new light on the question of his involvement in the invasion of Isabella and Mortimer in 1326. The volume includes the first part of Burghersh's institution register, comprising admissions of clergy to parochial benefices, appointments of heads of religious houses, and

ordinations of vicarages and chantries, in the archdeaconries of Lincoln, Stow and Leicester.
[Adapted from the Dust-Jacket.]

88

THE ACTA OF | HUGH OF WELLS | BISHOP OF LINCOLN | 1209–1235.

Edited by David M. Smith, Director of the Borthwick Institute of Historical Research, University of York. Pp. liii + 256. Published by The Boydell Press for the Lincoln Record Society. Printed by St Edmundsbury Press Ltd, Bury St Edmunds, Suffolk. Issued in 2000. ISBN 0–901503–65–7.

Content
Contents, 1 p. Dedication: 'IN MEMORY OF MY PARENTS', 1 p. Preface, 2 pp. Manuscript Sources Cited, 6 pp. Printed Books and Articles Cited, with Abbreviated References, 9 pp. Other Abbreviations, 1 p. Introduction, 27 pp. The Acta of Hugh of Wells, 217 pp. Appendix: Settlements, chirographs and final concords in which Bishop Hugh is a party, 3 pp. Index of Persons and Places, 29 pp. Index of Subjects, 5 pp.

Description
The diocese of Lincoln was the largest in medieval England, extending over nine counties, and the early thirteenth century saw considerable development in episcopal government and evident concern over Church reform in the aftermath of the Fourth Lateran Council of 1215. Hugh of Wells, who became bishop of the diocese in 1209, was an important royal official, familiar with the reforms in the chancery of King John, the experience of which he brought to his diocese in the twenty six years of his rule, most notably in the introduction of episcopal registration. His tenure of the see was marked by transition and innovation in the sphere of diocesan government, with particular emphasis on pastoral responsibilities at local level. This edition of his collected *acta,* or administrative correspondence, numbers over 450 documents or mentions of documents now lost, assembled from cathedral, monastic, and governmental archives. The collection supplements the surviving summary enrolments and reveals Hugh as an active and innovative diocesan at an important point in the history of the English Church.
[Adapted from Dust-Jacket.]

89

LINCOLN WILLS | 1532–1534.

Edited by David Hickman, Postdoctoral Research Fellow at the University of Sussex. Pp. xxviii + 474. Published by The Boydell Press for the Lincoln

Record Society. Printed by St Edmundsbury Press Ltd, Bury St Edmunds, Suffolk. Issued in 2001. ISBN 0–901503–66–5.

Content
Contents, 1 p. List of Maps, Tables and Figures; Dedication: 'For Richard and Susan Hickman, for their help and support during the preparation of this edition', 1 p. Acknowledgements, 1 p. Abbreviations, 1 p. Introduction, 20 pp. Lincoln Wills 1532–1534, 389 pp. Index of Persons and Places, 71 pp. Subject Index, 13 pp.

Description
Lincolnshire boasts an extensive archive of sixteenth century probate material, preserved in the registers of the consistory and archdeaconry courts of Lincoln, the peculiar court of the Dean and Chapter of Lincoln Cathedral, and the archdeaconry court of Stow. This volume continues the process begun by Canon C. W. Foster of publishing the county's probate records in as full a form as possible and the 585 wills included here bring publication up to the end of October 1534. Unlike the wills proved by the archiepiscopal probate courts of Canterbury and York, those from Lincolnshire reflect a population of lower social status. The overwhelming majority come from the ranks of husbandmen, yeomen or tradesmen, rather than the gentry. In this respect the wills offer a valuable source for the cultural and religious preoccupations of the 'middling sort' and those lower in the social spectrum on the eve of the Reformation. Equally, the detailed bequests of property, livestock and land provide an insight into the material culture and prosperity of the testators, as well as extensive genealogical and topographical information of interest to local, regional and family historians.
[Adapted from the Dust-Jacket.]

90

THE REGISTERS OF | BISHOP HENRY BURGHERSH | 1320–1342 | VOLUME II | INSTITUTIONS TO BENEFICES IN | THE ARCHDEACONRIES OF NORTHAMPTON, OXFORD, | BEDFORD, BUCKINGHAM AND HUNTINGDON, |AND COLLATIONS OF CATHEDRAL DIGNITIES | AND PREBENDS.

Edited by Nicholas Bennett, Vice-Chancellor and Librarian of Lincoln Cathedral. Pp. xi + 316. Published by The Boydell Press for the Lincoln Record Society. Printed by St Edmundsbury Press Ltd, Bury St Edmunds, Suffolk. Issued in 2003. ISBN 0–901503–67–3.

Content
Contents, 1 p. Abbreviations, 3 pp. Preface, 1 p. The Text, 208 pp. Appendix: Ordination of Cotterstock College, 8 pp. Index of Persons and Places, 92 pp. Index of Subjects, 8 pp.

Description
See LRS Volume 87.

91

THE LETTER BOOK OF | SIR ANTHONY OLDFIELD | 1662–1667.

Edited by P. R. Seddon, Lecturer in History, University of Nottingham. Pp. xxxiv + 76. Published by The Boydell Press for the Lincoln Record Society. Printed by Antony Rowe Ltd, Chippenham, Wiltshire. Issued in 2004. ISBN 0–901503–68–1.

Content
Contents, 1 p. Acknowledgements, 1 p. Abbreviations, 1 p. Introduction, 26 pp. The Letter Book, 49 pp. Appendix One: Taxation and Local Government, 6 pp. Appendix Two: Ecclesiastical Disputes at Spalding, 7 pp. Appendix Three, The Lincolnshire Deputy Lieutenants, 2 pp. Appendix Four, List of the Holland Troops, 3 pp. Index of Persons and Places, 6 pp. Index of Subjects, 2 pp.

Description
The threat of a Dutch invasion, the fear of challenges to the restored monarchy by supporters of the Interregnum regimes, and defiant Quakers were among the problems Sir Anthony Oldfield of Spalding had to face as a deputy lieutenant of the Lincolnshire militia. In the first decade of the Restoration the county militias were responsible for the internal defence of the realm and became the most important institution of local government. Oldfield's letters show in illuminating detail how the militia in England's second largest county was raised, trained, financed and deployed. As well as providing fascinating evidence about Restoration Lincolnshire, the letters enable an analysis to be made of the relations between the deputy lieutenants of a county militia and the Crown and Council. [Adapted from Dust-Jacket.]

92

HISTORIC TOWN PLANS OF | LINCOLN | 1610–1920.

Edited by D. R. Mills and R. C. Wheeler. Pp. x + 111. Published by The Boydell Press for the Lincoln Record Society with the Survey of Lincoln. Printed by St Edmundsbury Press Ltd, Bury St Edmunds, Suffolk. Issued in 2004. ISBN 0–901503–69–X.

Content
Opposite title-page, Dedication: 'IN MEMORY OF JAMES SANDBY PADLEY, KATHLEEN MAJOR', 1 p. Contents, 2 pp. Foreword, by Roger Kain, 1 p. Acknowledgements, 1 p. Abbreviations, 1 p. Introduction: Background (by D.

R. Mills and R. C. Wheeler), The Pioneers (by R. A. Carroll and J. A. Johnston), Early Nineteenth-Century Lincoln to 1845 (by R. C. Wheeler and D. R. Mills), Lincoln in the Railway Age: 1846–1920 (by R. C. Wheeler and D. R. Mills), 22 pp. Reproductions of Plans, 89 pp., plus 3 pp. unpaginated.

Description
Lincoln is fortunate to have a detailed record of its geography since 1610, when John Speed published the first surviving map of the area. At that time, Lincoln was still a relatively poor and under-developed city with only a small population. Despite some errors, Speed's map is a remarkably accurate work which bears testament to his abilities as a surveyor. His map was followed in 1722 by that of William Stukeley, the antiquarian and early archaeologist, whose map concentrated on historical features, and attempted to show the extent of the old Roman city, and medieval walls and monuments. The nineteenth century saw Lincoln mapped a number of times: William Marrat's work of 1814–17 brought a more rigorous mathematical approach, showing the city just before it finally began to prosper and develop. Around this time both James Sandby Padley and the Ordnance Survey published new maps, both with increased accuracy, though neither one was perfect. It was the electoral reforms of the 1830s that drove map-makers to define ward and parish boundaries, the details of which required a larger scale than previous works. So it was that in 1842 Padley published his remarkable Large Map of Lincoln, a map of such high quality that it matched anything in the country. The collection ends with the Ordnance Survey map of 1920, a detailed record of the city scaled at six inches to the mile. It shows an urban Lincoln much more recognizable to the modern eye: railways, terraced streets, industrial areas, roads, and much less empty space. This book collects together these maps and demonstrates their importance in describing the changing geography of the historic city. Together, however, the maps show more than just the development of Lincoln; they also show the history of cartography, the application of scientific techniques and the development of improved accuracy and precision.
[Adapted from Dust-Jacket.]

Reprint
2005 paperback edition, published by Boydell Press for the Lincoln Record Society and printed by 4edge Ltd, Hockley, Essex.

93

THE OVERSEAS TRADE OF | BOSTON | IN THE REIGN OF | RICHARD II.

Edited by S. H. Rigby, Professor of Medieval Social and Economic History, University of Manchester. Pp. xxxviii + 302. Published by The Boydell Press for the Lincoln Record Society. Printed by Antony Rowe Ltd, Chippenham, Wiltshire. Issued in 2005. ISBN 0–901503–74–6.

Content

Opposite title-page, Dedication: 'To Rosalind', 1 p. Contents, 1 p. Preface, 2 pp. Editorial Note, 3 pp. Abbreviations, 1 p. List of Documents, 2 pp. Introduction: The Boston Customs Administration in the Reign of Richard II, 24 pp. The Text, 215 pp. Appendix I: Samples of the Latin Text of the Documents, 4 pp. Appendix II: The Boston Customs Collectors and Controllers in the Reign of Richard II, 2 pp. Appendix III: Biographies of Boston Customs Collectors Appointed during the Reign of Richard II, 35 pp. Glossary of Weights and Measures and Glossary and Index of Imports and Exports, 24 pp. Index of Persons, 18 pp. Index of Places, 2 pp.

Description

In the fourteenth century, Boston was not only the outport for the major city of Lincoln, but was also one of the largest and wealthiest English towns in its own right. Yet, because the townsmen of medieval Boston lacked formal powers of self-government, there is no surviving local borough archive for the period before its incorporation in 1545, which means that the town has been relatively neglected by historians. Given this lack of a local archive, the port's Exchequer customs accounts now constitute one of the main sources for the history of medieval Boston. However, very few of these accounts have yet appeared in print even though they offer fascinating insights into Boston's trade with Scandinavia, the Baltic, the Low Countries and Gascony. They also provide important information about the merchants involved in overseas trade and about the work of the officials who administered the customs system. This volume provides an English calendar of all of the surviving accounts of the port's customs and subsidy collectors from Richard II's reign (a time when Boston was still one of the leading ports in England) along with all the surviving counter-rolls compiled by the customs controllers as a check on the honesty of the collectors. In addition, it gives translations of a number of other documents preserved in the National Archives relating to Boston during this period, which offer important information on the crown's regulation of overseas trade and the workings of the port's customs administration.

[Adapted from the Dust-Jacket.]

94

LINCOLNSHIRE | PARISH CORRESPONDENCE | OF | JOHN KAYE | BISHOP OF LINCOLN 1827–53.

Edited by R. W. Ambler, Senior Lecturer in History at the University of Hull. Pp. lxv + 494. Published by The Boydell Press for the Lincoln Record Society. Printed by Antony Rowe Ltd, Chippenham, Wiltshire. Issued in 2006. ISBN 0–901503–79–7.

Content

Contents, 1 p. Illustrations, 1 p. Acknowledgements, 1 p. Abbreviations, 4 pp.

Introduction, 50 pp. List of Correspondence Published in this Edition, 3 pp. The Text, 392 pp. Appendix: Handlist of the Lincolnshire Parish Correspondence of John Kaye, 16 pp. Select Bibliography, 6 pp. Index of Persons and Places, 49 pp. Index of Subjects, 31 pp.

Description

The five hundred and thirty-two letters that are published in this volume come from the extensive correspondence received from people in Lincolnshire parishes by John Kaye, Bishop of Lincoln between 1827 and 1853. They are important because they express the opinions and reflect the attitudes of lay people as well as clergymen: Kaye's correspondents ranged from members of the landed gentry to people who would usually have little direct contact with the bishop. These included a 'troublesome', 'deceptive' and 'pugnacious' village carrier disputing the fees charged for burial in his local churchyard, as well as the farmer who complained of the 'hill usige' that he had 'ricivid from the viker' of his parish. The correspondence reflects Kaye's work as a Church reformer, but it is also important for the way that it demonstrates the changing significance of the Church in the lives of local communities. The extent to which the Church and its affairs were the means through which the social relations of parishes were articulated and sustained was a measure of the continuing importance of the establishment. [Adapted from Dust-Jacket.]

95

'GRATEFULL TO PROVIDENCE' | THE DIARY AND ACCOUNTS OF | MATTHEW FLINDERS | SURGEON, APOTHECARY AND MAN-MIDWIFE | 1775–1802 | VOLUME I ~ 1775–1784.

Edited by Martyn Beardsley and Nicholas Bennett. Pp. xxv + 166, plus 16 pp. of plates. Published by The Boydell Press for the Lincoln Record Society. Printed by Antony Rowe Ltd, Chippenham, Wiltshire. Issued in 2007. ISBN 978–0–901503–59–6.

Content
Contents, 1 p. List of Illustrations, 1 p. Acknowledgements, 1 p. Editors' Note, 1 p. Abbreviations, 1 p. Flinders Family Tree, 2 pp. Introduction, 11 pp. The Text, 166 pp.

Description
The diary and account books of Matthew Flinders, surgeon and apothecary at Donington in south Lincolnshire, are published here for the first time. His son, also Matthew, a navigator and sailor, became a central figure in the early history of the Australian nation, and much is revealed about the early life of the young Matthew in his father's diaries. There is a wealth of detail about the home, the family and the village in which the future explorer grew up. The daily routine of business, socialising with neighbours, unusual events such as the beaching of a

whale near Boston, or the visit to Donington of Mr Powell the famous fire-eater, are recorded alongside family joys and sorrows, the births and deaths of children, the passing of Flinders's beloved wife Susanna and his subsequent remarriage. The childhood and schooling of the young Matthew are a recurring theme, and the recording of the purchase of a two-volume edition of Robinson Crusoe in 1782 perhaps gives a hint of things to come.

[Adapted from the Dust-Jacket.]

96

MAPS OF THE WITHAM FENS | FROM THE THIRTEENTH | TO THE NINETEENTH CENTURY.

Edited by R. C. Wheeler, Honorary Secretary of the Charles Close Society. Pp. viii + 173. Published by The Boydell Press for the Lincoln Record Society. Designed and typeset by The Stingray Office, Manchester. Issued in 2008. ISBN 978–0–90150–383–1.

Content

Contents, 1 p. Acknowledgements, 1 p. Abbreviations, 1 p. Introduction, 21 pp. Cartobibliography, 44 pp. Reproductions of Maps, 100 pp. Select Bibliography, 1 p. Index of Persons, 1 p. Index of Places, 4 pp.

Description

The low-lying parts of Lincolnshire are covered by an array of maps of intermediate scope, covering a greater area than a single parish but less than the whole county. Typically produced in connection with drainage or water transport, and considerably predating the Ordnance Survey, to which many are comparable, they go back as far as the medieval period and continue to the late nineteenth century. This volume covers the Witham Valley, with the East, West and Wildmore Fens north of Boston, reproducing the most important of the maps and listing the less useful ones. The history of the drainage of the area is unusually dramatic. By 1750 the Witham was a failed river: the winter floods were worse than they had been for centuries and navigation from Boston to Lincoln had ceased. Over the following sixty years, local interests, aided by some able engineers, brought both navigation and drainage to a state of perfection that made Lincolnshire prosperous and fed the industrial north. These maps, reproduced here to a very high quality and in both colour and black and white, are an essential tool for understanding this history, and the volume thus illuminates certain episodes that have previously been opaque. The maps are accompanied by a cartobibliography and introduction.

[Adapted from the Dust-Jacket.]

97

'GRATEFULL TO PROVIDENCE' | THE DIARY AND ACCOUNTS OF | MATTHEW FLINDERS | SURGEON, APOTHECARY AND MAN-MIDWIFE | 1775–1802 | VOLUME II ~ 1785–1802.

Edited by Martyn Beardsley and Nicholas Bennett. Pp. xiii + 305, plus 16 pp. of plates. Published by The Boydell Press for the Lincoln Record Society. Printed by CIP Antony Rowe, Chippenham and Eastbourne. Issued in 2009. ISBN 978–0–90150–385–5.

Content
Contents, 1 p. Acknowledgements, 1 p. List of Illustrations, 1 p. Editors' Note, 1 p. Abbreviations, 1 p. Flinders Family Tree, 2 pp. The Text, 240 pp. Appendix 1: The Will of Matthew Flinders, 6 pp. Appendix 2: Flinders's Annual Income, 3 pp. Index of Persons and Places, 40 pp. Index of Subjects, 15 pp.

Description
This volume completes the edition of the diary and account books of Matthew Flinders, surgeon and apothecary of Donington. His son, another Matthew, who later won renown as the first circumnavigator of Australia, appears here as a schoolboy, choosing not to follow his father as an apothecary but pursuing instead a career at sea. The diary records the social life of Donington - magical deceptions at the Bull and the visit of a theatre company - and the joys and sorrows of family life. Flinders's success in business led to investments in land and government securities, yet his fear of poverty was never far away and his wish to sell up and retire was never realised. The war with France is a recurring theme, both in the ever-increasing taxes imposed to pay for it, and in the local patriotism evoked by Nelson's victory at the Nile, and that of the 'Glorious First of June' in which the young Matthew took part. The king's recovery from madness in 1789 was celebrated by the illumination of the whole town, while at Christmas 1792 Flinders joined his neighbours in burning an effigy of the hated radical, Thomas Paine.
[Adapted from the Dust-Jacket.]

98

BUILDING | A RAILWAY | BOURNE TO | SAXBY.

Edited by Stewart Squires and Ken Hollamby. Pp. 151. Published by The Boydell Press for the Lincoln Record Society with the Society for Lincolnshire History and Archaeology. Design by Simon Loxley. Printed by Print-Wright, Ipswich. Issued in 2009. ISBN 978–0–9015038–62.

Content
Dedication: 'To the memory of Charles Wilson and all those unknown workers

who together built the Bourne to Saxby railway', 1 p. Contents, 1 p. List of Maps and Drawings, 1 p. Introduction, 2 pp. Charles Stansfield Wilson 1844–1893, 6 pp. The Photographs, 82 pp. Appendix A: National Archives RAIL 491/548 (Extract from Contract No 2), 2 pp. Appendix B: Album Details, 4 pp. Appendix C: *Bourne to Saxby* by John Rhodes, 35 pp. Select Bibliography, 2 pp. Index, 8 pp.

Description
Charles Stansfield Wilson was the engineer who supervised the civil works on the railway line from Bourne to Saxby. A keen amateur photographer, he took a series of photographs during the construction phase of the line from 1890 to 1893, seventy-two of which were mounted in an album: this is a priceless survival, as photographs of the construction of a railway in Victorian England are extremely rare. This volume presents a selection of these illustrations, accompanied by full and extensive captions which tell the story of the construction, and detail the work of the men and machines involved. There are pictures of the various stages of construction, of temporary and permanent engineering structures and of the locomotives themselves. The volume also includes other contemporary photographs of the Wilson family; colour photographs of what can be seen of the line today; explanatory text, describing the significance of the photographs in railway and social history; a biography of Wilson; a history of the line and its construction, and a new edition of John Rhodes's 1989 history of the line.
[Adapted from the Dust-Jacket.]

99

THE | CORRESPONDENCE | OF THE | SPALDING | GENTLEMEN'S SOCIETY | 1710–1761.

Edited by Diana Honeybone and Michael Honeybone. Pp. xxx + 272. Published by The Boydell Press for the Lincoln Record Society. Printed by CIP Antony Rowe, Chippenham and Eastbourne. Issued in 2010. ISBN 978–0–901503–87–9.

Content
Contents, 1 p. List of Illustrations, 1 p. Acknowledgements, 1 p. Abbreviations, 1 p. Introduction, 22 pp. The Text, 203 pp. Illustrations, 11 pp. Appendix 1: List of Correspondents in alphabetical order, 6 pp. Appendix 2: Brief Biographies of Correspondents who were members of the Spalding Gentlemen's Society, 17 pp. Appendix 3: The Original Eighteenth-Century Filing System used by the SGS for its correspondence, 17 pp. Appendix 4: Letters from the 1760s relating to the SGS, 3 pp. Appendix 5: Family Tree of the Johnsons of Spalding (Simplified), 2 pp. Index of Persons and Places, 6 pp. Index of Subjects, 4 pp.

Description
One of the more remarkable survivals from sociable eighteenth-century England

is the Spalding Gentlemen's Society. Founded in 1710 in Spalding in the south Lincolnshire Fens by the local barrister Maurice Johnson to encourage the growth of 'friendship and knowledge', it received hundreds of letters from correspondents across Britain and overseas. These, concerned with antiquities, natural philosophy, numismatics, mathematics, literature and the arts, were collated by Johnson to provide material for the Society's weekly Thursday meetings. This detailed calendar brings together the 580 letters to survive from 154 correspondents. Of these, 119 were members of the Spalding Society, including well-known figures of the intellectual world: Martin Folkes, Roger Gale, William Stukeley, many Freemasons and three secretaries of the Royal Society and the Society of Antiquaries. The letters are annotated and indexed; fifty-four are transcribed in full. They provide a vivid picture of the interests of the 'curious' and demonstrate how knowledge spread during the eighteenth century.

[Adapted from the Dust-Jacket.]

PARISH REGISTER SECTION

1

THE | PARISH REGISTERS | OF | BOSTON | IN THE COUNTY OF LINCOLN | VOLUME I | 1557–1599.

Copied by F. Besant, M.A., F.R.A.S., F.R.G.S., Vicar of Sibsey, and edited by C. W. Foster, M.A., F.S.A., Vicar of Timberland and Canon of Lincoln. Pp. xi + 227. Printed by W. K. Morton & Sons Ltd, Saltergate, Lincoln. Issued in 1914. For the year ending 30 September 1913.

Content
Contents, 1 p. Introduction (Timberland, Lady Day 1914), 4 pp. Errata and Explanations, 1 p. Register, 142 pp. Schedule of the Bishops' Transcripts from Michaelmas 1561 to Michaelmas 1599, 2 pp. Index of Persons, 79 pp. Index of Places, 1 p. Index of Subjects, 1 p.

2

THE | PARISH REGISTERS | OF ST MARGARET IN THE CLOSE | OF | LINCOLN | 1538–1837.

Edited by C. W. Foster, M.A., F.S.A., Vicar of Timberland and Canon of Lincoln, with an Introduction by R. E. G. Cole, M.A., Canon of Lincoln. Pp. xvi + 184. Printed by W. K. Morton & Sons Ltd, 27 High Street, Horncastle. Issued in 1915. For the year ending 30 September 1913.

Content
Frontispiece: North-east view of the Church of St Margaret in the Close, Lincoln (from a drawing in the Willson Collection in the Cathedral Library). Contents, 1 p. Preface (Timberland, Midsummer 1915), 1 p. Introduction (Lady Day 1915), 7 pp. Errata, Abbreviations and Explanations, 1 p. Register, 153 pp. Schedule of the Bishops' Transcripts preserved in the Muniment Room of the Dean and Chapter of Lincoln, 3 pp. Index of Persons, 19 pp. Index of Places, 7 pp. Index of Subjects, 2 pp.

3

THE | PARISH REGISTERS | OF | BOSTON | IN THE COUNTY OF LINCOLN | VOLUME II | 1599–1638.

Copied by F. Besant, M.A., F.R.A.S., F.R.G.S., Vicar of Sibsey, and edited by C. W. Foster, M.A., F.S.A., Vicar of Timberland and Canon of Lincoln. Pp. xi + 227. Printed by W. K. Morton & Sons Ltd, 27 High Street, Horncastle. Issued in 1915. For the year ending 30 September 1914.

Content
Contents, 1 p. Introduction (Timberland, 3 June 1915), 1 p. Errata and Explanations, 1 p. Register, 206 pp. Schedule of the Bishops' Transcripts from 1 October 1599 to 25 March 1639, 2 pp. Index of Persons, 28 pp. Index of Places, 2 pp. Index of Offices and Occupations, 2 pp.

4

THE | PARISH REGISTERS | OF | GRANTHAM | IN THE COUNTY OF LINCOLN | VOLUME I | 1562–1632.

Edited by C. W. Foster, M.A., F.S.A., Vicar of Timberland and Canon of Lincoln, with an Introduction by Gilbert G. Walker, M.A., Rector of Somerby with Great Humby and Rural Dean of South Grantham. Pp. xv + 228. Printed by W. K. Morton & Sons Ltd, 27 High Street, Horncastle. Issued in 1916. For the year ending 30 September 1915.

Content
Contents, 1 p. Preface (Timberland, Michaelmas 1916), 2 pp. Introduction (Somerby Rectory, Grantham, 18 August 1916), 6 pp. Errata, Abbreviations and Explanations, 1 p. Register, 188 pp. Schedule of Signatures in the Parish Register and Bishops' Transcripts, 5 pp. Certificates written at the foot of the first nine folios of the present Register testifying that it is a true copy of the original Parish Register, 2 pp. Schedule of the Bishops' Transcripts from 1 October 1562 to 24 March 1632, 2 pp. Index of Persons, 25 pp. Index of Places, 2 pp. Index of Subjects, 2 pp.

5

THE | PARISH REGISTERS | OF | ALFORD & RIGSBY | IN THE COUNTY OF LINCOLN | COLLATED WITH AND SUPPLEMENTED BY THE | BISHOPS' TRANSCRIPTS | A.D. 1538–1680.

Edited by Reginald Charles Dudding, Rector of Saleby. Pp. xv + 209. Printed by W. K. Morton & Sons Ltd, 27 High Street, Horncastle. Issued in 1917. For the year ending 30 September 1915.

Content
Contents, 1 p. Introduction (18 August 1916), 7 pp. Errata, Abbreviations and Explanations, 1 p. Alford Parish Registers, 163 pp. Rigsby Parish Registers, 15 pp. Bishops' Transcripts of the Parish Registers of Alford from Michaelmas 1561 to Lady Day 1681, 4 pp. Bishops' Transcripts of the Parish Registers of Rigsby cum Ailby from Michaelmas 1561 to Lady Day 1681, 3 pp. Index of Persons, 20 pp. Index of Places, 2 pp. Index of Subjects, 1 p.

6

THE | PARISH REGISTERS | OF | GAINSBOROUGH | IN THE COUNTY OF LINCOLN | VOLUME I | 1564–1640.

Edited by C. W. Foster, M.A., F.S.A., Canon of Lincoln and Vicar of Timberland. Pp. xi + 276. Printed by W. K. Morton & Sons Ltd, 27 High Street, Horncastle. Issued in 1920. For the year ending 30 September 1916.

Content
Contents, 1 p. Introduction (4 August 1920), 3 pp. Erratum, 1 p. Abbreviations and Explanations, 1 p. Registers, 242 pp. Bishops' Transcripts of the Parish Registers of Gainsborough from Easter 1599 to Lady Day 1623, 2 pp. Index of Persons, 25 pp. Index of Places, 2 pp. Index of Subjects, 4 pp.

7

THE | PARISH REGISTERS | OF | BOURNE | IN THE COUNTY OF LINCOLN | 1562–1650.

Edited by C. W. Foster, M.A., F.S.A., Canon of Lincoln and Vicar of Timberland. Pp. xxi + 245. Printed by W. K. Morton & Sons Ltd, 27 High Street, Horncastle. Issued in 1921. For the year ending 30 September 1917.

Content
Contents, 1 p. Introduction (Timberland Vicarage, Lincoln, 11 September 1920), 11 pp. Errata, 1 p. Abbreviations and Explanations, 1 p. Registers, 215 pp. Bishops' Transcripts of the Parish Registers of Bourne from 6 April 1562 to Lady Day 1641, 3 pp. Index of Persons, 22 pp. Index of Places, 3 pp. Index of Subjects, 2 pp.

8

THE | PARISH REGISTERS | OF | ST PETER AT GOWTS | IN THE CITY OF LINCOLN | BAPTISMS 1540–1837 | BURIALS 1538–1837 | MARRIAGES 1826–1837.

Edited by Reginald C. Dudding, Rector of Saleby. Pp. xvi + 142. Printed by W. K. Morton & Sons Ltd, 27 High Street, Horncastle. Issued in 1923. For the year ending 30 September 1918.

Content
Contents, 1 p. Preface (Timberland Vicarage, Lincoln, 1 May 1923), 1 p. Erratum, Abbreviations and Explanations, 1 p. Introduction (Saleby Rectory, 26 May 1922), 8 pp. Registers, 126 pp. Index of Surnames, 14 pp. Index of Places and Subjects, 2 pp.

9

THE | PARISH REGISTERS | OF THE | CITY OF LINCOLN | MARRIAGES | A.D. 1538–1754.

Edited by C. W. Foster, M.A., F.S.A., Canon of Lincoln and Vicar of Timberland. Pp. xiii + 290. Printed by W. K. Morton & Sons Ltd, 27 High Street, Horncastle. Issued in 1925.

Content
List of Publications of the Society: Parish Register Section, 1 p. Contents, 1 p. Abbreviations and Explanations, 1 p. Introduction (Timberland Vicarage, Lincoln, 6 December 1925), 4 pp. Appendix: Schedule of Bishops' Transcripts, 3 pp. Parishes in the City of Lincoln: St Benedict, 16 pp., St Botolph, 9 pp., St John in Newport, 1 p., St Mark, 9 pp., St Martin, 32 pp., St Mary Magdalene, 12 pp., St Mary in Wigford, 21 pp., St Michael on the Mount, 15 pp., St Nicholas in Newport, 1 p., St Paul in the Bail, 37 pp., St Peter at Arches, 25 pp., St Peter in Eastgate, 12 pp., St Peter at Gowts, 13 pp., St Swithin, 20 pp. Index of Persons, 52 pp. Index of Places, 14 pp.

INDEX

[The following abbreviations are used: CWF (Charles Wilmer Foster); KM (Kathleen Major); LRS (Lincoln Record Society); PRS (Parish Register Section).]